C.G. Jung: Face to Face with Christianity

Conversations on Dreaming the Myth Onward

Jakob Lusensky

CHIRON PUBLICATIONS • ASHEVILLE, NORTH CAROLINA

www.ChironPublications.com

Interior design by Danijela Mijailovic
Cover design by Aletta Wetterstrand
Front cover image: ETH Library, Public domain, via Wikimedia Commons
Edited by C. Claudia Galego
Printed primarily in the United States of America.

ISBN 978-1-68503-221-0 paperback
ISBN 978-1-68503-222-7 hardcover
ISBN 978-1-68503-223-4 electronic
ISBN 978-1-68503-224-1 limited edition paperback

Library of Congress Cataloging-in-Publication Data Pending

"For now we see through a glass, darkly; but then face to face: now I know in part; but then shall I know even as also I am known."

—1 Corinthians 13:12, King James Version

"No one must look too long at the difference, so that, cowardly or arrogantly, he forgets that he is human; no man through his special dissimilarity is an exception to the fact of being human, but he is first human and then he is the specially different."

—Søren Kierkegaard, *Works of Love*

Contents

Acknowledgments

My sincere gratitude to all the contributors whose conversation makes up the chapters of this book. A special thank you goes to Murray Stein, who from the first stumbling steps of this project has generously supported me in recommending conversation partners and further reading, and whose thorough research in this field has laid a foundation for my own.

I would like to express heartfelt appreciation especially to my editor and conversation partner, Christina Galego. Your thorough editing has helped transform my broken written English into a pleasant reading experience. More than that, throughout this whole endeavor you have been there with me, deeply listening, passionately discussing, deeply engaging and guiding me in a dialogue at the intersection of Christianity and psychology. Without you I am afraid this book would not have come into being.

I want to thank my life partner, Lea, for her support, love, and patience throughout this at times painstaking process. In your being there with me through the ups and lows, you embody the language I try to encapsulate in thinking, words, conversation. Rosa, my co-writer in the early mornings, without you as inspiration there would be no words.

Finally, thank you to Hans-Jörg Rösch, David Marcus Schmid, and all others who have met me in private, often passionate, discussions at the fruitful place where psychology meets the cross.

Introduction

by Jakob Lusensky

In the experience of analysis—first as a patient and today as a Jungian psychoanalyst myself—I have often been confronted with the unavoidable suffering a human life entails. The analytical room has shown me that the questions Jung faced in his lifelong wrestling with Christianity are just as alive for individuals in our own time. Many people are first introduced to Jung through his psychological concepts and analytic theory, which can and do provide a helpful map for those in emotional pain. Jungian psychology opens to the existential and spiritual dimensions of life, yielding the possibility of interpretive depth in the search for meaning. As a depth psychology, it enables a more holistic understanding of the underlying significance of suffering—and of the psyche's potentials for healing.

But the experiences of an individual's life or analysis are not always founded on or explainable by psychological concepts and theoretical formulations. In the midst of anxiety, despair, and depression, psychological concepts offer handrails at best to help us position ourselves in the encounter. At worst, as renowned Jungian scholar Sonu Shamdasani observes, the same vocabulary can become a kind of guardrail or safety net, "vital for some, no doubt, for protection," but that may "block access to the very experiences in question."[1] In the analytical room, in our lives, in the process of individuation, we are often left naked: too wounded and vulnerable for concepts to become illuminating for us. Like Jung, we too

[1] Sonu Shamdasani, *Carl Gustav Jung and the Red Book (Part I)*, (symposium presented at the Library of Congress, Washington, DC, June 19, 2010), video, https://www.loc.gov/item/webcast-4909.

must struggle alone with the unresolved complexes of childhood, with the unanswered questions of living, and with an often bewildering imperative to find language for these experiences.

As analysis deepens, or as we mature into life, we can learn to listen to what Jung refers to in *The Red Book* as "the lament of the dead": not only to our individual unresolved complexes, unanswered questions, and unlived life, but to that of our parents and ancestors. Understanding how parts of our suffering are linked to a past that goes beyond personal history—generational trauma, as it is often called today—can become a way to broaden the story we tell ourselves about ourselves and why we suffer. Listening to the lament of the dead can in this way help us find more compassion for the people we grew up with and the suffering they caused, as well as for ourselves, for the wounds inflicted internally in relation to them. If we consider the human self as like a sapling growing through life into a tree, we can begin to connect to this broader story—in noticing the depths of our roots, the soil in which we have been planted, and the seed that was our beginning. We can begin to appreciate the trees that grow around us.

But there is a level of human suffering that lies beneath the personal and generational, beyond the laments of the dead. It is the painful confrontation with the limits of human life itself. It is the inevitable tragedy that everyone and everything we love will be taken from us. Classical psychoanalysis speaks, with its atheist ethos, of the necessity of adapting to the *reality principle*; in Christianity, the paradox and painful limits of human life and the self are symbolized by the cross.

At the center of the Western imaginary, there is Christ on the cross. A figure of the unavoidable suffering in a human life. A painful reminder that our psyche's defense mechanisms invent the most creative ways of avoiding facing what we must. No one will be free from accident, disease, death. It is at this raw level of human existence, at the imagined or real threat of loss, separation, sickness, poverty, suffering, and death, that the questions of faith and belief—the questions of religion—often first become relevant. It is as we are waiting on the examination results from the doctor; as our child is suddenly stricken with illness; as our vehicle collides head-on with two others; as a loaded gun is pointed at our head that we find ourselves turning to pray, to a faith that is able to become part of our reality. Looking into reality's tragic face, depth psychology cannot save us. Standing before reality, we have reached a limit, an impasse, a crossroads: the cross at the end of the road, the choice of whether or not to pick it up.

Where do Christ and Christianity fit into a new psychology?

James Hillman, well known for his archetypal psychology and emphasis on the importance of a polytheistic approach to the human psyche, may be an unlikely person to voice the question: "Where do Christ and Christianity fit into a new psychology?"[2] The question emerged in a 2010 public dialogue between himself and Shamdasani, who answers, "Well, it's the central figure for Jung. It's the central figure in his personal iconography, but also, as you say, for much of Western culture, given the effects that Christianity has had, as Jung says in the work, upon the soul."[3]

The question of Christ—the message of Christ, the meaning of *imitatio Christi*—is a central question for Jung in *The Red Book* and in the conversations presented in the book you are now reading. It is, if you like, the cross around which these thirteen dialogues ambulate, as well as the crossroads where psychology and Christian faith intersect. It is a well-known fact for many Jungians that Jung understood Jesus Christ psychologically, as a symbol of the Self—or rather, an incomplete symbol of the Self, since Jung viewed Christ as too perfect and one-sided, as having lost his shadow. In a letter to Adolf Keller on March 21, 1951, Jung puts it bluntly: "If Christ means anything to me, it is only as a symbol. As a historical figure he might just as well be called Pythagoras, Lao-tze,

[2] James Hillman and Sonu Shamdasani, *Lament of the Dead: Psychology after Jung's Red Book* (New York: W. W. Norton & Company, 2013), 219.
[3] Hillman and Shamdasani, *Lament of the Dead*, 219.

Zarathustra, etc. I find the historical Jesus completely unedifying, simply interesting because controversial."[4] For Jung , Jesus of Nazareth of two thousand years ago was of little importance, whereas Christ had become for him one symbol of many in a pantheon bearing witness to Jung's psychological theory of individuation.

The question C.G. Jung

In recent years, I have had the opportunity to lecture in introductory courses on Jungian psychology for master students of psychoanalysis in Berlin. I usually start the lecture by letting the students freely associate and share what first comes to mind when hearing the words *Jungian psychology*. The responses are usually somewhat the same: archetypes, the collective unconscious, individuation, complexes, shadow, anima, self, introversion, extraversion.

In a similar way, when you ask today's most powerful algorithm to associate (in other words, if you google *Jungian psychology*), the first results you will find are links to the same well-known concepts—illustrations of Jung's theories of the psyche, quotes of his writings, and black-and-white photos of the wise old man smoking his pipe. Since Jung's passing in 1961, analytical psychology has established a powerful persona in the cultural discourse, not least through the increased presence of the internet and social media, making Jungian concepts and theory an integral part of the psychologized vocabulary of the *Zeitgeist*.

The idea behind the conversations with Jungian scholars and analysts that form this book has been to go beneath the theory and concepts Jung left behind, to unearth the underlying existential questions he wrestled with in his own life. Unearthing the questions that lie below Jungian concepts is like pulling a plant from its soil to study the roots.

---

[4] C.G. Jung and Adolf Keller, "Letter 31," in *On Theology and Psychology: The Correspondence of C.G. Jung and Adolf Keller*, ed. Marianne Jehle-Wildberger, trans. Heather McCartney and John Peck (Princeton, NJ: Princeton University Press, 2020), 143.

Such roots are the questions about the purpose of human existence that Jung would ask himself, questions with which philosophy, theology, and religion have always grappled. Jung , through the new science of psychology, found a language in which to try answering them.

In old age, Jung famously summarized the meaning of his life for Aniela Jaffé in *Memories, Dreams, Reflections*: "The meaning of my existence is that life has addressed a question to me. Or conversely, I myself am a question which is addressed to the world."[5] Jung explained that his life task was to communicate an answer to the question that was himself, in order not to depend on the world for an answer. He continued: "Perhaps it is a question which preoccupied my ancestors, and which they could not answer."[6] Considered this way, what we are left unearthing—the plant whose roots are studied by the conversations in this collection—are not only the questions beneath Jung's concepts but the question of Carl Gustav Jung himself.

The naked Jung

With the publication of Jung's *The Red Book: Liber Novus* (2009) and *The Black Books: 1913–1932, Notebooks of Transformation* (2020), we find an intimate account of Jung's passionate struggle with the questions life had addressed to him. Imagining Jung as a question asked by life itself, we become witnesses to his reckoning with parts of his Self, his complexes, the lament of his ancestors, and a religious tradition and God in which he could no longer believe. Beginning with his break with Sigmund Freud and intensifying after the release of *Psychology of the Unconscious* (published in 1912), Jung found himself in an existential vacuum. In the book, he treats the myths of peoples of the past—myths that had long helped such peoples orient their lives. In his own day, Jung had, himself, to face the question, *in*

---

[5] Aniela Jaffé and C.G. Jung, *Memories, Dreams, Reflections*, ed. Aniela Jaffé, trans. Richard Winston and Clara Winston (New York: Random House, 1961), 350.
[6] Jaffé and Jung, *Memories, Dreams, Reflections*, 350.

what myth might man live now? "In the Christian myth, the answer might be, 'Do *you* live in it?' I asked myself. To be honest, the answer was no."[7]

Jung's wrestling takes the form of an inner dialogue in which he is summoned to engage with the characters of his unconscious. Painstakingly he takes account of his encounters in his *Black Books* journals. The initial entry on November 12, 1913, begins with a petition: "My soul, my soul, where are you? Do you hear me? I speak, I call you—are you there?"[8] What we witness today with new access to these intimate personal accounts is a raw, naked, vulnerable portrayal of a man in existential crisis—a Jung without any helpful psychological concepts to hold onto. A Jung without clothes, if you like. A person in emotional pain who, recognizing that his myth has lost meaning for him, sets out in despair on a process of self-experimentation, actively allowing images and visions to rise from the unconscious. Carefully noted in his *Black Books* entries and later illustrated and calligraphed in his *Red Book*, these are the visionary experiences that, late in life, Jung would admit were the *prima materia* for his psychological thinking and theory-building.

A few years after the publication of *Liber Novus*, Shamdasani, professor at the Welcome Trust Centre for the History of Medicine at University College, London, along with Jungian analyst James Hillman, published their forementioned conversation and commentary on the importance of *The Red Book* for our own time. In *Lament of the Dead: Psychology After Jung's Red Book* (2013), they emphasize that the questions Jung attempted to work through in *The Red Book* were intimately related to Jung's personal life and Reformed Protestant heritage but could also be understood as Jung's wrestling with the unanswered questions of his parents and ancestors.

Hillman points to personal biography when observing Jung confronting his own inheritance: Jung is "wrestling with his actual father,

[7] Jaffé and Jung, *Memories, Dreams, Reflections*, 195.

[8] C.G. Jung, *The Red Book: Liber Novus*, Reader's Edition, ed. Sonu Shamdasani, trans. Mark Kyburz, John Peck, and Sonu Shamdasani (New York: W. W. Norton & Company, 2009), 238.

he's wrestling with the Church, he's wrestling with the world he grew up in, with nineteenth-century Christianity as he knew it in Switzerland, and with theologians."[9] Shamdasani proposes in his 2010 Library of Congress lecture celebrating *Liber Novus'* release that we understand it as Jung's articulation of a "theology of the dead."[10]

In his theology of the dead, human redemption takes the form of Jung taking up the legacy of answering the unanswered questions of the souls of the dead. Shamdasani, in his conversation with Hillman, highlights a footnote in *The Red Book* in which Jung writes: "Not one item of the Christian law is abrogated, but instead we are adding a new one: accepting the lament of the dead."[11] It is a statement clarifying the extent both to which Jung himself saw his confrontation with the unconscious as unfolding within a Christian context, and of his having wished to add to it the psychoanalytical principle of learning to listen to (and attempt to answer) the unanswered questions of our ancestors' unresolved complexes.

The specific questions that Jung's unconscious lamented and that he attempted to work through in his years writing *The Red Book* between 1914–1930 (he would resume writing at the end of his life only to put it down again and not finish it), and later in his psychological concepts and theory-building, are summarized by Shamdasani: Throughout the work, the question for Jung is what does it mean to be a Christian? How are we to understand the Christian ideal of imitating Christ today? Does it still have meaning?[12] For Shamdasani, such questions reveal Jung attempting to recover a genuine experience of being a Christian.[13]

Essential questions these were for Jung, and in my opinion, they remain essential both to Jungian psychology and Christianity in our time. I decided to bring these and other questions to my interlocuters in the conversations that make up this book. The purpose of these conversations

---

[9] Hillman and Shamdasani, *Lament of the Dead*, 123.
[10] Shamdasani, *Carl Gustav Jung and the Red Book (Part I)*, 2010.
[11] Jung, *The Red Book*, 297.
[12] Jung, *The Red Book*, 213.
[13] Jung, *The Red Book*, 213.

has been to ambulate around, to analyze, to linger with the same questions Jung himself wrestled against. Each conversation is singular, unfolding and standing on its own. Readers are invited to explore the world of each dialogue in whatever way suits their subjective disposition.

Jung's wrestling with Christianity

For anyone who has spent time with analytical psychology, it is not news that Jung's unconscious was steeped in Christian soil or that many of the questions he wrestled have their roots there. Shamdasani and Hillman's analysis of *The Red Book* merely highlights anew the importance of Christianity and Christ in this formative period of Jung's life and for his psychological theory-building. Shamdasani summarizes: "One of the most striking things about *The Red Book* when one first encounters it is the extent and the character of Jung's involvement with Christianity. The central character of the work is Christ."[14]

As the story goes, C.G. Jung was born , raised, and buried as a Christian. His father was reared in a Swiss Protestant family and worked as a pastor of the Reformed Church, as did his maternal grandfather and six of his uncles. Jung was baptized, took communion in, married, and was laid to rest in the Protestant Reformed Church of Switzerland. He understood himself culturally to be a Christian, and so, he believed, was his unconscious. Jung stresses his life mission as being fundamentally linked with Christianity, writing: "My problem is to wrestle with the big monster of the historical past, the great snake of the centuries, the burden of the human mind, the problem of Christianity."[15]

The problem of Christianity and its linkage with the existential questions Jung was asking himself—about the loss and recovery of a myth to live by—would accompany him through childhood and adolescence

---

[14] Jung, *The Red Book*, 213.

[15] C.G. Jung, *The Symbolic Life: Miscellaneous Writings*, Vol. 18 of *Collected Works of C.G. Jung*, ed. and trans. Gerhard Adler and R. F. C. Hull (Princeton, NJ: Princeton University Press, 1976), ¶ 279.

until his later years. But it was after his visit to India in 1937–1938, and an impressive dream about the search for the Holy Grail, that there was a clear turn of focus in his writing, and he shifted his attention more firmly to topics related to Christianity. From his *Terry Lectures on Psychology and Religion* in 1937 onward, Jung produced a series of works aimed at working through Christian ideas and concepts. These ideas and concepts had long been present as questions in Jung's personal life, and were those he grappled with in the active imaginations collected in *Black Books* and *Liber Novus*.

It was in this *Red Book* period of actively writing down, illustrating, painting, and working through his active imaginations that Jung would start looking for ways to translate these experiences into theoretical and psychological language. In his 1918 essay "The Role of the Unconscious," he analysed a patient's dream to illustrate the idea that Christianity in its traditional form can have a repressive psychological effect on the unconscious, instinctual side of man.

In 1923, he returned to the theme of Christianity's prohibitiveness in fourteen summertime seminars held at the small seaside resort Polzeath, on the southeast coast of England. The latter part of these seminars focused on the historical and psychological effects of Christianity, on what Jung reiterated is traditional Christianity's repression of the unconscious.

Jung distinguished between ecclesial Christianity and what he understood as *real* Christianity, the former of which, he said, does not work in order to inspire individuals anymore. He goes on to address how Christianity has repressed part of our human nature, has tried historically to exclude the animal side in humanity, what Jung referred to as the *inferior man*. He highlighted how more traditional or doctrinal Christianity especially attempted to suppress man's individual capacity for fantasy and symbol formation, which the Church had seen as a threat to its power that would often be labelled heretical.

Jung attacked traditional Christianity with the voice of a Protestant Reformer, but also presented his own revisioning of a Christianity that might yet transform if it were to be open to integrating a depth-psychological approach:

> If the old Christianity can assimilate the new powers from the unconscious which analysis has made available, it will go on, having gained a fresh understanding of the teachings and renewed power. The Jesuit spirit may well take over analytic methods, and in the future the Church may become the greatest exponent of analysis.[16]

Before an audience of about thirty participants, Jung passionately proclaimed that the fire of the Holy Spirit is at work in the analysis between analyst and analysand within this early movement of analytical psychology. He ended these lectures by speaking about how individual relationships lay the foundations of what he calls the *invisible church*—a term Jung was very fond of and that Murray Stein expands on in the first conversation of this book.

Alchemy as the Christian unconscious

Jung's turning back to Western culture in the late 1930s, his commencing the working through of his own Christian tradition, was accompanied by his growing interest in alchemy. Jung understood alchemy not only as the chemical process of trying to distill gold, but as the psychological process of the individual alchemist trying to redeem their soul. Jung came to understand the alchemical tradition's symbolism as having a psychologically compensatory function to what he believed was the too-one-sided Christian tradition's at times reductive symbolism and dogma. Throughout the 1930s and until late in his life, Jung would write and lecture on alchemy to reveal its compensatory function for the Christian man. This started with him writing

[16] M. Esther Harding and C.G. Jung, TS (27 leaves) of lecture "Human Relationships in Relation to the Process of Individuation," July 1923, *Cornwall Seminar, July 1923, C.G. Jung: Unauthorized Notes / by M. Esther Harding*, Kristine Mann Library, C.G. Jung Center, New York, leaf 20. https://collections.library.yale.edu/catalog/10076043.

a psychological commentary on the Chinese text *The Secret of the Golden Flower*, which was sent to him in 1928 by Christian Sinologist and missionary to China Richard Wilhelm (1873–1930), who would later become his friend. In his later book *Psychology and Alchemy* (1941), Jung summarizes the link between Christianity and alchemy, noting that "alchemy seems like a continuation of Christian mysticism carried on in the subterranean darkness of the unconscious."[17]

In 1930, Jung had stopped working on *The Red Book* and focused more of his attention on the comparative study of the individuation process. The lectures he gave at the Swiss Federal Institute for Technology in Zürich (ETH) between 1933 and 1941 would become the mainstage for this. These lectures were open, the audience comprised of students of the ETH, the general public, and Jung's followers who had moved to Zürich in the last two decades. The ETH lectures were the locus of Jung's theoretical attention through this decade, and many of the ideas that would take the form of books in the last decade of his life were introduced and elaborated in these lectures.

In the semesters of 1939–1940, leading up to start of the Second World War, after Jung had delved into comparative studies between individuation and Eastern spirituality, Tantric Yoga, and meditation, he decided suddenly to turn west more specifically to Europe, and his interpretative lens to *The Spiritual Exercises of Saint Ignatius of Loyola.*

Saint Ignatius of Loyola lived and worked in sixteenth-century Europe. As the founder of the Jesuit order, he had put together a structured form of spiritual exercises practiced by Christians to this day. Jung, who had prepared his lectures while examining Eastern spiritual practices and their relationship to active imagination and the process of individuation, suddenly shifted focus to what he saw as a specifically Western form of meditation.

Jung would, as in the earlier lectures, use his own psychological theory and concepts to explain the exercises. He paid special attention to the visions Loyola reports to have had in the latter's semi-autobiographical

[17] C.G. Jung, *Psychology and Alchemy*, Vol. 12 of *Collected Works* (1968), ¶ 452.

account "Reminiscences," indirectly comparing them to his own visions and active imaginations of 1913, and to his writing in *Black Books*. Interestingly, at the time of preparing these lectures and meditating on Loyola's exercises, Jung himself had a vision of Christ that he later describes to his secretary and longtime collaborator Aniela Jaffé in the following account (June 27, 1957):

> When I was engrossed with psychology and alchemy—no, to be more precise, it was when I was giving the seminar on Ignatius of Loyola—once, in the night, I had a vision of Christ. One night I awoke and there, at the foot of the bed, I saw a crucifix. Not quite life-sized. It was very clear and couched in a bright light. In this light, Christ was hanging on the cross and then I saw that it was as if his entire body were made of gold, as if of green gold. It looked wonderful. I was scared to death by it.[18]

The late Jung

It is in the important late decade of Jung's life that his wrestling with and working through Christianity finds full theoretical expression. Well known to Jungians is his work *Aion: Researches into the Phenomenology of the Self*, which aims at a psychological understanding and thoroughgoing interpretation of the Christ image. In the foreword of this book, Jung writes: "I have been requested so often by my readers to discuss the relations between the traditional Christ-figure and the natural symbols of wholeness, or the self, that I finally decided to take this task in hand."[19]

The hypothesis that Jung presents in *Aion* is that the symbol of Christ represents the Self, but only partially, because the Self had been

---

[18] Martin Liebscher, "Introduction to Volume 7," in *Ignatius of Loyola's Spiritual Exercises*, Vol. 7 of *Lectures Delivered at ETH Zürich*, ed. Martin Liebscher, trans. Caitlin Stephens (Princeton, NJ: Princeton University Press, 2023), xlvii.

[19] C.G. Jung, *Aion: Researches into the Phenomenology of the Self*, Vol. 9 (Part II) of *Collected Works* (1969), x.

split into good and evil components. "Nevertheless the Christian symbol lacks wholeness in the modern psychological sense, since it does not include the dark side of things but specifically excludes it in the form of a Luciferian opponent."[20] For Jung, the Christ symbol represents only one side of human nature, the other being shown by his enemy, the Antichrist or Satan. The result of this, argues Jung, creates a doctrine, tradition, and ultimately a Christian culture and collective unconscious that is split, characterized by unreconciled oppositions in man.

The book is a return to and clarification of ideas Jung had broached earlier on, especially in his essay "A Psychological Approach to the Dogma of the Trinity" (1948). It was there that Jung had spelled out theoretically his hypothesis of a disproportionate Christian theology, which he contrasted with his own vision of human wholeness, namely a wholeness stressing the importance of including the dark side of God by adding "a fourth" to the doctrinal Trinity.

In Jung's late, much- discussed work *Answer to Job* (1952), he draws an arc back to questions he had been formulating and attempting to answer in *Black Books* and *Liber Novus.* Murray Stein describes *Answer to Job,* also known as a "psychotheology,"[21] as Jung's working through of the Christian image through his own countertransference. "What Jung presents in *Answer to Job* is both an analysis of himself—of his father complex and unresolved transferences to his father Paul Jung and Sigmund Freud —and a therapeutic analysis of the biblical Christian image of God through the counter-transference."[22]

A leitmotif throughout the book is the idea of reintegrating evil back into the godhead, and Jung's lifelong difficulties with the Christian concept of *privatio boni*—evil as merely the absence of good. The basic notion of this doctrine is that evil has no substance; only the good exists

---

[20] C.G. Jung, *Aion*, 41.

[21] See James W. Heisig, *Imago Dei: A Study of C.G. Jung's* Psychology of Religion (Lewisburg, PA: Bucknell University Press, 1973).

[22] Murray Stein, *Jung's Treatment of Christianity: The Psychotherapy of a Religious Tradition* (Asheville, NC: Chiron Publications, 2015), 165.

on its own power. Evil exists only insofar as there is possibly deviation from the good. In the course of Christian theology, the development of the dark side of human existence was, for Jung, deprived of substance and thereby regarded as the absence of good. Jung viewed this development as the byproduct of psychological denial. The end result was that certain unwanted aspects of our psychological reality had to be repressed, relegated to the unconscious. According to Jung, Christianity had suppressed evil from self-awareness, and so too did we, as Western individuals equipped with an unconscious informed by such repressions. It would become part of the task of analysis and individuation to transform parts of these repressed elements.

Murray Stein writes that, in Jung's view, ecclesial Christianity had unmoored evil from reality: "Theologically it denied evil the status of ontological reality, in the doctrine of God as *Summum Bonum* and in the understanding of evil as *privatio boni*."[23] In *Answer to Job*, Jung returned to what had also been a major theme of *Liber Novus*, offering a theodicy in trying to answer the question of why a good God permits the manifestation of evil. Jung's rendering is a passionate critique of the nature of God as the " highest good." In Jung's mind, God is beyond the human categories of good and evil. The religious task for contemporary man, says Jung, is to prepare for the next development of human incarnation and the integration of the dark side of the God-image through the process of individuation.

Imitatio Christi

Another leitmotif of Jung's *The Red Book*, one he returned to in his late works, is the *imitatio Christi*. In Christian tradition, the imitation of Christ is the practice of following the example of Jesus Christ. It is the development in one's own life of an attitude inspired by Christ's way of living a life of self-sacrifice in service and brotherly love. Jung's wrestling with and working through this central pillar of Christianity leads him

[23] Stein, *Jung's Treatment of Christianity*, 151.

to propose, rather than a literal following or imitation of Christ (which he believed the traditional Church and most theology emphasized), an exclusively psychological interpretation.

For Jung, Jesus became an ideal of how to live life as an individual, as authentically as Christ did. Jesus' life could thus be read as an analogue for our psychological development toward individuation. Jung wrote in his commentary on *The Secret of the Golden Flower*:

> *The imitatio Christi* has this disadvantage: in the long run we worship as a divine example a man who embodied the deepest meaning of life, and then, out of sheer imitation, we forget to make real our own deepest meaning—self-realization . . . . The imitation of Christ might well be understood in a deeper sense, namely as the duty to realize one's best conviction, which is always also a complete expression of the individual temperament, with the same courage and the same self-sacrifice as Jesus did.[24]

In a 1940 lecture, he elaborated:

> This is a critical point: the question of the *imitatio Christi*. Should it be an imitation of the life of Christ such that one even gets the stigmata, like Saint Francis, or does it mean that each person should live life to the full, in their own way, until the bitter end, as Christ did? Those are two very different paths. It is clear that for medieval and more recent Christianity it was certainly a matter of the *imitatio Christi*, not about living one's life *sine imitatione*—without imitation.[25]

In *Answer to Job*, Jung questioned the Church's teaching that the incarnation was a unique historical event; he formulated instead a

[24] C.G. Jung, *Alchemical Studies*, Vol. 13 of *Collected Works*, ¶ 80–81.
[25] C.G. Jung, "Lecture 16," in *Ignatius of Loyola's Spiritual Exercises*, 229–39.

psychologically-informed Christology, where the incarnation did not cease with the ascension but continues through the Holy Spirit in man. In the final paragraph of the book, he explained that this process, the "indwelling of the Holy Ghost, the third Divine Person, in man, brings about a *Christification of many*."[26] Jung proposed that we understand Christ as an archetypical pattern of how God continues to incarnate in the human being.

The *mysterium*

Jung's last major work, to which he dedicated more than a decade, finishing it in his eightieth year, is *Mysterium Coniunctionis: An Inquiry into the Separation and Synthesis of Psychic Opposites in Alchemy* (1955). It summons the work he had begun on alchemy twenty-five years earlier with his commentary on *The Secret of the Golden Flower*—and much of Jung's late works besides. This work extended the dream of healing Christianity's one-sidedness by attending more deeply to the psychologically compensatory symbolism of alchemy. Herein he examined and interpreted classical alchemical texts in detail, focusing his investigation on the alchemical process of separation and synthesis of chemical substances, which he understood as a symbolic language for the process of psychological integration and individuation.

As the subtitle indicates, its focus is on the *coniunctio* and the preceding stages leading up to a synthesis of opposing elements. Jung regarded the alchemical process also as an analogue for the psychotherapeutic process, a process of transformation of *chaos* and *prima materia* into what the *lapis philosophorum*—the philosophers' stone—is able to shape. The *lapis* was the substance that alchemists observed could turn base materials such as mercury into gold. Jung's own thesis was that the *lapis* is not only parallel to the Christ figure, but also a symbolic image

[26] C.G. Jung, *Psychology and Religion: West and East*, Vol. 11 of *Collected Works* (1970), ¶ 758.

of the whole Self. He saw both the alchemist's laboratory and the analytical room as a vessel where psychological transformation can take place: the unfolding of the human Self.

Jung's social conscience

In one of his last well-known public works "The Undiscovered Self" (1957), Jung considered how the deeply personal, the depth- psychological, has also a political dimension. This essay, written at the escalation of the Cold War—the clash between communism and capitalism alongside imminent threats of nuclear disaster—is as relevant today as it was in the late 1950s. In it, Jung argued that individual self-knowledge, the fostering of religious development through a process of individuation, is necessary to counterbalance the collectivist totalitarian and technocratic ideologies of the day. He wrote:

> The individual who is not anchored in God can offer no resistance on his own resources to the physical and moral blandishments of the world. For this he needs the evidence of inner, transcendent experience which alone can protect him from the otherwise inevitable submersion in the mass.[27]

What is required for resistance to collective forces is a depth psychology that can help facilitate the transformation of individual selves through reconnection with one's unconscious dreams and symbols. Through cultivation of the inner world of an individual, resistance to the collective erasure of difference in the name of communist and capitalist ideology can take form.

Another of Jung's last essays emphasizing the social conscience of Jung's thinking, and which in my opinion has been too little discussed by Jungians, is the essay "A Psychological View of Conscience." Written in 1958, three years before his death, it was published as part of a collection of

[27] C.G. Jung, *Civilization in Transition*, Vol. 10 of *Collected Works* (1970), ¶ 511.

essays entitled *Das Gewissen*, released by the C.G. Jung institute in Zürich. In it, Jung continued to explore the link between individuation and the collective, specifically the role of *conscience* in psychological development.

In the essay, Jung differentiated between two levels of conscience, *the moral* and *the ethical.* He related the former to Freud's theory of the superego, and the latter to his own theory of individuation, the archetypes, the *Pax Dei*, and the voice of God. In essence, Jung argued for how individuation can best be understood as a process of *making one's conscience conscious.* He argued that it is through the development of the individual's conscience—through learning to listen to the inner voice of God—that they might transform into a human Self.

> If the voice of conscience is the voice of God, this voice must possess an incomparable higher authority than traditional morality. Anyone, therefore, who allows conscience this status should, for better or worse, put his trust in divine guidance and follow his conscience rather than give heed to conventional morality.[28]

Altogether, this brief overview of Jung's wrestling with Christianity should help clarify to what extent Christianity forms a touchstone of Jung's lifework and psychological theory. We remember that Jung imagined himself a question posed by life itself; we can appreciate in this light how trying to answer this question became his vocation.

Jungians wrestling with Jung's Christianity

It is helpful to have some understanding of what has been done in the research field of Jungian–Christian dialogue since Jung's passing in 1961. That Jung wrestled with Christianity is nothing that we became aware of for the first time with the publication of *Liber Novus*. But what the book does help highlight is the extent to which his psychological crisis, and later psychological concepts and theory, are intimately related to his working through of Christianity.

---

[28] C.G. Jung, *Civilization in Transition*, ¶ 840.

In the half-century that has passed since Jung left the scene, a small group of independent Jungian scholars and analysts have made important individual contributions. This introduction will not exhaust the important research in the field, but it hopes to inspire you as a reader to continue your own explorations. Nonetheless, a few persons behind the research at the nexus of analytical psychology and Christianity should be mentioned insofar as their respective insights inform the conversations contained herein.

Murray Stein, who himself contributes the first conversation in this collection, argued almost forty years ago, in his seminal work *Jung's Treatment of Christianity: The Psychotherapy of a Religious Tradition* (1985), that Jung's psychology can be understood as an attempt at treating the ailing Christianity Jung had experienced as a child and adolescent growing up in a Reformed Protestant family. Stein presents the hypothesis that Jung acts as a therapist for the healing and transformation of Christianity: "Jung's stance toward Christianity was fundamentally that of a psychotherapist, and so the goal of all his efforts with this 'patient' Christianity was its psychotherapeutic transformation."[29]

According to Stein, throughout Jung's life, Jung took on the role of psychotherapist of what he argued was a psychologically too-one-sided Christian tradition—a tradition that had lost its therapeutic effect of offering a sense of psychological wholeness to its believers. Viewed through this lens, Jung's analytical psychology can be understood as a possible treatment plan aimed at helping Christianity in its psychotherapeutic transformation. "This image of Jung as a psychotherapist to an ailing religious tradition accounts for what he was trying to do with Christianity and why he made the specific recommendations he did for fundamental changes in Christian doctrine."[30]

Murray Stein's collected writings are a trove of insights for our field of research. Most notably mentionable here are Jung's writings

[29] Stein, *Jung's Treatment of Christianity*, 18.
[30] Stein, *Jung's Treatment of Christianity*, 18.

on the topic edited in the volume *Jung and Christianity* (Princeton University Press, 1999) and Stein's own 2015 book, *Solar Conscience, Lunar Conscience: An Essay on the Psychological Foundations of Morality, Lawfulness, and the Sense of Justice.* The latter discusses the forementioned late essay of Jung's, "A Psychological View of Conscience," and the role of conscience in psychological development and individuation, a topic of concern in some of the conversations presented in this book.

Stein studied at the University of Chicago with Peter Homans, his main professor and dissertation advisor for the thesis that became Stein's 1985 book on Jung's treatment of Christianity. Homans had already analyzed Jung's relationship to Christianity from a more traditional psychoanalytic and sociological lens in his book *Jung in Context: Modernity and the Making of a Psychology* (1979).

Homans was interested in how Jung's psychology fit into the picture of modernity, how psychology in a sense replaces religion for some people. *Jung in Context* situated Jung's work in the context of the nineteenth and twentieth century, examining psychology and its connection to the decline of religion. For our research on Jung and Christianity, Homans's book offers rich insights and a nuanced picture of the complex relationship Jung had with the Christian tradition he grew up in, the faith of his father, and his own attempt to reconcile them.

Not being an analyst himself, Homans was nonetheless unafraid to put Jung on the couch. He showed how Jung's relationship to his father appears at times to have tainted his interpretations of Christian theology and faith. Drawing closely from Jung's life, Homans showed how Jung's childhood and adolescent experiences were inseparable from his experience of religion. In Homans's words, "To study the former is to become preoccupied with the latter."[31]

Foremost, Homans elucidated to what extent Christianity is a foundation for Jung and those of us trying to decipher his psychological

[31] Peter Homans, *Jung in Context: Modernity and the Making of a Psychology* (Chicago: University of Chicago Press, 1979), 115.

project. "While it is true that at one level he repudiated [Christianity], it is equally important to recognize that, at another level, he also attempted to assimilate elements of it; for that religion was also, in part, the *experiential matrix* out of which his psychology emerged."[32] Homans described how, as a child and adolescent, Jung experienced this matrix in two fundamentally different modes: through the Protestant Reformed tradition as his father, family, and culture had taught it; but also through his own personal and mystical experiences as a child and young adolescent. He explained this as Jung's having a *double relation* to Christianity in both assimilating and repudiating it.

This double relation might help to explain some of the ambivalence toward Christianity expressed throughout Jung's writings and teachings, a psychological tension coming to life both in his attacks on traditional forms of Christianity and in his desire to reform and dream the Christian myth onward.

Jung on evil

It is around the doctrine of evil and the dark side of the God-image that Jung gets into conflict with theologians, and many Christians alike will have to start their wrestling with Jung there. For Jung, the human Self, as the symbol or image of God in man, psychologically encapsulates both good and evil. "For in the self good and evil are indeed closer than identical twins!"[33] To clarify Jung's position and how it differs from a Christian view, we turn to Jungian analyst and Episcopal priest John A. Sanford (1929–2005), and his mentor and analyst Fritz Künkel (1889–1956).

Sanford, influenced by Künkel's position, described it as Jung's having misunderstood the *privatio boni* to mean a denial of evil. Instead, explains Sanford, the Christian doctrine shows how evil came into being and what kind of existence it has.

---

[32] Homans, *Jung in Context*, 131.

[33] C.G. Jung, *Psychology and Alchemy*, ¶ 24.

He contends the existence of evil is not denied in this doctrine; the scripture is full of examples of it and the devil is seen as a real and active agent in human life. Evil is allowed for the higher purposes of God and relates rather to the freedom and choice given us as humans. Künkel's position differs fundamentally from the Jungian in that it does not ascribe evil to the human Self but to the *egocentricity* of the human being.

Evil is not understood as an intrinsic part of God or in its reflection in the human self of man. Rather, evil is to be found in deviation from the Self, from our center and totality, in the focus on our ego's longing to fulfill its endless desires and needs related to our position and status in the world. Egocentricity is an individual's going beyond God's will, putting himself instead at the center. In contemporary terminology, it is our narcissism that produces evil, not God. The origins of evil are not God-given nor born into human selves, but found in our childhood traumas, in our own grappling with egocentric fears and longings.

Jung in correspondence

Another way to illuminate the intimate and at times complex nature of Jung's working through of Christianity is to consider his private letters of correspondence. Throughout his life, Jung was an active correspondent. It is in his letters that one often finds a more uncensored voice, one that expresses itself freely on matters close to the heart, and without deference to an audience or his scientific persona.

Jung's friendship with Dominican priest Victor White (1902–1960) has been thoroughly documented, analyzed, and interpreted by another Jungian scholar and conversation partner in this book, Ann Conrad Lammers. Her book *In God's Shadow: The Collaboration of Victor White and C.G. Jung* (1994) brings to life the tender, fruitful, and complicated exchange between the two friends and colleagues, providing a view to a pioneering exchange between the fields of Catholic theology and analytical psychology.

Jung—initially excited about the learned Catholic theologian, Thomist, and scholar showing interest in and appreciation for his psychological thought—wrote to White early in their correspondence: "You are to me a white raven inasmuch as you are the only theologian I know who has really understood something of what the problem of psychology in our present world means. You have seen its enormous implications."[34]

Significantly, Lammers places Jung as working within the context of the Protestant Reformed tradition. She writes that "Jung's own path was through the wilderness of Protestantism,"[35] and further, that "Jung was thus genuinely a Protestant, not in the sense that he regularly went to church . . . but by temperament and ingrained intellectual habit."[36] This decisive placement of Jung's work within the spirit and tradition of Protestantism are points that Murray Stein also emphasizes in some of his writing.

Though Lammers and Stein largely agree on Jung's formative influences, Lammers does not subscribe to Stein's hypothesis of Jung as a psychotherapist of Christianity. Acknowledging that Jung at times viewed himself as a therapist of the Christian faith, she reminds us of the guiding principles he had established for himself as a clinician: first, the patient must be *seeking* treatment; the therapist, moreover, must learn and use the language of the patient. On the discrepancies at issue in Jung's approach, she remarks: "First, the institution of the Western church did not come to Jung asking for help, and so was not truly accessible to his care. Second, Jung could not act as a therapist if he failed in one of the basic conditions he required of himself as a doctor . . . we have seen that to a great degree he rejected the church's language."[37] Jung's proposed treatment, Lammers suggests, may have been originally biased by his outright refusal of the "conceptual coinage of theology."[38]

Lammers's book offers rich insights into Jung's own rendering of Christianity, but also highlights the difficulties of bridge-building between

---

[34] C.G. Jung, *C.G. Jung Letters*, Vol. 1, *1906–1950*, ed. Gerhard Adler and Aniela Jaffé, trans. R. F. C. Hull (London: Routledge Kegan & Paul, 1973), 383.
[35] Ann Lammers, *In God's Shadow: The Collaboration of Victor White and C.G. Jung* (New York: Paulist Press, 1994), 135.
[36] Lammers, *In God's Shadow*, 138–39.
[37] Lammers, *In God's Shadow*, 151.
[38] Lammers, *In God's Shadow*, 151.

the field of analytical psychology and theology. The creative collaboration and bridge-building between White and Jung would eventually break down following White's critical review of *Answer to Job*, although the two would privately reconcile their friendship before White's early death.

Another important lifelong correspondence of Jung's that centers on the exchange between Christian theology and analytical psychology—this time with the Protestant side of the Christian tradition—is documented in the book *On Theology and Psychology: The Correspondence of C.G. Jung and Adolf Keller* (2020), by Swiss historian Marianne Jehle-Wildberger. Adolf Keller (1872–1963) was a lifelong friend of Jung's, a celebrated Protestant theologian in his time as well as a pioneer of the modern ecumenical movement. Their friendship spanned half a century, and their correspondence documents and offers unique insight into the development of Jung's psychological theory, and especially its relationship to Christianity.

Their private and rich exchange is full of insights into how analytical psychology and Christian faith can enrich one another, but also how they at times stand in conflict. The tension between knowledge (*gnosis*) and faith (*pistis*) is at times put in flesh in these two individuals, who learn to agree to disagree on fundamental positions. In response to receiving one of the first copies of *Answer to Job* in August of 1951, Keller, always gentle but unafraid of confronting Jung, asks a poignant question: "Will the religious motif of integration, or totality, possess the same religious binding power as the need for forgiveness, for personal fellowship, for salvation instead of for insight, for sanctifying transformation instead of for complementary 'becoming whole'?"[39]

To my mind, this is a question as significant for Jungians and Christians to ask today as it was fifty years ago. With the publication of the

[39] C. G. Jung and Adolf Keller, "Letter 42," in *On Theology and Psychology: The Correspondence of C.G. Jung and Adolf Keller*, ed. Marianne Jehle-Wildberger, trans. Heather McCartney and John Peck (Princeton, NJ: Princeton University Press, 2020), 179.

Keller–Jung letters, we have access to a correspondence that promises to continue to inspire and offer rich insight for further research in our field of study.

Jung's dream of the temple

Regarding more contemporary scholars working in this field, I would like to single out the writings of Berlin-based Jungian analyst and scholar Wolfgang Giegerich. In Giegerich's collected works, *Dreaming the Myth Onwards: C.G. Jung on Christianity and on Hegel* (2020), one finds a collection of essays offering poignant points of critique of many of Jung's central interpretations and reformulations of Christian thinking. In particular, I have found his essay "Jung's Millimeter: Feigned Submission—Clandestine Defiance: Jung's Religious Psychology" particularly helpful in preparing questions for the conversations in this book.

The essay offers an analysis of a dream shared in *Memories, Dreams, Reflections*, which Jung himself claimed led him to write *Answer to Job*. In the later part of this dream, Jung's dream-protagonist is together with his father, who to Jung's surprise is presented as a distinguished scholar of theology, inside what looks like the exact replica of the *divan-i-kaas* (the council hall of Sultan Akbar at Fatephur Sikri, which Jung had visited during his trip to India), the whole forming a gigantic mandala.

From the center, Jung's dream-I sees a steep flight of stairs ascending to a spot high up on the wall, "which no longer corresponded to reality." At the top of the stairs is a small door, and Jung's dream-father announces, "Now I will lead you into the highest presence." His father kneels and touches his forehead to the floor. "I imitated him, likewise kneeling, with great emotion. For some reason I could not bring my forehead quite down to the floor—there was perhaps a millimetre to spare."[40]

Suddenly, Jung understands (perhaps his father had told him, he explains) that the upper door led to the solitary chamber where lived Uriah,

---

[40] Jaffé and Jung, *Memories, Dreams, Reflections*, 245.

King David's loyal general, whom David shamelessly betrayed in the Old Testament[41] to steal Uriah's wife, Bathsheba. Jung offers an interpretation of this scene wherein he likens Uriah to a prefiguration of Christ, the God-man—like Job, abandoned by God. Only later, Jung explains, did he understand that this allusion to Uriah in the dream signified that Jung would have to speak publicly about the ambivalence of the God-image in the Old Testament, and that his wife Emma would be taken from him in death. Jung appears to identify with Uriah, writing: "These were the things that awaited me, hidden in the unconscious. I had to submit to this fate, and ought really to have touched my forehead to the floor, so that my submission would be complete."[42]

But what about the millimeter? Jung's thinking about what prevents him from bowing entirely to the floor, being a millimeter away, is that it was human freedom: "Something in me was defiant and determined not to be a dumb fish." He likens his own to Uriah's and Job's faith: If there were not something of the sort in free men, no Book of Job would have been written. "Man always has some mental reservation even in the face of divine decrees. Otherwise, where would be his freedom? And what would be the use of that freedom if it could not threaten Him who threatens it?"[43] Jung concludes his self- interpretation by observing that the dream discloses the idea of the creature that surpasses its creator by a small decisive factor. The relationship between Jung's ego and the God-image becomes one that appears to involve a certain competition.

Let us now turn to Giegerich's radically different interpretation of this important (for our topic) late dream of Jung's. In Giegerich's interpretation the sincere submission to the authority of God enacted by Jung's dream-father was not accessible to Jung's dream-I at the time of this dream. Touching his forehead to the ground would have meant a complete submission bowing down to the suffering God-man Uriah (whom he

[41] 2 Samuel 11:1-12, 23

[42] Jaffé and Jung, *Memories, Dreams, Reflections*, 246–47.

[43] Jaffé and Jung, *Memories, Dreams, Reflections*, 247.

interestingly enough never sees in the dream; faith is belief in the invisible). "Jung, condoning and ennobling the defiant behavior of the dream-I as its demonstration of freedom, is not ready to show the humility that would be a prerequisite for acknowledging the image of suffering man as '*the highest presence*.'"[44] There is still some reservation, a lack of humility: a millimeter remains between Jung and surrender to what the dream describes as the highest presence.

In order to further illustrate his point about Jung's faith (or lack thereof) in the dream , Giegerich borrows a theological concept from the great Protestant reformer Martin Luther: his "theology of the cross" (*theologia crucis*) versus a "theology of glory" (*theologia gloriae*). Giegerich writes: "If it would not have been Uriah but a majestic God who was the highest presence, Jung could have willingly touched his forehead to the ground without hesitation."[45] He goes on to say that in his whole psychological thought, Jung could not go the "way of Uriah." He could not face a "psychology of the cross" (*psychologia crucis*) within the spirit of *kenosis* and self-emptying, and thereby access the humility necessary to bow down to the suffering God-man (Uriah as a refiguration of Jesus). In Giegerich's interpretation, "He [Jung] went the way of the numinous God-image in the psyche, represented by mandalas and other splendid symbols"[46] and a psychology of glory.

To summarize, Jung's dream-I refused to humble himself before God. In Jung's own interpretation, he identified instead with the suffering Uriah; that is, his fate would be like Uriah's: betrayed and without his wife. He feigned total submission and hailed his resistance, which takes the form of a defiant attitude, in terms of human freedom. Defiance is Jung's final answer to the God who takes the form of a suffering servant—and to his millimeter distance from accepting a psychology of the cross.

---

[44] Jaffé and Jung, *Memories, Dreams, Reflections*, 247.

[45] Wolfgang Giegerich, *Dreaming the Myth Onwards: C.G. Jung on Christianity and on Hegel*, Vol. 6, *The Collected English Papers of Wolfgang Giegerich*, ed. Wolfgang Giegerich (London: Routledge, 2020), 13.

[46] Giegerich, *Dreaming the Myth Onwards*, 13.

The conversations

The conversations published in this book were initially recorded and made available for the podcast *Psychology & The Cross*. The podcast is an initiative I started a few years back as part of my own research and writing within the field of Jungian psychology and Christian faith. It became a medium for establishing a dialogue with Jungian analysts and scholars who have spent much more time than I have wrestling with these matters.

The decision to put some of these conversations into print has also to do with the limits of the podcast medium, and the realization that some of the insights brought to light in these recorded meetings merit further study and I believe more attention also from the Jungian community. Publishing edited versions of these conversations in printed form is an attempt to plant seeds in firm soil so that they might continue to engage a wider range of individuals within the Jungian community, as well as people further interested in the fields of theology, philosophy, and Christian faith.

Each of these thirteen conversations starts with a background story, with the scholar sharing a little bit about their engagement with analytical psychology and eventual relationship to organized religion. The conversation then goes deeper, into the specific area of study of a given interlocutor, before it begins to ambulate around Jung's engagement with Christianity, the questions he was asking, and his attempts at answering them throughout his life.

Given its importance for Jung, the concept of the *imitatio Christi* and Jung's rendering of it is a recurring theme to which many of these conversations circle back. In some of these conversations, specific dreams from Jung's life are discussed, such as the one- millimeter dream analyzed by Giegerich, as well as his provocative statement later in life, in answer to BBC journalist John Freeman, when asked in an interview filmed at his home in Küsnacht:

Freeman: Did you believe in God?

Jung: Oh, yes!

> Freeman: Do you now believe in God?
>
> Jung: Now? Difficult to answer . . . I know. I don't need to believe; I know.[47]

As you will learn from the following conversations, no two scholars make the same sense of Jung's claims about God here. The wrestling continues.

Participating analysts and scholars

Murray Stein, renowned Jungian analyst, scholar, and author, is my former teacher at ISAPZürich and was the first person I invited to engage in a conversation about C.G. Jung and Christianity. In our exchange, Murray shares his story of growing up as the son of a pastor, and his journey into Jungian psychology. He offers a dynamic perspective on how analytical psychology and Christian faith can be complementary to each other, and shares key insights from his seminal work *Jung's Treatment of Christianity: The Psychotherapy of a Religious Tradition* (1985).

Ann Conrad Lammers and I discuss the correspondence between Dominican friar Victor White and C.G. Jung, which she meticulously considered in her excellent study *In God's Shadow: The Collaboration of Victor White and C.G. Jung* (1994). Ann explains how the relationship between White and Jung developed, what questions they wrestled with in their fifteen-year friendship, and what difficulties they faced in venturing to build a bridge between psychology and theology. In this conversation, Ann reveals parts of her personal experiences working through Christian faith and Jungian psychology.

---

[47] C.G. Jung, "Face to Face: Carl Jung," interview by John Freeman, *Face to Face*, BBC, October 22, 1959, video, 38:00, https://www.bbc.co.uk/iplayer/episode/p04qhvyj/face-to-face-carl-jung.

Sean J. McGrath is a colleague from my training in Zürich, where he was doing research at the Jung Institute. A former Catholic monk, he has published widely on the history of the ideas and the philosophy of religion, most recently *Political Eschatology* (2023). He is professor of philosophy at Memorial University of Newfoundland and an adjunct professor of religious studies at McGill University. He helps in our conversation to correct some misunderstandings in relation to Jung's view of evil and the feminine. He illuminates where psychology ends and faith begins, and warns us of psychological absolutism when addressing these matters.

Jason E. Smith released a very insightful book with Chiron Publications in 2020, entitled *Religious but Not Religious: Living a Symbolic Life*. In reading the book, I was moved by his authentic account of a very personal wrestling with the Buddhist and Christian traditions. Jason generously shares some parts of his personal story before helping us get a deeper view on Jung's engagement with Christianity and the possibilities of interplay between the worlds of analytical psychology and Christian faith.

Amy Cook has written one of the most insightful books I have read about Jung in the last year, entitled *Jung and Kierkegaard: Researching a Kindred Spirit in the Shadows* (2018). Jung dismissed Kierkegaard, but Amy shows that if he had taken the time, there could have been great overlaps and possible syntheses between their works. We discuss their respective renderings of the *imitatio Christi*, and the question of whether analytical psychology represents a break with Christianity or a possible continuation of it.

Bernard Sartorius was my first analyst during my Jungian training in Zürich. He has a background in the Christian ministry and long experience as a scholar of theology and Islamic Studies. His book *The Orthodox Church* was included as the tenth volume of the series *Les Grandes Religions Du Monde*. Our conversation steps around the psychological differences between Christian and Muslim faith. We discuss Jung's view on Islam, the psychological motive of surrender, and Jung's statement, in the notorious BBC interview, about God: "I don't need to believe; I know."

David Tacey is a celebrated Jungian scholar who has written more than fourteen books at the intersection of analytical psychology, spirituality, and religious faith. David is someone I had long wanted to have a conversation with, ever since I read his critiques of the work of James Hillman. David shared a few stories about his analysis with Hillman prior to the conversation recorded in this book (such anecdotes may yet be found in the relevant podcast episode). In our conversation here, he delves into his understanding of Jung as a prophet for a new age, revealing his views on the problems Christianity faces today.

Kenneth Kovacs is a pastor in the Presbyterian Church (U.S.A.), author, and a Jungian analyst-in-training. He received his doctorate in practical theology from the University of St. Andrews, St. Andrews, Scotland. I first met Kenneth at a small symposium on analytical psychology in Rome. Kenneth has researched the important collaboration and correspondence between Jung and his long-term friend and correspondent, the Swiss theologian Adolf Keller. Kenneth shares with us some of the insights from their conversation, warns us of the dangers of a literal imitation of Christ, and shares his thinking about how the Church and analytical room can mutually enrich their exchanges.

Donald Carveth is not a Jungian but a renowned psychoanalyst in his own right, who has written extensively on the question of conscience, superego, and guilt in the psychoanalytic room. In 2013 he published the book *The Still Small Voice: Psychoanalytic Reflections on Guilt and Conscience* (Karnac Publishing). The conversation with Donald enlarges the discussion to include how the psychoanalytic process can be understood alongside the Christian story. This conversation left me with a taste for more, so I invited him to have a separate conversation with Sean McGrath and myself, on Jung's forementioned essay "A Psychological View of Conscience."

Paul Bishop is a renowned scholar of C.G. Jung, Friedrich Nietzsche, and Johann Wolfgang Goethe. I have had two separate conversations with him for the podcast, the first one about *Faust* and Friedrich Nietzsche's influence on Jung, the second about Jung's late provocative work *Answer to Job.* This latter conversation I decided to publish in this book, as it will help us better understand this important work of Jung and its place within the Jungian canon.

Pia Chaudhari holds a doctorate in theology from the Department of Psychiatry and Religion at Union Theological Seminary in New York. Her research interests include theological anthropology, depth psychology, processes of healing, and the engagement with aesthetics and beauty. She is a founding co-chair of the Analytical Psychology and Orthodox Christianity Consultation (APOCC). Her book *Dynamis of Healing: Patristic Theology and the Psyche* was published in 2019 by Fordham University Press.

Jung's Treatment of Christianity, with Murray Stein

"You know, the reason I became an analyst—I was ordained as a minister—and it wasn't that I lost my faith, or went sour on the Christian ministry. It was because I felt that Jungian psychology went deeper into the source of people's needs and problems. And as an analyst, I could go there with them."

—Murray Stein

JL: Dear Murray, could you share something about how you yourself first got in contact with Jung's psychology, and what your own experience of Christian faith has been?

MS: Well, I was born into a Christian family. My father was a Baptist preacher. And so I grew up in a parsonage, very much in the Church. We attended church three times a week: Sunday morning, Sunday night, and Wednesday evening. And I memorized a lot of bible verses. The Bible was my geography more than where we lived, because we moved around quite a bit to different places as my father went up the ladder in the ministry. And so I became very familiar with the Bible. When I visited Israel some years ago, I felt very at home there because of the names. It's a familiar territory, because I grew up in and with Bethlehem and Jerusalem and Jericho—and all those places—Egypt, the Promised Land. When I went to college, of course, I was exposed to the modern intellectual world in a very powerful and convincing way. Before that, in high school—I had some very good teachers—we studied Greek tragedies and world history and philosophy, but university studies open the mind to the world of the great thinkers in a more expansive way. And so my baseline perspective began to change, and I became oriented more to that world of Western modern thinking than to biblical perspectives. I still maintained a connection to the Church and attended Sunday services regularly at Battel Chapel in Yale University, where I listened attentively to the great preacher William Sloane Coffin, who was all about social action.

This was in the [19]60s, right in the midst of the civil rights and the anti-war movements. It was a very dramatic and emotionally engaging time to be young in America. After graduating with a bachelor's degree in English, I went up the hill to Yale Divinity School, and it was at that time that I began to hear about Jung. One of the professors taught a course in psychology and religion, and he offered a course comparing Augustine's *Confessions* and Jung's *Memories, Dreams, Reflections*. Jung was being studied in the religious studies departments of universities but was not welcome in the psychology departments. This is still largely the case in American universities.

Between my second and third years at the Divinity School—this was 1967–68—I took a sabbatical year and went to Washington, DC, where I was an intern at the Church of the Savior and worked in the War-on-Poverty program that was in full swing at that time. On the staff of the church, whose pastor was the charismatic Gordon Cosby, there was a person named Elizabeth O'Connor who had recently published a book titled *Journey Inward, Journey Outward*. In her work, she used Jung's ideas a lot and connected them up with her Christian commitments to an inner life of prayer and reflection and an outer life of engagement on behalf of social justice. At a Sunday afternoon garden party, sometime in early 1968, out of the blue and in response to our talk about the causes of war so endemic to human history, she suggested that we look to Jung for insight into shadow projection as a possible cause of war among peoples and nations. The next day I went to a local bookstore and found *Memories, Dreams, Reflections*. I took it home and couldn't put it down. I was hooked instantly, and I confess I have never turned back. To this day,

I find that book, composed by Aniela Jaffé out of passages from Jung's works and conversations with her, utterly captivating.

At the same time, there was a small work group at the Church of the Savior engaged with the question: *where am I?* It was my first experience in this kind of group. It was not quite a therapy group, but it was open to sharing personal experiences and questions about where one found oneself in life at this particular moment. I had never reflected on my life in a psychological way before, and this too was an eye-opener. It was the combination of this type of personal reflection and reading *Memories, Dreams, Reflections*, where I became aware of the significance of dreams for the first time, that really drew me powerfully to Jung. And so, really, it was in this Christian context that I became exposed to Jung.

When I went back to Yale Divinity School with my wife—I had gotten married during the year in DC—the first person I ran into on campus was a professor named Russell Becker. He was in charge of Pastoral Psychology and was also just back from a sabbatical year that he had spent in Zürich, Switzerland at the C.G. Jung Institute. And he came back to his work all fired up about Jungian psychology and how it could be applied in his pastoral counseling ministry. He offered and I accepted instantly to go into therapy with him. Through the rest of the academic year, we met twice a week and worked on my dreams. And also I took a half-time job at the New Haven Mental Health Center, which was run by Yale Medical School, and worked on a team with psychiatrists, social workers, and psychologists treating in-patient and out-patient clients in what was called a therapeutic community. Here I was exposed to the world of *mental health*, something that was entirely foreign to my previous work and life experience. And in that year, too, I became acquainted with Jungian training programs. I had no idea such a profession existed before this time. As book review editor for a newly created YDS journal, I read and reviewed a book titled *Insearch* by James Hillman. It was James Hillman's contribution to psychology and religion—still my favorite book by Hillman. At the time, he was Director of Training at the Jung Institute in Zürich. After reading his book, I wrote to him and asked if it would be possible for me to come and study in

Zürich, and he replied with a very positive and welcoming invitation, so that's how I came to leave for Zürich after graduation from YDS in 1969.

Looking back, I see this all as a synchronistic process. Without conscious planning or knowing, one thing simply led to another, doors that I didn't even know existed opened in front of me, and in the end, I was able to study at the Jung Institute in Zürich for four years, from 1969 to 1973. I then came back to the United States, began practicing as an analyst, and ended up in Chicago, where I took a doctorate at the University of Chicago—in a department called Religion and Psychological Studies—under Peter Homans's direction. While I was in the program at the U of C, Peter Homans wrote a book called *Jung in Context*. He had previously written a book titled *Theology After Freud*, and now he was taking up the cultural context of psychoanalysis with specific reference to Jung. He wasn't a Jungian by any means, but he was interested in how Jung's psychology fit into the picture of modernity and in how it is, in a sense, a product of modernity. The U of C was heavily influenced by the *social construction of reality* idea, which looks at cultural movements like psychoanalysis as byproducts of cultural forces. It is somewhat deterministic and reductive, but Homans handles these ideas sensitively in his book on Jung. He argues that depth psychology replaces moribund religions for some people in modernity. *Jung in Context* situates Jung's work within the context of modernity as it was developing in the nineteenth and twentieth century. As religion declines in the West, psychology (and psychoanalysis) takes off and develops its concepts and practices, and this becomes attractive to people who are looking for a new way to fulfill their spiritual needs. These are now fulfilled by analysis rather than by traditional religious activities.

That was my early experience as a Jungian analyst in the making. I loved Jung, and I could identify with Jung. He was also the son of a pastor and grew up in a parsonage. However, my father didn't have the problems with religion that Jung's father had. He was passionate about his ministry as a pastor, and he really believed in the gospel he preached three times a week. My mother was beside him and also was a believer. So I didn't have the same problems that Jung had with his father and mother. While I had quite a positive relationship to my father, I felt I outgrew him in a way, because he was very contained within the evangelical Christian framework. I stepped into the modern world, on the other hand, and became a Jungian psychoanalyst, a member of a very modern profession. My father did not discourage me from going there, but I don't think he understood what I was doing.

And so, I had to separate a bit from my father and his religion. But I took with me a lot of the things that I had been taught as a child, and particularly an appreciation of the Bible. I still like to read the Bible. I've written a book about the Bible, *The Bible as Dream*, which is an interpretation of the biblical narrative from Genesis to Revelation as an individuation process of a people.

JL: I would love to delve into your book that you wrote in 1985, Jung's Treatment of Christianity. *And in the acknowledgements of this book, you're thanking your wife for faithfully accompanying you on the long march to securing a very old dream. Could you say something about how that came about? And a little bit about the book, a lovely book?*

MS: Well, the dream was to somehow try to bring Jungian psychology and Christianity together under one cover. The very first book of Jung's that I was ever exposed to was *Psychology and Religion*. And that was by accident. I was looking through the shelves of a public library in Detroit, Michigan, where I finished high school, and I saw a book whose title interested me, *Psychology and Religion*. This was Jung's Terry Lectures that he gave in 1936 at Yale. I took the slim volume home and tried to read it. I had already read Freud's *Interpretation of Dreams*, and I thought, wow, this would be interesting, psychology and religion. But I couldn't understand any of it. It was way over my head. And it took me years to understand and appreciate it. Today, I think it's a marvelous work. Some twenty-five years later, I wrote *Jung's Treatment of Christianity*, which came about as a result of my doctoral studies at the University of Chicago. I had to write a dissertation, and Peter Homans was willing to accompany me on that and act as my advisor. He really let me do what I wanted.

My thought setting out to investigate Jung's writings about Christianity was to ask the question, *what was he doing?* Why did Jung write so much about Christianity, especially after 1938? That year was a turning point, as I discovered. He traveled to India, and while there he had a dream in which he was about to go in search of the Holy Grail. In the dream, he needed to recover the Holy Grail, and he felt that this meant that he had a mission to somehow contribute to the spiritual crisis of modernity by using his knowledge and skill as a psychotherapist. The subtitle of my book is *The Psychotherapy of a Religious Tradition*.

Following his return from India to Europe, he began writing with particular focus about Christian themes: in 1940, he lectured on "A Psychological Approach to the Dogma of the Trinity"; in 1941, he lectured on "Transformation Symbolism in the Mass." Both of these Eranos lectures were extensively reworked and published in later volumes. In 1951, he published *Aion*, which is an interpretation of the Christian tradition from its beginning to the present day, and in 1952 there followed his highly controversial *Answer to Job*, an interpretation of the Bible. After that dream in India, he really becomes much more engaged in Christian themes. In a sense, all of his late works are very occupied with the topic of Christianity.

And I wanted to know, what was he trying to do? This was for [Jung] obviously not a mere intellectual exercise. Then one day, suddenly, I realized that he was applying his therapeutic method to Christianity. He was taking Christianity as a patient and was relating to Christianity as a patient who is suffering from the problem of one-sidedness, the source of neurosis. Christianity has divided psychic wholeness and created a split between the anima and the animus (the masculine and feminine) and good and evil. It has in its collective mentality identified with one side and rejected the other: masculine *logos* over feminine *eros* and the good over evil. The opposites do not disappear; they are repressed and cause psychological conflicts that lead to neurotic behavior. This is what Jung saw in his father and in the tradition. As a healer, it would be his task, then, to offer his analysis and interpretation and to show a way forward to an integration of the opposites. This would be a further development of the Christian collective personality toward the state of wholeness, the final terminal of the individuation process.

If you look at Dante's *Commedia*, for instance, there are the three levels of Afterlife: the *Inferno*, where the souls of unrepentant sinners are condemned for eternity (that's the realm of Satan); the *Purgatorio*, where the repentant sinners' souls are going through a cleansing process and gradually moving upward toward Heaven; and *Paradiso*, where the graduates of Purgatory and the Saints dwell with the Godhead. Dante makes his way through all these levels, and finally he has his great vision of the Trinity and his experience of Divine Love at the end. In a sense, he is integrating the levels as he goes, but the souls in Hell are forever cut off from the souls in Heaven. The base level (shadow and evil) is never connected or brought into relationship with the upper levels. Darkness and light remain forever apart. That's the medieval worldview, and that's what Christianity had developed. Modernity of course abandoned all of that mythology and declared the transcendent world null and void. Materialism replaced spirituality, and that's where we are today. But Jung wasn't satisfied with the modern spirit and sought to reach back to the ancient revelation and bring it into the postmodern worldview. This was his mission, his quest for the Holy Grail.

So the question he asked was, Is there a way for Christianity to take a further step on the road to wholeness? To move from the Three to the Four? The individuation process begins in wholeness and ends with wholeness. The opposites that develop during the process are united once again in the final stage of individuation. In the middle, the task is one of holding the tension of the opposites in anticipation of the mandala of wholeness that will bring them into harmony. That's where we are today with Christianity. The opposites are still in tension and we need to hold them so until a resolution can emerge. Actually, that is anticipated in the Book of Revelation, where John is shown a vision of a New Heaven and a New Earth and the descent of the Holy City of Jerusalem descending like a Bride from Heaven to Earth, uniting spirit and matter, above and below, with the Transcendent dwelling in the midst of it. But that state of wholeness has not yet occurred within humanity or in the Christian tradition. We still wait for it.

In the last chapter of my book, I speculated on how Christianity might move forward toward this state of wholeness concretely, by recognizing the feminine in the Godhead and in the Church's practices, and by facing the shadow and working further to integrate evil. That was a big one for Jung: the problem of evil and what to do with it, how we think about evil, and how to relate to evil in a way that embraces rather than represses it. Jung felt that evil was a very powerful force, and the problem was how to be with it, how to deal with it, and how to bring it in relation to the good. That's the problem.

JL: It's thirty-six years since your book was published. I was wondering about how you look at the treatment and Jung's treatment. And if you look at it—if your view has changed somewhat, or if it still stands.

MS: My view of what Jung was doing in these late writings hasn't changed. My personal view of what's going on in Christianity today is very limited. I have not followed the theological trends after Barth, Bultmann, and Tillich. To me, it now looks very divided between right-wing and left-wing political trends, especially in the United States, with such strong support of people like Donald Trump, on the one hand, and pro-choice, BLM, and LGBTQ supporters on the other. And yet you have the mainstream Protestant churches, and the part of the Catholic Church that supports what Pope Francis is talking about, helping the disadvantaged, trying to decrease the huge gap between the rich and the poor that exists in the world today, integrating diversity and bringing women more into the foreground of the Church's authority. In some of the Protestant churches there are a lot of women clergy now; that was never seen before. When I was a student at Yale Divinity School, I think we had only three or four female students in my class who were studying for the Master's in Divinity (MDiv). That was the basic degree that would qualify one for ordination as a minister in the Protestant churches. Nowadays, YDS classes are more or less evenly divided between women and men. Of course, the same thing happened in the medical school and law school. Many women have entered the professions as a result of the feminist movement, and the Protestant clerical ranks have been affected. To a lesser degree in the Catholic Church, but still significantly nowadays, women are being elevated into positions of more authority and higher levels of participation.

JL: In your book Jung's Treatment of Christianity, *you also say something. I will quote it and I thought it was very interesting. You say:* . . . [W]*hat Jung foresaw as the future evolution of the Christian tradition could perhaps most accurately be thought of as the child of Christianity and the grandchild of Judaism. It would be at this generation of this great Judeo-Christian religious tradition, Jung would have hoped that a new religion would represent, I have suggested, a therapeutic transformation of Christianity: partially Christianity's child, and partly quite different from its own unique religious tradition.*

MS: Well, I think I had in mind certain movements within Christianity that were a departure, and yet not—that maybe went in the direction of New Age spirituality—that combined Buddhist practices (for instance, meditation practices) with Christian piety—and that this evolution toward a kind of world religion would come out of Christianity, would combine elements of Christianity with other religious traditions and form something new. That isn't an idea unique to me at all.

There's a much-quoted letter from Jung to Max Zeller, a student of his who had sent him a dream, in which Jung speculated that a new religion would form in about six hundred years. In the meantime, he said, individuals are creating their own spiritualities from their inner work on their dreams and using active imagination. Eventually, this will become a new world religion. So I think that was in the back of my mind, that for Christians this new religion, which combined private inner work whether in formal analysis or not and used dreams and active imagination, and also related that to the traditional Christian background of belief in Christ, would eventually produce a new form of religiosity that would be a grandchild of Judaism and a child of Christianity. I look at Christianity as the child of Judaism. It comes out of the Jewish tradition. All the—Jesus and the apostles—were all born as Jews, and assumed this new religious attitude, formed a child (Christianity). And then there would be a grandchild in this next stage.

JL: Some years ago, when I was going deeply into [Martin] *Luther, I contacted you with some questions, and you shared with me this beautiful paper that you wrote that I didn't know of, "Jungian Psychology and the Spirit of Protestantism." And could you share a little bit about in what way you see Jungian psychology as working within this spirit of Protestantism? And maybe we could also touch a bit on Jung's rendering of this Christian concept of the imitation of Christ—which I find very, very interesting, how you explore that—and Jung's interpretation of that.*

MS: I start with the fact that Jung grew up in a very Christian Protestant context—not Lutheran, however, but Swiss Reformed as shaped by the theology of John Calvin in Geneva and Ulrich Zwingli in Zürich. Jung's his father was a pastor in this denomination, and he had six uncles who were ministers as well. His maternal grandfather, Samuel Preiswerk, was a very well-known figure as head pastor (known as the antistes) in the Basel Minster, the most important Swiss Protestant Church in Basel and for that matter in Switzerland. As a child and young man, Jung was steeped in Christian tradition, and he absorbed this influence deeply. It shaped him as a thinker, without doubt. When he set about doing his creative psychological work, that is, after Freud, it was inevitable that some of those religious and theological constructs would play a background role. One feature of Jung's mature psychological theory and practice was that it focused very much on the individual and the individual's relationship with the Self. That is precisely the Protestant attitude about the relationship between the individual and God: the individual's relationship to God is direct and unmediated by priest or community. You communicate directly with God in prayer, and God sees you as an individual and relates to you as such. This was a central feature of the Protestant Reformation in all of its forms, Lutheran, Reformed, Anabaptist, and all others.

This emphasis on individual responsibility and access to the Divine is very much a feature of Protestantism, and when Jung gets around to doing his type of psychoanalysis, he underlines this point over and over again. He values the numinous experience of the individual above all else, and he is guided by revelations of the Divine will that come to the individual in dreams and active imagination. In addition, he argues that individual consciousness is a higher form of consciousness than collective consciousness. You go into any collective, be it into a mob, a political rally, a church, or a meditation center with a guru in charge, the level of consciousness in people is reduced. It becomes controlled by collective attitudes and influences, and Jung rates this a lower form of consciousness that pertains when the individual is alone. The individual's consciousness is the highest form of consciousness. Individuation is a project carried out by individuals, albeit in relation to other people and to the collective. The individual is the final arbiter of value and personal meaning.

Jung also brings the idea of destiny into his psychological theory. We are born with a destiny. That idea is shared with Calvinism, where the individual is eternally predestined to be one of the chosen for salvation or not. When he speaks about the destiny of the individual, he is referring to guidance of the individuation process from a quasi-divine source, the Self. The Self is in charge of the individuation process. Jung's concept of synchronicity, too, is very close to what I grew up with as *answers to prayer*, or *divine interventions in history* or *grace*. It's like this: You're going down a certain path in life, and suddenly something happens by accident that's very meaningful, and your direction changes utterly. And this turns out to be your future. Most of our big turning points in life come about through synchronistic events, meaningful coincidences. It's how we meet our partners; it's how we choose our careers. When Jung's MDR fell into my hands at the chance comment of Elizabeth O'Connor, it changed my life. When I read it, I thought, wow, this is a whole new world I want to look into, and it led me to Zürich and into my now fifty years as a Jungian psychoanalyst.

Jung's emphasis on the individual and his negative feeling about collectives have carried over into the Jungian world, where a sense of community is rather undernourished. Jung experimented a bit with the notion of community among the analyzed in founding The Psychology Club in Zürich, where his patients and students could come together and meet with each other, listen to lectures, and interact. They also enjoyed parties at Christmas and other occasions, so there was an amount of socializing and hilarity among them, as we see in photos. It was an attempt to form a community of people who are doing their individual work in analysis and otherwise in isolation. It wasn't a big success. There was such an emphasis on the individual work rather than the relational aspect of psychological life. This is part of our heritage from Jung. And in a sense, that is Protestantism.

JL: Looking the other way around, in your mind, what could Christianity offer analytical psychology?

MS: I think what Christianity offers Jungian psychology would be a clear vision of the relation of the Divine to the human, or as we say in Jungian psychology, the relation of the Self to ego. The gospel is clear that we are not the Master, but we can be in relation to the Master. The clarity of this perspective on the correct relation between ego and Self is so critically important for psychotherapy generally. The danger of a psychotherapy without this perspective is that it creates individualistic monsters, people so ego-powered that relations to the *other* take second place, if even that. James Hillman called this out in his critique of modern psychotherapy. It favors ego-building to the neglect of the archetypal, the myth that gives life meaning, the religious, the numinous. Christianity places centrality on the revelation of God in Christ, with all else falling into place behind or around that numinous point.

Jung well recognized that for the West, Christ is the central symbol of the Self, but he argued that it is not a symbol that embraces the whole of the Self. It excludes, by dogmatic design, the dark, the shadow, evil. It is too cleaned up and too one-sidedly spiritual. It leaves out the body, the material aspect of the Self, and the instinctual. So he proposed a revision. This would be a Christ figure that includes the totality of the psyche. I believe Christian input would be essential in formulating a new self-symbol for the West.

I think another way in which the Christian Church can be helpful to analytical psychology is in developing a sense of community. The idea of an invisible community without boundaries in time and space is needed by the Jungian movement in the world. Jung sometimes spoke of *the invisible church*, that is, a sense of being in community with others not necessarily bounded by an explicit organizational feature or the requirement to get together regularly for rituals, but that exists to foster a sense of unity, or *oneness with others* who are working along the same lines, who are at the same level of consciousness, and are working on themselves in similar ways.

What Christians also have and really prize above all else is their faith in an invisible power, a spiritual source of inspiration, of grace, of comfort, that will always be present to them. I think Jungians could learn from that to strengthen their conviction that faith is necessary for conducting effective Jungian psychoanalysis. As analysts, we place our faith in the Self, in the psyche, such that when we sit down with a patient and conduct analysis, we believe that the answers to the patient's questions and needs will emerge out of their inner world, out of their dreams, and out of the dialogue. That's an act of faith. And I think that needs to be very much stressed in the training programs, namely, that the analyst doesn't have the answers. What the analyst has is faith that the answers will come in due course if we are attentive and patient. Without this faith, you can't work as an analyst.

JL: Coming back to the idea of individuation and the imitatio Christi *that you write about in your paper on Jungian psychology and the spirit of Protestantism. What* [do you think] *about Jung's understanding and rendering of the* imitatio Christi? *Because I think the Christ has something to do with the question of community, no? What does my individuation and becoming who I am, have to do with you and your process? I have a quote from Jung here to share with you. He says:*

> *The* imitatio Christi *has this disadvantage. In the long run, we worship as a divine example a man who embodied the deepest meaning of life. And then, out of sheer imitation, we forget to realize our own highest meaning. The imitation of Christ might well be understood in a deeper sense, namely, as the duty to realize one's best conviction, which is always also a complete expression of the individual temperament, with the same courage and the same self-sacrifice as Jesus did.*

MS: That's the way Jung understood the human being, Jesus of Nazareth, that Jesus had his vocational calling and followed it faithfully to the end. He made his experiment, and he lived it completely. That is what Jung advocates: live your experiment, live your destiny, live your vocation to the best of your ability, no matter what it costs. In Jungian psychology, we talk about myths to live by. Jung tells us in *Memories, Dreams, Reflections* that when he broke with Freud, he reflected on his life and he realized that he didn't know what his myth was. So he needed to discover his myth. Now we have *The Red Book* to study how he pursued his quest for a myth. Along the way, he found many interesting figures in his inner world, and he said these adventures in active imagination were the *prima materia* for his working out his personal myth. Once he found it, he followed it faithfully. In this sense, he was following the understanding he had of the *imitatio Christi*: not following Christ's path, but his own vocational path, as his destiny to its conclusion.

JL: And what happens to Christ, then? I'm just wondering what happens to these values symbolized by Christ as a figure, as we're interpreting it in the way that Jung did?

MS: I think what happens is, if you go deeply into yourself, you find values and images that aren't so different from what Jesus found. In other words, Jesus was living an archetypal pattern and living it out to its fullest extent. We too will find an archetypal pattern that won't be so different from his, but in following it we're not imitating him. If you imitate somebody, you look at what they're doing and then you imitate it, so you're trying to become like them. You don't try to become like yourself, you try to become like them. And this alienates you from yourself. You get cut off from yourself. You cut off large pieces of yourself as a result of imitation. You may gain something from it, of course. People who practice the *imitatio Christi* in the traditional way—experiencing the stigmata, lacerating themselves, carrying the cross—do gain some sense of identification with Jesus in his suffering. But it really alienates them from their own suffering, from their own history, from their childhood, from their parents, from their families. It creates a kind of fictional identity. So they end up living a fantasy life, imagining that they are this man who lived two thousand years ago in a very different culture, a very different time.

That's the problem with literalization of the *imitatio Christi*. I don't think Jung meant to say that it's not good to pay attention to the great values that Jesus talked about, his teachings. Those are all very positive values and represent a very high level of consciousness and what Jung called in his last book, *Mysterium Coniunctionis*, the achievement of a level of consciousness, what Gerhard Dorn called *unio mentalis*. *Unio mentalis* requires separating the soul from the body and connecting it to the spirit, so that you have control over your instincts and you're able to think about them and reflect on them and live them in a conscious way. In this state of consciousness, you have a sense of others as well as yourself and a sense of spiritual values. All of that is a very positive development in a person's life. So Jung isn't against that. He's against the idea of alienating yourself from your own concrete life and history and trying to become something else. He had similar objections to people trying to become Buddhists, or practicing kundalini yoga, or something else that's not in their own tradition. Stick with your tradition, was his advice, live out of your own history and develop that. That's more authentic, and it won't alienate you from yourself and your personal history.

It's interesting that Christ does appear in *The Red Book* right at the end, in Jung's garden literally, behind his house in Küsnacht, which he refers to in the text as Philemon's garden. There is a fascinating conversation between Christ and Philemon, in which Philemon recognizes the superiority of Christ. Christ recognizes Philemon as the Gnostic magician, Simon Magus. In the final line of *The Red Book*, as we have it, Christ declares that what he brings is not a return to Paradise, to peace and harmony, or to a life that is not tormented by the problem of evil. His gift is "the beauty of suffering." It is a telling moment in Jung's realization of his personal myth. It includes a lot of suffering.

I think Christ was an important symbol for Jung. He carried a Bible in his pocket all his life, his grandson told me, and sitting on the train to Zürich, he would pull it out and read a passage. You can see from his writings that he was immersed in the biblical texts, in the biblical world. For Christians like myself—people with a Christian background—Christ will continue to be an important figure in private meditations and religious practices. And I don't personally place him as a figure within the pantheon of symbolic images that the Jungian psychology considers as archetypal figures. For me, personally, he transcends them. But that's my own personal myth speaking. A Hindu or Jewish or Muslim or Buddhist Jungian analyst wouldn't feel the same about Christ. They would put a figure from their religious tradition above the others as a superior figure. I can live with that, and I trust they can live with my preference. We can have friendly dialogues on that understanding, I think.

JL: Much of Jung's legacy seems to me to have to do with his universal psychological theory that he left behind, in these concepts, whether the archetypes, whether the collective unconscious. But could one imagine how Jung's life and psychological project could have looked different if he would have stayed working more within the Christian tradition?

MS: Russell Becker, who was my mentor at Yale Divinity School, once said to me that it's too bad Jung was born in Switzerland. Had he been born in America, he would have had a better appreciation for the Church. The Church in his Swiss experience was so cold and so uninteresting to him. It was so bereft of Spirit. Jung tells us in MDR that when he took his first communion, he returned home disappointed. He was surprised that nothing numinous happened to him. The wine was bitter and the bread was stale. He couldn't really participate in that church.

He felt God had abandoned his Church and was not elsewhere. That's why he had to find a new myth for himself. Somebody once asked him why he didn't become a Roman Catholic, because he showed so much interest in the symbolism, and in wrote response he an essay, "Why I am not a Catholic." He couldn't become a Catholic because he was a Swiss Protestant. Swiss Protestants can't become Catholics. It's impossible. They've been fighting Catholics for centuries. He wanted to go to Rome late in his life, but he fainted at the train station. He couldn't go there.

He outgrew his religious background very early in life. But he always appreciated elements of Christianity. If you read his Zofingia papers, you can see he very much valued the mystical elements in Christianity, of which there is nothing in Swiss Protestantism. Swiss Protestantism took the statues and the stained-glass windows out of the churches and stripped them bare. Everything became focused on theological ideas and the Word. On Sunday mornings, intellectual sermons were presented, and morality was stressed, but the spirit that is carried by symbolism was lost. Jung was sensitive to that. He couldn't really stay within his Protestant tradition.

Other Jungians like John Sanford were able to work within the Christian tradition. John Sanford was a well-known Jungian analyst in the United States and remained an Episcopal priest in San Diego, California to the end of his life. He practiced Jungian analysis as a part of his pastoral work in the Church. And the books he wrote use Jungian psychology to interpret and really make more interesting certain Christian ideas and biblical texts. He was working from inside, not to reform but to add a psychological depth of meaning to the tradition. I've enjoyed his books and have recommended them often.

Coming back to Europe, the debate between Luther and Zwingli was in part and maybe quite largely about a question: Is Christ really present in the communion? The Swiss reformer, Ulrich Zwingli, said decisively, No, this is a memorial service: we are remembering what happened fifteen hundred years ago. Martin Luther, the great German reformer, disagreed: It's a real presence, he stoutly affirmed. Luther thereby retained the mystical element in his Protestant church. The celebration of communion in the Lutheran Church therefore has a numinous quality that the communion service in the Swiss Reformed churches lack. And Jung missed that sense of mystery. At heart, Jung was a mystic. Had he grown up in a more mystical tradition—maybe as a Lutheran in Germany, just across the border from Basel—it would have been more possible for him maybe to work within the received Christian tradition and contribute his psychological work without departing from it or at best contributing from the outside. But Jung was also very much a modern man, and he had broad interests in all the world religions and all human cultures. I think he, in a sense, exceeded all the traditions in history in his thinking. That's the meaning of the theory of archetypes. They are universal, not particular, and all have numinous features. But in his personal practice and in his life, I think Jung stuck pretty close to his ground and to his origins.

JL: I'm also thinking, just to share with you before we end: I think that the title of this podcast will be Psychology and the Cross.

MS: Psychology and the Cross?

JL: Yes, and then something with Jungian underneath. I think it would be something in that vein.

MS: Let me share a story about Jung and the cross. The founder of the Jung Center in Houston, Texas was a woman named Ruth Thacker Fry. She was somewhat eccentric but also quite charismatic, a big woman with flaming red hair. She had met Jung when she studied at the Jung Institute in Zürich in the 1950s. At the celebrations of Jung's eightieth birthday in 1955, which she attended, she was able, after standing in a long line, to shake his hand. She was wearing a necklace with a big cross hanging from it. As Jung recognized her, he took the cross in his big hand and held it there for a moment. And then he said some words that she never forgot: "You know where the place to live is? Right in the center. That's where the opposites come together, right in the center. That's where you must live."

The White Raven: Victor White and C.G. Jung, with Ann Conrad Lammers

"What does it mean for Jung to be a Christian? Those symbols of the Christian Church continued to matter to him deeply. The crucifixion remained a central image in his thinking. And the idea of resurrection, well, he reframed it in terms of winning through to a resurrected body while one is still alive. But that is the kind of language that he would not use if he had abandoned the Christian mythology, the Christian story."

—Ann Conrad Lammers

JL: How did your journey into Jungian psychology, and your scholarship in Christianity, begin?

AL: How did it start? There've been so many chapters in my relationship to C.G. Jung. I think my first hint about him probably came while I was a senior in high school. So, seventeen years old. The wife of one of the senior faculty at the boarding school where I was studying put me up to thinking about Jung's writing about the feminine, because I had given myself an assignment to write an independent study paper, a scholarly paper that was far beyond me. It was more than I knew how to do at that age, but I was fearless and I jumped in. I wanted to write about how women are portrayed in literature. (*Laughs.*) Rather a small topic.

Once I got to studying in seminary, I gravitated immediately to courses on theology and psychology. By that time, I was already a mother of two children, and divorced, and quite invested in the prospect or possibility of ministry, especially therapeutic—therapeutically understood— healing. How would healing come to people from both the psychological and the theological side? I took more than one course on schools of depth psychology, in relation to theology. And that gave me a chance to sink my teeth into some of Jung's writings in graduate-school context, where it was possible to ask difficult questions and get some kind of guidance in how one would approach those answers. It was Jung that took me by the lapels and dragged me deeper; I couldn't stop reading. When I began to think about further graduate study, I was still not through digging into the marriage or bridge or combination that I wanted between theology and psychology. By the time I had done three years at seminary, I had a fair idea about schools of theology. I knew how many different voices there were in the room, even to do any kind of exegesis of a biblical passage. There were many voices in the room.

I was in my later thirties when I began doctoral work at Yale, in their religious studies department. Bless them—they gave me lots of rope to hang myself with. I did an independent program that was permitted under their generous understanding of what their department was for. It included some pretty demanding theological seminars for which I'm ever grateful. And I had to decide for myself what to do about the psychological side of my study program. Well, it was going to be C.G. Jung—there was no question about that. I needed to find some way to make the theology side of the equation and the psychology side talk to each other. And that meant I had, essentially, to find a case study. I was guided to the letters that Jung wrote to Victor White. At that point, we only had Jung's side, and only three quarters of Jung's letters to White had been published. But that was already a lot.

JL: For the people who don't know much about Victor White, maybe only that he was a priest, or that he was a Dominican [priest], *or maybe not even that: Could you give a short introduction to Victor White?*

AL: Victor White was the son of an Anglican priest. He and his father were estranged. There are some clues that make me think that his father was a pretty hard man: hard to love, a hard man to be the son of. And White, who had a calling from early on toward theological study and the ministry, decided to become a Catholic, and did. By the time he was nineteen, he was already a Dominican. He had joined the Dominican order, and he was getting a thorough grounding in philosophy (four years of philosophical coursework before three years, I think, of theological coursework), the very rigorous training that Dominicans were given who came into the order as young people, as White did. He was born in Croydon, part of London now, but his resting place, his permanent place to do his study and teaching, was the Oxford Blackfriars house.

Victor White was a systematic theologian. He was a good, orthodox Thomist. He had done a fair amount of study in neo-scholastic writings, but his own leaning was toward a part of St. Thomas's teaching that prepared him, in a way, to work with Jung, because one of his very important papers was on the concept and process of affective knowledge. Most of St. Thomas's writings are propositional and discursive and logical and rational. But there was a side of Aquinas that dealt in direct, intimate knowledge of God, a leaning toward mysticism, if you like. And it was known for Victor White's purposes as *affective knowledge*. This was very important to White. It prepared him to be open to the experiential and experimental side of learning that made Jung's work congenial to him. And it made him congenial to Jung.

White went through some personal turmoil during the Second World War and began doing Jungian analysis with an analyst in London. John Laird was rather a colorful personality, and he was helpful to White when White first went to see him. It was really an eye-opener for White, who hadn't heard of Jung before. John Laird began informing him about concepts like the shadow.

Well, during the Second World War, which is when all this is going on, you couldn't send a letter to Switzerland, or a package. The mails were not open during the war. It wasn't until 1945—August—that White was able, finally—he'd been preparing himself to write to Jung, and he finally got his chance. He sent Jung four off-prints of papers that he had written about Jung's thought and about Thomas Aquinas. He tried to make a blend, or to bridge over between orthodox Catholic thought in the Thomistic world, and Jungian psychology, depth psychology.

He found several ways that Jung and Aquinas were soulmates. They're both teleological in their thought. They're looking at a final cause. For Jung, the Self is pulling the ego toward its wholeness. That's teleology—the *telos*, the goal. And for Aquinas, following Aristotle, God works teleologically. The whole salvation history is teleology. It's all going toward the ultimate revelation of the kingdom. For White, the payoff would have been that he wanted to make Catholicism—orthodox, theological Christianity—acceptable, usable, helpful to modern human beings, human beings as they are today. Not as they were in Aquinas's day, but as they are now. And so he wanted to bring Jung into his Thomistic world in much the way that Thomas Aquinas brought Aristotle into his theological world. Only problem was, Aristotle had finished his writings by the time Thomas got to him. C.G. Jung was very much a work in process, a man in process. He was still working on things.

JL: And when Victor White reached out to Jung with the first letter, what was Jung seeing in Victor White, then?

AL: When Victor White showed up and sent him those four papers that he had written, Jung thought this was it: He had the collaborator he'd been looking for. Victor White was open to the experimental and pragmatic and empirical science of psychology. Victor White would hear him without distorting the message. And he would learn, in turn, how to use the language that Victor White was an expert in applying. So both of them had a sense of urgency. (Jung, because he was reaching the last years of his life already. Their relationship lasted for fifteen years at the ends of both of their lives. White died very young, of cancer—well, pretty young, in his fifties. And Jung died of old age. They died within a year of each other.)

When they began their collaboration, they both thought that they could save the Christian West—putting it very boldly. They wanted to help the culture, help the civilization, which had just come through this terrible war.

JL: So what about the white raven? Jung's description of Victor White?

AL: Well, he's making a nice little pun. But he's also referring to the passage in Kings, I think, the first book of Kings, where Elijah is fed by ravens. He's out in the wilderness, dying, and ravens bring him his food. So White was a gift from God, bringing Jung, out in the wilderness all alone (the voice of the prophet who is not wanted in his own country), his sustenance. That's why White is a white raven. And of course, it's important that it should be a white raven, not a black one. Black ones are bad luck, as we know, and a portent of death.

JL: Right. When you said that now, I thought of that famous picture, the photo of the two, that you also have printed in your book. Victor White is in his black dress and Jung is dressed in white.

AL: Yes. And when Victor White looked at that photograph, according to one of his friends, Aelred Squire, he pointed to that picture and made a wisecrack about it. He said, "There's God and the unconscious." *God and the Unconscious* is the name of one of Victor White's books. So here's a picture: Jung is God; White is the unconscious, the one in the shadow.

They had about five years of really positive collaboration. What happened right away was that, extraordinarily, Jung invited White to come and stay with him at Bollingen, at the tower. That just didn't happen off the bat, with every stranger who wrote to him. That tells you something about how earnestly Jung wanted to engage with this man. And White was delighted, and came, of course, and they spent time talking to each other and sailing. And White went home from that visit with a dream, that he wrote to Jung, that they were out sailing. And Jung was smoking his pipe, not paying attention to the helm. He was just letting the wind carry them. And they were being carried through rocks. And Jung wasn't upset about that, in the dream. And they somehow or other came up on the shore. The boat had developed wheels and rolled on the shore—it was amphibious! So this was how White's unconscious greeted the relationship. And Jung wrote back, saying it is indeed a dangerous—an exciting but a dangerous—journey that we are on. And the wind is in charge. Which, to a sailor, would be a horrifying conclusion. You don't let the wind be in charge, you keep your hand on the helm, and you work your sails, and you guide your boat, especially if there are rocks. But Jung himself was a bit euphoric, I think, about the prospects of this relationship. After this, they both did a good deal of important writing.

Victor White chose to ignore certain things in Jung's writings that he had access to. There was a lecture that Jung had given at Eranos, about the Trinity, that White got hold of and read. And he chose to overlook the section of that lecture that says the Trinity is incomplete without the fourth; and the fourth has to include evil. Well, that was going to be extremely problematic, and White ignored it at that point. In 1948, when Jung was busy writing his lecture for Eranos for that summer (the title was "Über das Selbst," "About the Self" or "On the Self"). That was another of his writings that went pretty deep into the issue of God needing, or God having, an evil side, God being both good and evil, *complexio oppositorum;* Victor White couldn't make sense of it. White was being shown, at that point in 1948, a kind of red-hot revelatory process that Jung was going through, that Jung was very excited about, and it fell with a thud. White could not assimilate it. He couldn't make sense of all these positive and negative polarities within what was meant to be sacred. That just didn't scan for White's orthodox Thomistic mind. He couldn't make it—he couldn't assimilate it and digest it. He couldn't greet it with joy, which is what Jung would have hoped for, I think.

What White did instead was to write an extremely critical review of "On the Self." He said, Jung is falling into Manichaeism: he believes that there are two Gods, a good and a bad. Or something like that. It's a dualistic error, a heresy, basically. In his review, he gave Jung some advice about readings that he might do that would straighten him out. And it is so condescending, what White wrote. It sounds like the kind of advice that you would give to a first-year theology student who hasn't done his assignment. Jung's next letter to White took White's argument apart in rather angry terms—he resented very much being called a Manichee. Things did not get better after that; their letters get really almost incomprehensible at a certain point.

And then, while this was going on, White was also encountering crisis in his life as a Dominican, because Jung came out with *Answer to Job* shortly after , in 1952, and White read it. At first, White's understanding was that this was a piece of writing that Jung would share with his inner circle. By no means was it going to be published. But that was never really Jung's intention.

"I love it. I've never seen anything better." And that was White's first reaction to *Answer to Job*, when he thought it wasn't going to be published. But it was published. And then, in 1954, it was published in English. And now White really had a problem, because his colleagues were reading it. As long as it was only in German, it could fly under the radar. But now, his English Dominicans could read *Answer to Job* in English. And White had already hitched his wagon so firmly to Jung's that he couldn't separate his career from Jung's writings.

Answer to Job was a problem for White's colleagues, and therefore for his superiors, and therefore for White's career. White was supposed to have become the Regent of Studies, which is a position that he earned and needed to have and should have had, and would have been good at. He would have controlled the whole curriculum for Oxford Blackfriars, for all the young men who were coming in. He would have been in charge of their learning, and he would have done a great job. But also, through an accident of history, a very highly placed Dominican in Rome, who was sympathetic to White, had died in a car accident and was replaced by the next man in line for that job—who was extremely conservative and didn't like White's work or White's reputation or White's connection to Jung, at all. And all of a sudden, White was not going to be the Regent of Studies. In fact, he had to go take a sabbatical in California. He was kind of exiled from England. This crash in his career came at the same time that Jung's wife was dying of cancer, and the combination of White running into a brick wall in his professional life and being sent away, and Jung encountering the final illness of Emma Jung, meant that neither man had any libido left.

JL: You, who have spent so much time (maybe more than most of the people on this planet) with these two men and this correspondence, this hopeful collaboration that started so enthusiastically from both sides: You speak in your book about "bridge makers," and also that they are using the metaphor, in their conversation, of building bridges, or bridge-building. I'm wondering, how do you look at the collaboration?

AL: Well, in my view, if one could abstract the collaboration away from the biographies of the two men, so that they would have infinite amounts of energy and time to commit—because they loved each other, they were real friends. You could see that at the end, when they reconcile as much as possible before the deaths of both of them. If this whole explosion around the time of 1954 had not been made more difficult or even inevitable by White's decision not to leave his order—he was a captive at that point: he wasn't going to make it in the outer world, he was going to stay on as a Dominican; and now he had been denied the promotion that he ought to have had. So White was very angry; but he couldn't get angry at his superiors, not if he was going to stay in the order. The anger that flowed was toward Jung. But Jung had a wife who was dying in 1955, and he had no more patience for this argumentative cleric who had turned on him.

What if they had had infinite amounts of time and patience? What if they had not been, each in their own way, suffering so much in 1955? I don't know if they would have had to fall into the silence, the distance, that they were forced into at that point. Jung basically said to White, Don't write anymore, don't contact me. The next question is, but what about matters of principle? Could they, in fact, have built a bridge between their two starting points? In my book, *In God's Shadow*, I made it my job to try and sort that out. And I came to the conclusion that because of the differences of epistemology—how do you know what you know?—they were never going to create a simple or harmonious connection between their two systems of thought.

That wasn't really within the realm of possibility from the time they began. They both got a bit carried away by their hopefulness and their excitement about finding each other. And White's willingness to just gloss over the things in Jung's writing that he really couldn't agree with—I think he thought that eventually he could bring Jung around, because he underestimated how deeply rooted those statements of Jung's were in Jung's experience and his thought. He wasn't going to leave behind—Jung wasn't—the concept of God as the complex of opposites. And the opposites include, for Jung, evil. White couldn't go there, and Jung couldn't be elsewhere. So I think in the end it was not a bridge that anybody could have built, not from their starting points.

JL: In your book, you comment on Murray Stein and others, this presentation of Jung as a doctor of Christianity. Jung tried to treat it as you would treat a patient, and you write that, in a way, he did not really follow the method he had established for himself, which was that first, you need to get to know the patient, and listen to the patient—learn the language of the patient—before any treatment can actually take place.

AL: I think Jung wished he could be a doctor to the Christian West, tried his hardest to be, but the patient wasn't asking for treatment, of this kind, from him. Or maybe, some were, just as the institution that White belonged to had a power shadow. Most churches do. I don't think you can be a doctor to an institution unless the institution has hit a crisis point and asks for someone to come in and sort them out. And then you can help to a point, but I don't know that you can do that kind of healing and reform from outside.

JL: When I read your book, or at least that chapter, I get the sense that you're saying that maybe he wasn't interested in learning all the details, for example, around the theology. Was he interested enough in the patient, or did he have a genuine interest in healing the patient?

AL: I think when it came to individuals, he certainly was interested in healing the patient. But I think there's something a little grandiose and maybe—well, let's just leave it at that. Just a little grandiose, thinking that you can heal a tradition or heal an institution. Unless you're inside it.

JL: You have to be in the institution. You have to be inside.

AL: Well, I'd like to hear somebody tell the story of how an institution was reformed from the outside.

JL: I'd also just like us to spend a few minutes on something we come back to in the previous conversations with other Jungian scholars and analysts. Jung's BBC interview at the end of his life, and when asked about his faith, answering, "I don't need to believe; I know."

AL: In principle, Jung knows and often repeats that God is un- knowable. This was something on which he and White agreed, by the way. One of White's books is titled *God the Unknown*. So he can't mean that. He can't be reversing himself on that point. So what is it that he's saying? I think he's talking about what he elsewhere says is the impact of direct experience, direct personal experience. His encounters with the unknown God: He knows what he himself has lived, and he doesn't rely on a system of belief. He has no doubts and therefore he doesn't need to believe, because the experience was direct, and personal, and intimate. It's part of him.

When Jung says he doesn't need to believe, that he "knows," this could be self-validating, a self-validating position. If you imitate Jung, if you take this as your standard of how to approach the Divine, then any convincing experience is self-validating. You become the authority, because you had the experience. And that could become delusional. I think we have to look at the shape of Jung's life to decide, was he being delusional ? Or was he just saying, *this is where I stand, based on my experience?* Well, I guess what I'm saying is that any individual imitating Jung needs to be part of a validating community. There needs to be more wisdom here than just my estimation of my own mission in life. I may get a sense of calling, but I need to have it validated by the group. There needs to be a trustworthy circle. Jung said, for heaven's sakes, Don't imitate me; be yourself.

JL: I'm wondering, do you then, yourself, view Jung as a Christian?

AL: Yes, I do. Because I think he was capable of being more than one thing. What does it mean for Jung to be a Christian? Those symbols of the Christian Church continue to matter to him deeply. The crucifixion remained a central image in his thinking. And the idea of resurrection. Well, he reframed it, in terms of winning through to a resurrected body while one is still living, while one is still alive. And that's a figure of speech. I'm not sure how it applies to Jung himself, or how it applied to any of his followers who heard him say it. But that is the kind of language he would not use if he had abandoned the Christian mythology, the Christian story. So he's still living in the Christian myth.

JL: And is there a way for you to see his project as a sort of attempt to reform Christianity?

AL: I think John Dourley [Jungian scholar] is perfectly right. That he wanted to transcend Christianity: reform it, if he could, but also transcend it. He thought it might take another six hundred years.

JL: Is there room for Christ in that vision of Jung's?

AL: Jung never abandoned referring to Christ. He never gave it up. He never rejected that central figure of Christianity. So how could one answer that? Is there room? There was for Jung. It's just that he reframed everything in terms of the soul's individual experience. And so for the individual psyche, the individual soul, that image of Christ is a powerful inner person, a powerful inner presence. Unless it's not, unless your roots are planted somewhere else. But if your roots are planted in Christian soil, why should the image and person of Christ be irrelevant to you?

JL: Well, I guess some people might argue that Jung relativizes Christ, makes him one symbol of many.

AL: Oh, yes, I think that's perfectly true. And if one begins from a perspective of absolute dedication to—how to put it?—propositionally defined Christian thought, then Jung becomes unappetizing, unacceptable. It's not acceptable to relativize; Christ can't be just one symbol of the Self. I would say what one wise priest once said to me: I think God knows more than we do. God knows what there is room for. I would love to see some spaciousness of personal conscience in this discussion. And for my conscience, there is room for Jung's relativized idea of Christ. I don't know if it's how I will end my days on earth, appealing to Jung's relativized Christ, but there is room for that in the discussion.

Depth Psychology is Not the End of the Road: Jung and Theology, with Sean J. McGrath

"At the end of the day, psychological integration is not salvation. And I think that most people who have done the work will be ready enough to concede that. This is not the end of the road. It's not salvation. What do we want? We want not just integrated individuals, but we want a redeemed order of being. We want justice on earth. And Christianity has from the beginning been about that. Not justice in some Never Never Land—that's a myth. Christianity from the beginning was about justice on earth. The Kingdom of God on earth, as it is in heaven."

—Sean J. McGrath

JL: How did your journey on the spiritual path begin?

SM: In many ways, I feel like I had a second childhood there at the monastery, and that everything I really know about life, I learned in those five years. They were the greatest years of my upbringing—without a doubt. I didn't only learn about mediaeval mysticism and contemplative Christianity, and how to meditate, and so on. I also learned how to harvest wood, how to build a house. So there was a lot of practical skill that I learned there. But most of all, I learned what it means to tend to the soul, to care for your soul. Why it's important, for example, to have a vibrant intellectual life, but also to have an outdoor life at the same time. And also to leave space in your day for nothing whatsoever, for just what they used to call *holy leisure*. Without that kind of attention to your life, religion just remains a theoretical project. And that was something that I would never have known had I not experienced it.

JL: I also know that you actually spent some time in Zürich, and that you did get interested in Jung and spent some time at the Jungian Institute.

SM: It's not at all unrelated to the monastery. So, five years in the monastery, from the age of twenty-three to twenty-eight: You can imagine it was a tumultuous time for me as a young man. And I went through a lot interiorly. And, in fact, I had a psychological crisis. I think it was more or less the day after I made my simple profession—took my vows, took my habit—I fell in love with a young retreatant, a young girl who was on retreat there. And I had such a powerful attraction for her. It led to nothing but long-protracted conversations with my spiritual director, but I didn't understand what was happening to me. I did not understand how my soul could go upside down like that. I didn't understand what I was feeling, because I had never been in love before. And it was in that context that I started to read Jung to save my life.

And I was reading Jung on *anima* and *animus* originally, and discovering: *What should you do when you fall in love?* Well, you should tend to yourself; you should look after your garden. It has to do with some kind of pressing need for an integration. This was my salvation at that time. So I would get up very, very early in the morning to study Jung. And, of course, I was not discouraged from doing so. But I didn't have anybody in the monastery who knew anything about it, but they were open to many things. And one thing led to another. And I realized it wasn't just *anima*, *animus*, but the whole issue of the unconscious became a real living experience for me: to profess your life to a religious order, and celibacy, and so on. And then the next day to have yourself tripped up by a powerful, powerful feeling that you didn't understand. And it was coming out of nowhere, and it almost had a religious quality to it. This was a kind of wake-up call: that I have an unconscious, so to speak.

There are other ways to describe it. We don't have to use the term the unconscious, but that language helped me to realize that there's work to be done. So, after I left the monastery, I was deeply involved in psychoanalytical work in a certain way. And I had an analyst for some years, as I was a new professor. And I began to teach psychoanalysis in my philosophy classes, at an introductory level. And then at some point, I decided to go more deeply into it. And I thought, well, I'm going to do some research in this. I applied for a Humboldt grant, to do research in the philosophical background of psychoanalysis, particularly the nineteenth-century sources of psychoanalysis.

As you probably know, psychoanalysis didn't drop from the sky, but it had a long history in philosophy—particularly in German idealism, which made it possible for people like Freud and Jung to do the work they did. They received some concepts from a tradition that I researched as a Humboldt stipendiate in Germany for about three or four years. And while I was doing that work, I wasn't far from Zürich. I was in Freiburg, in Germany. I realized that in order to really understand psychoanalysis, I needed to train . . . . I could not simply do this from the outside—I could not simply just do this as an analysis, although I was undertaking intense analysis at the time. I needed to train—I needed to become completely immersed in the paradigm. Of course, I was also open to the possibility that I was called to do psychoanalytical work, but the primary motivation, or at least the decisive idea there, was that in order to do my research, I need to train to become an analyst, even if I don't become an analyst. And that's how I ended up at the C.G. Jung Institute in Zürich. And that's how we met.

JL: So moving on a little bit to the actual theme of discussion, psychology and the cross. I would like to speak to you about the Christian concept of the imitatio Christi *(the imitation of Christ), and how Jung is linking that to his own idea of individuation.*

SM: First of all, my least favorite part of Jung concerns precisely this. I find Jung to be misleading, at best, on religion and theology. So with regard to the *imitatio Christi*, here's one thing I would say: It needs to be better theologically informed. If we're going to have a psychology of *imitatio Christi*, I think it's a great idea, but we need to be a little bit more attentive to the sources. For example, if we actually look at the source texts of Christianity, we'll see that Christ is not primarily a model. That was a heresy: the idea that we already have everything we need *in potentia*, in our soul, and we just need somebody to model it for us, and along comes Christ, and we suddenly realized, *oh, we just have to imitate him and we'll become saved*. That was called Pelagianism—this was not original Christianity. Christ was not primarily a model; he was a savior.

So if we think about the early texts, the first text, things that were written before any gospels were written, the letters of St. Paul: there is no *imitatio* without first a transformation of the soul by *grace*; not by effort, not by practice, not by the law, not by meditation, not by spiritual exercise, but actually by a kind of intervention—a divine intervention—that transforms the soul. And then the imitation follows. This is the first gospel.

And there is an important analogy here with other traditions, I think—in particular, with Mahayana Buddhism. They talk about *other power*, that at a certain point, all the sitting in meditation in the world is not going to—you're not going to break through if you're just relying on your own energy. Something else is going to happen, there's going to be an extra-egoic power that is going to more or less transform you, invade you, make it possible.

So it's not by effort that the practitioner, whether Buddhist or Christian, breaks through illusion. And it's for this reason that we really need to be careful when we start talking about, say, a psychological *imitatio Christi*. We need to make a distinction, I think, between psychological integration and religious experience, and I find that Jung is continually blurring this distinction. And it becomes even worse with the second, third, fourth generation of Jungians, when there really is no attention to the distinction. Psychotherapeutic work becomes religious experience, and we no longer need grace. All we need is the right kind of attention to our complexes, and to our dreams, and so on. No, and we'll get there on our own steam. That's not the gospel, and that's not the Christ.

JL: So, when Jung says that the idea is not following Jesus as a role model, but that you have to live your life as fully as Jesus did—

SM: It's a beautiful idea. But the first point we have to realize, when we look at the texts, is that Christ is not only a teacher. He's not even primarily a teacher, as Kierkegaard says: *In Christ, the teacher is the teaching*. That's Kierkegaard, and he's very faithful to the Pauline sources of Christianity here. That is, the point is not to follow the beatitudes, and so on. The point, rather, is to see in the Christ the teaching itself. And what do we see in the Christ?

We see the crucified Savior, we see God with us, God among us. He's absolutely unique—at least he was experienced as absolutely unique by his contemporaries. We're not talking about an archetype walking around. We're talking about a human being who lived two thousand years ago. We have far more reason to believe in the existence of Jesus of Nazareth than we do, for example, in the existence of Homer.

So, this is somebody who lived—and who had a practice that transformed the world, that transformed the Roman Empire, made modernity possible. And so we need to realize that there's a history here that we have to contend with. So what did the first Christians see in Christ? Did they see a model for a moral life or for psychological integration? On the contrary, they didn't see that at all. What they saw was God among us in an absolutely unique way. And it was not experienced as projection. It was not experienced as the alienated self, projected on somebody who happened to be walking down the road, as though it could be anybody. Now, I'm not suggesting that psychology needs to subscribe to that. On the contrary, psychology doesn't have to be religious. It could be perfectly atheistic. And I think that psychology, atheist psychology, has helped many, many people. But if it's going to talk about the *imitatio Christi*, then it needs to be a little more attentive to what those terms mean.

And, of course, once we are transformed and saved, the imitation of Christ follows, but if you look at the great imitators of Christ, they do so in such a unique way that there's no two that are the same. Think of St. Francis, one of the great imitators of Christ. But St. Francis doesn't act like Jesus of Nazareth. He acts in a completely different way. And when some of his followers tried to follow Francis, they said: Francis, I want to do what you're doing; I want to be like you. He said, *No, you can't do what I'm doing. If you do what I'm doing, it's going to be wrong. You've got to do your own thing, go your own way*. Each of us is intended to incarnate the Divine in an absolutely unique way. So the imitation of Christ, it doesn't have to do with doing what he did, or speaking the way he did, but with being open to the Father, to God. And that was Christ's consciousness: not my will, but the will of God. And then, you become a new Christ. That's the point: a completely different kind of Christ, maybe a Christ that doesn't look anything like Jesus of Nazareth.

JL: Isn't this also Jung's rendering, in a way? Don't follow Jesus ; live your life as fully as Jesus did. It sounds very Jungian to me, when you speak about it like this.

SM: Well, I do think that Jung understood something about Christianity . . . One of the things that I find really interesting is how Jung says, Okay, I'm in India now. And there's all kinds of wonderful archetypal stuff going on. But I have to go back home and deal with the Christ. That's the content of my Western European soul. I thought this was a very good idea. And in many ways, he does. He endeavors to do with Christianity what Freud did with Judaism. He deals with the Christian unconscious. There is such a thing as the Christian unconscious, I think. I think this is all excellent. And this is precisely what needs to be done.

But what happens—and this is related to perhaps other things we might talk about with regard to psychology and its limits—is that there's a kind of usurping of the theological by Jung. The theologian no longer has anything really to say about this: it all becomes psychology. And this is when things go a little funny. Psychology that has no outside, let's say: theology is outside of psychology in some respects, or even philosophy or metaphysics. Psychology that has no outside—and this is precisely so with the psychology of [Wolfgang] Giegerich—is psychological idealism. It is an absolute psychology. And I think, properly speaking, it's an atheist psychology, because if there's nothing outside, then there's certainly no transcendent God. So at some point, in the many writings of Jung on Christianity, this kind of move happens, whereby the Christ of theology, the Christ of history, becomes insignificant. And all we're talking about is the Christ of the unconscious, or the Christ of the European unconscious, underneath which there is a collective, and so on, in the Self.

I think that Jung is a fabulous guide on individuation. The integration of the internal diversity of the Self is a great representative of the psychology of productive dissociation, which is the psychology of the nineteenth century, Romantic psychology. In many ways, he's a conservative, because Freud comes along and tries to rid psychology of its philosophical, theological, romantic heritage. And Jung says, *you can't do that; that is a distortion*. So all of this, I'm entirely on board with. But when we go back to the nineteenth-century sources of psychology or psychoanalysis, and we look at some of Jung's nineteenth-century predecessors, we'll find a much more nuanced understanding of the limits of psychology—the limits of psychology, and that which transcends psychology, and the transcendent as understood no longer merely as the unconscious but (perhaps this is Nikolai Berdyaev) the superconscious: not just something underneath us, but something above us, something that cannot be contained by our psychology. And it's only really with those kinds of categorical statements in place that we can properly make sense, let's say, of what Paul is describing when he speaks about Christ as the image of the invisible God.

JL: Staying a little bit more with Jesus Christ: In my own conversations at times, with Jungians or in my own training, when one tries to discuss Jesus, it often has come back to statements like, Jesus is a symbol of the Self. Is there something more that you could share about Jung's relationship to Jesus Christ? You wrote to me in an earlier correspondence that "Christ is at the heart of Western imagination."

SM: Because Christ is at the heart of the Western imagination. Christ is the heart of European civilization. I believe this is true. I believe that modernity, for example, with its emancipatory politics, wouldn't exist without Christianity, without the gospel, that the secularization of the gospel is what produced the best aspects of our modern culture. And I might add, some of the worst aspects. So there's no way of understanding Europe and its consequences, without understanding Christianity. And I think Jung understood this very well.

So this is why I think Freud's psychology of religion is so useless, really, because of the marginalization of the central psychological fact of the West, which is the Christ. That said, I have no difficulty with the psychology of the Self. I think the emphasis on the Self is extremely important. Otherwise, when we have no psychological center-point, when there is no unconscious unity driving the development of the psyche, we will just end up with a plurality, which is just a carnival. I think this is what happens in Hillman [James Hillman], for example. I think Hillman is actually de-Christianizing the Jungian model. And I think the repercussions of that are very severe. So, no difficulty whatsoever with the idea of a self as the center of the psyche, which is somehow teleologically or finalistically directing the development of the individual.

But when we talk about the symbols of the Self, here I think attention to the sources gives us a little bit of precision. So what does Paul say about Christ? He says that Christ is the image of the invisible God—that's Colossians 1:15—the image of the invisible God. Now that sort of sounds like the symbol of the Self. But let's think a little more carefully. We also know that the human being is made in the image of God—that's in the book of Genesis. So we have to ask ourselves, What's the relationship of this Christ image of God and this human image of God? And there we find a very rich tradition of reflection, particularly in the Church Fathers, where the thesis is essentially that the being that we are meant to be only comes into perfection in the Christ.

So in Christ we know not only who God is; we know for the first time who we are, or more specifically, who we ought to be. So if that's the theological thesis in a probably inadequate generalization, let's look for a moment at the psychological claim that Christ is a symbol of the Self. As we know, there are plenty of symbols of the Self: whenever there's a God symbol, a religious symbol, it's a symbol of the Self. So it might be the Buddha, it might be the Tao, it might be a mandala. All symbols being equal, of course, that's a legitimate approach to religion from a psychological perspective. But at some point, we need to go from the commonalities of all these things and look at the differences, and this is, I think, extremely important.

It's very important to notice how different the Buddha is from the Christ, and you can't really know the differences between Buddha and Christ unless you read Buddhist scriptures and Buddhist commentaries on scripture and Buddhist philosophy—similarly with Christianity—and then it's in the differences that everything comes to life in a certain way. And I think that what we see in the Christian revelation of the Christ is that Christ is not primarily a symbol of the self. He's a symbol of God. He's a symbol of God, and God is not the self. The self, then (we'd have to say from a Christian perspective), that unconscious center of the soul: the self is an image of God. And Jung says as much, he says, it's *imago Dei*, it's an image of God. We have that in Genesis. And so it points toward God. But Christ doesn't simply express the human reality; he does that, of course, but he also expresses the divine reality. We get both. This was a big debate in Christology in the fifth century: fully human, fully divine. So you can't tear one from the other. And you can't confuse them—you can't say that to be fully human is simply to be fully divine. That's not true.

But neither can you say that to be fully divine is to be something unhuman. That's not true either. So what you have in the Christ is not just the human reality come to concrete expression, but we have the Divine itself revealed. Paul will say, for example, that we really don't know anything else about God but what we see in the Christ, and this is found also in the Gospel of John. Nobody has seen the Father except for the Son, and what you see in the Son is the Father. This is a radical, radical claim, that the Christ becomes a kind of—the only—concrete focal point for the religious aspirations of the human community longing for God. Longing for knowledge of God—looking in the Torah, looking in wherever, in mystery religions—and only here—this is the scripture, this is the Christian account, of course—only here do we see who God is. So Christ is primarily a symbol of God. That's, I think, crucial. That's the crucial point.

And if he is a symbol of the Self in some kind of general, religious science kind of sense—like Buddha, whatever—it's in this very specific difference that we truly understand who the Christ is for. You would never say that about the Buddha, for example. The Buddha is not a symbol of God. Buddha said, there is no God. Buddhism is, if it's not atheistic, it's *a-monotheistic*, right? So there's a striking difference there. I would say that the Buddha has far more credentials for being understood as a symbol of the Self in the Jungian sense than the Christ does.

JL: Do you have anything to say about how you understand Jung viewing this God-man, or how he was viewing Jesus? Do you think that he looked at him enough?

SM: I feel that he really stopped looking at a certain point. And he dealt only with what he learned as a young man growing up in the Reformed Church, I think it was, with a father who had religious problems. He was not particularly interested in theology, or what theologians had to say. And we can see this in the dispute that he had with Victor White about evil. Victor White was a very generous and sympathetic and uncombative kind of interlocutor. He was a Thomist, of course, and a trained theologian, but he had a great deal of interest and openness to what Jung was doing. Unfortunately, it wasn't shared. Jung was not interested in what White was doing. And that was a discussion that really couldn't happen because of Jung's, I think, prejudices about theology. So there is something unintegrated about Jung's Christianity. And I think that's what confuses things. So at the moment, I'm having a hard time thinking of a really important point that Jung makes about the Christ. I can't think of a single one, honestly; maybe there is one, but certainly the things he says about the Christ in the *Answer to Job*, for example: absolutely, absolutely mixed up. So there's far too much of Jung's unintegrated Christian heritage in Jung's psychology of Christianity, and not enough Christianity.

JL: You spoke of the conversation Jung had with Victor White, and the question of evil. In our previous conversation, you mentioned to me that you see that somehow Jung is misunderstanding evil. You also say that there's no place for it in God. Could you maybe help us to understand Jung's view on evil and your critique of that?

SM: So it's not entirely true to say that there is no place for evil in God. It all depends on what you mean by God, of course, right? There are different notions of divinity. I'm not saying there's only one. Now I'm a Christian theologian; I speak as a Christian theologian. And my sources are, as I said, people like Paul, Maximus the Confessor, Thomas Aquinas. I realize there are different ways of looking at these things. I just offer what I know, or what has been most illuminating for me on these issues.

It seems to me that if you look at the question of evil—and I really salute Jung for making it such a central question—it really is a central question. And I also salute Jung for recognizing that, psychologically speaking, it's absolutely crucial for the analysand or the individuating soul to reckon with the reality of evil. And I think that we've forgotten that in so much self-help industry. I hear far too much, *It's all good*, and not enough, *This is bad; this shouldn't be*. Now, that said, with regard to the question of evil, it is perhaps the oldest question and it is certainly the central question of Christianity. People don't recognize that the problem of evil is not an objection to Christianity. The problem of evil is the presupposition of Christianity. Think about the central symbol of Christianity: it is the crucified Savior. Or if you don't want Christ as the Savior, call him the best man who ever lived: crucified and rejected by the community. What could be more evil? And this symbol is now the symbol of our salvation. So sometimes people think that, *oh, yes, because of evil, we can't believe in Christ*. I would say the opposite, actually. Only if you believe in evil can you understand the Christ—but that's perhaps a complicated story. And I don't really want to go into it; I wanted to say something different.

I wanted to say that, historically, coming out of the ancient world, the Western tradition, we have three models for speaking about evil. And these are not properly distinguished in Jung and they need to be. The first is the Neoplatonic model. This is the tradition of evil as a privation of goodness—this was at the heart of the discussion with Victor White. And Jung doesn't like this, for good reasons. Because to say that evil is nothing but the privation of good is to undermine its psychological reality: it's nothing, it's just an illusion or something like that. Now, that said, Neoplatonic Christianity, like in St. Augustine, is quite different from pagan Neoplatonism. In pagan Neoplatonism, you get the thesis that Jung objects to—that evil is nothing. In Christian Neoplatonism, it's modified. But nevertheless, there's that problem of saying evil is just nothing. That's Neoplatonic. Then you have the opposite perspective in the ancient world, which is the Gnostic perspective. And this turns out to be the one that Jung ends up subscribing to, for reasons that are actually inconsistent with his own psychology.

In the Gnostic model, you have good and evil as both real, but as sort of equal and opposing cosmic forces. I like to think of this as the theology of George Lucas: the dark side of the Force, the light side of the Force, and they're always battling it out, they're always duking it out. One's always getting the upper hand, only for the other one to take the upper hand, and somehow rather recognizing the two as dialectical pairs, that one will never be without the other. This is some kind of enlightenment experience and salvation. Now the problem here of course is if good and evil are equal and opposing forces, then they are really two parts of something higher that is neither good nor evil. So, the Force is really, in itself, neither good nor evil, but as these two modalities; and so the Divine, on this Gnostic model, really has to be understood as beyond good and evil. In which case, you no longer have this real problem of evil, do you? Right, what you see in evil is really just divinity in another way, another shape and form. There's no particular reason, I think, to object to it definitively. And I think this is the direction Jung goes with the idea of integrating evil and so on.

But there's a third tradition, and the third tradition is the one that is most maligned, most badly represented by Jungians. And that is the monotheist tradition. And this is what Victor White was trying to argue for. And in the monotheist tradition, you don't say evil is nothing, but neither do you say that it's an equal and opposing force to the good. You make a distinction between goodness as infinity, goodness as the unlimited perfection of divinity—completely out of proportion to evil—and evil as created, if you like (that's a bit difficult)—but a feature of the created world or more actually a finite perversion of creation. And according to monotheism, evil is permitted for God's inscrutable reasons, ultimately to do with freedom. It's permitted to infect the world for a time, but in the end, it shall be cast out. But the most important point is that there is no balance between them. John 1:[5]: the light shines in the darkness and the darkness does not comprehend it. There's no proportion between good and evil. An ant has more in common with a human being than evil has with God. So there's no dark side of God in the sense of an evil twin to the Trinity or something. The devil is not God's other personality or something that Christians have repressed. On the contrary, if there is such a thing as evil, which I fully believe there is, and so does Jung, then it has something to do with us and the created world.

Now what, with regard to the Jungian/Gnostic matter of integrating the dark side? I don't think that Jungians are accurately describing their own psychology here. Because plainly they're not talking to you about committing crimes or abusing others. And that's what I mean by evil. What I mean by evil, what the tradition means by evil, is using somebody as a means. The devil is the one person who recognizes no other outside themselves, neither God above nor another person. Everybody is an object for him: using other people, but as a means to your own self-aggrandizement. Think about this as somehow taking a grotesque form in Nazi Germany, where everything becomes a means to the end of the glorification of the German state. Jungians are not talking about integrating that, they're not talking about becoming more like an early-twentieth-century Satanism, becoming more deliberately bad, wicked, selfish. They're talking about becoming more honest about your desires, more honest about your failings, about the shadow, the inferior side of yourself, instead of projecting it onto others. That's all excellent psychology. But the integration of that is not an integration of good and evil in this cosmic sense. This is rather humility. And this is perfectly compatible with Christianity. This is the recognition that you're not perfect, that you're not God, that the things that you most hate in others are things that you have disowned in yourself.

To make it a little more simple: what Jung has done is he's objected to the thesis that evil is nothing, which comes out of Neoplatonic Platonism. It's also a feature of some oriental systems, for example, Taoism. Jung is not on board there. There's a psychological reality of evil. This immediately puts him on the terrain of, let's say, monotheism—or Gnosticism, perhaps, and then Jung takes another step further, and he says monotheism is repressive of evil and denies the divinity of evil or something like that, the shadow side of God. And so then Jung takes a Gnostic approach, and we end up with good and evil as equal and opposing forces. So ultimately, if Gnosticism is the theology of George Lucas, Jungianism, at its worst, is the psychology of George Lucas.

JL: If we continue on looking at what you view as maybe some misunderstandings of Jung or maybe the followers of Jung, there's also the idea of the fourth element or the feminine element missing within Christianity, the embodiment of the feminine as a part of individuation. You also see that as a misconception of sorts.

SM: Yes. I think here what we see is Jung dealing with the repressive, misogynistic , popular Christianity of the [19]50s, particularly in a European context—the European Protestant context, but also elsewhere. There was lots of repression and misogyny in Roman Catholicism, too, in the [19]50s. He's taking this admittedly skewered and inadequate expression of Christianity—but every age of the Church is inadequate to the revelation—and he's making it into dogma. And this is a complete confusion.

So it's a very good idea to deal with misogyny and repression. I think we should kick it out wherever we find it. But let's go back to the sources. Now, here's the question: is the feminine actually rejected by Christianity? And I would say openly, right out, on the contrary, on the contrary: Christianity has been or is perhaps the central religious force that has led to the emancipation of women. I would go so far as to say that without Christianity there would have been no emancipation of the feminine—that the recognition of the equality and the difference of the feminine is central to the New Testament.

We know, for example, that Jesus admitted, among his followers, women. This was extremely countercultural at this time; some of them perhaps were deaconesses in the Church, they were involved in roles of leadership. We know that Paul—who is often given a hard time for saying women should wear head dresses in church and so on—believes that, ultimately, men and women are equal, that there is no man, there's no woman, there's no free person, there's no slave, but we're all one in Christ. This was an absolutely radical breakthrough. This is a kind of universalism that exists nowhere else in the ancient world. It changed history. And at the center of it was a recognition of the feminine as equal and other to the masculine. And even in the Divine.

So I said that Jung projects his own cultural prejudices onto the division and falsely concludes that the feminine is the rejected other of

God. That's simply not true. It's a complicated story. But let's just think for a moment of how the feminine then becomes identified with evil in Jung, because they're both rejected. And then we call for a reintegration of the feminine / the devil into the Trinity. First of all, notice that Jung is in fact perpetuating the cultural problem of identifying femininity with evil. He hasn't changed it at all. He said, actually, no, the feminine and evil, yeah, we have the devil there, we get the Virgin Mary, we can have a whore there, we could have a monster—the whore, the monster, the Virgin Mary, the devil—they are the fourth. So there's a confused identification of femininity with evil there, which is totally against his impulse.

And then secondly—more importantly, I think—Jung betrays how little he knows about Trinitarian theology. There is a long history of discussing the feminine side of God in relationship to Trinitarian theology, and it goes back—in fact, it's even earlier than Trinitarian theology. It goes back to the Shekhinah in Judaism, which is the feminine aspect of God, the material aspect of God, or Sophia, the wisdom figure discussed in the Old Testament, who is feminine, who plays before the throne of God and visits humanity with knowledge. These figures were at the center of the discussion of the first Christians—theologians—thinking about who God is, given that the fullness of God dwells in the Christ. There are others too: the Spirit, for example, is feminine. This is something that early Trinitarian theologians were thinking about, and more recently, feminist theologians have been thinking about. In Hebrew, the word for Spirit, *ruha*, is feminine. There's even a tradition of speaking about Christ as androgynous, that he has a feminine side to himself: we call it Sophia.

In any case, there's everywhere a recognition that archetypal masculinity, archetypal femininity have equal place in divinity. There's an active and there's a passive element to the Divine. There's a receptive and there's a more initiating aspect to divinity. And these questions are not easy to resolve. There're plenty of debates about them, but they run right throughout the tradition. It wasn't as though we were all waiting for Jung to say, *hey, we've got to put a fourth person in the Trinity, and it's going to be maybe the devil or maybe the Virgin Mary, or maybe both, because there's no femininity in the Trinity*. This is simply not true. Trinitarian theology has been discussing this point for a long time. And now there is actually a great resurgence of interest in what they call Sophiology, particularly coming from the Eastern Church, with a feminine figure, the feminine figure of Sophia, as a kind of divine counterpart, a divine helper from the beginning, who is not one of the persons of the Trinity, but somehow the whole Trinity manifest to itself, the mirror of God's wisdom. This is becoming a real theme, I think, among theologians today who are interested in recovering some of the mysticism, and some of the more cosmic-oriented theology of the Eastern Orthodox Church. None of this stuff has anything to do with Jung. Many of these people don't even read him . There it is: they find their way into the divine feminine simply by being faithful to the record of Trinitarian theology.

JL: I want to end with the question of whether Jungian psychology (which I also brought up with Amy Cook when we discussed Søren Kierkegaard) [see Chapter 5] *can be viewed as a continuation of Christianity or is it a break? Sometimes one feels Jung is coming out almost as a reformer of Christianity, bringing the old wine into new bottles. And I wonder how you view that. Is analytical psychology a continuation? Or does it aim at surpassing Christianity?*

SM: Well, I think that it all depends on how it's practiced and thought. It certainly could be a continuation. Historically, I think it is what the Germans would call the *Wirkungsgeschichte*. It's the historical effect of Christianity. And I think Jung understood this very well. So this is why people who are training in analytical psychology have to learn something about religion in general, but also Christianity in particular—there's something, let's say deeply, essentially Christian about Jungian psychology. I wouldn't deny this. But does it surpass it? Certainly not.

And with regard to Kierkegaard, here you have an excellent example of a psychologist, every bit as astute an observer of the human soul and the unconscious as Jung, who refuses to absolutize psychology.

Kierkegaard is perhaps the best example of a meta-psychologist of the finite. Psychology not as idealism, but psychology as realism: realistic psychology, which means a psychology that knows that there is something more than psyche at work in the world. So I think every practitioner is going to find his own way. You don't have to be a Christian to be a Jungian, obviously; you simply have to understand something of Christianity to understand Jung, just like you need to understand something about Judaism to understand Freud, or something about Catholicism to understand Lacan. These people are human beings. They bring their religious heritage into their meta-psychology. You'll have no critical purchase on the thing unless you understand these things.

What I would love to see is that psychology becomes something like meditation, yoga, eating your vegetables. You can do it in any religious register you like; it's a good thing. It's a good thing to care for the soul. We had all kinds of other practices for caring for the soul in the ancient world. Paul is very affirmative of them. The early Christians were quite affirmative of some of the practices of the mystery religions, in terms of therapeutics of the soul, or a Stoicism, or so on, Epicureanism. There were a lot of practices of soul care in the world when Christianity appeared, and Christianity could affirm what was best in them without ever being confused about what it was, namely, that Christianity is not just a therapeutics of the soul. It's much, much more than that. And in that regard, it's compatible with a great variety of therapeutics—yoga, for example, or psychoanalysis.

JL: What could Christ or Christianity bring to the world of analytical psychology today? Is there something that Jungians really need to look at here?

SM: I'm tempted to say what Christianity or Christ—let's speak about Christ because Christianity is much more amorphous and pluralistic and problematic than the Christ—what does Christ bring psychology? I think Christ brings salvation. And I don't think psychology does. And on the other hand, beware theologians and would-be mystics who have not done their psychological work, because they have done a lot of damage to a lot of people. So it's not a one-way street. Religion absolutely needs—modern religion—needs psychotherapy. It might be the case, as Jung himself said, that mediaeval religion didn't need it. It had its own methods of dealing with the confusions of the soul and the neuroses that rise in the life of an ordinary person. But modern religion needs psychoanalysis and psychotherapy.

But at the end of the day, psychological integration is not salvation. And I think that most people who have done the work will be ready enough to concede that this is not the end of the road, it's not salvation—that somehow, rather, we want more. And we want more for the world, too. We want justice on earth. The world is, I think, far more dangerous now than it was when Jung was writing. We have tyrants who are now impervious to democratic critique. They just ignore mass protests and violate human rights as they wish. It's not at all clear that goodness prevails in history.

So, what do we want? We want not just integrated individuals, but a redeemed order of being. We want justice on earth. And Christianity has from the beginning been about that. Not justice in some Never Never Land—that's a myth. Christianity from the beginning was about justice on earth. The kingdom of God on earth, as it is in heaven. That was the Lord's prayer. Almost every scholar believes that at least this much we know he said: on earth, as it is in heaven.

JL: But wouldn't Jung say that the kingdom is to be found within?

SM: Yes, and there are passages where Christ says something similar. But how are we to understand that? Does it mean that the kingdom is simply a state of inner quiet, such as we might attain through a Buddhist practice? That's not the biblical Christ. If you look at what Christ did, he didn't say, *oh, let's all learn a spiritual practice now, so that we can find inner quiet*. In fact, he also has very little to say about prayer—just that we should do it, we should do it quietly by ourselves. But what did he do? He healed people. He healed people, he criticized power, he turned the logic of the world upside down. There's something hugely extraverted about the Christ. And this is a striking difference from the Buddha. This is not an inward path: close your eyes and find the center. This is actually an outward path: overthrow injustice, resist it—non-violently, of course—offer yourself for it, lay down your life for others. So if Christ has a kingdom-within path to teach us, it is a path that proceeds within by going without, or in other words: lay down your life for your community. And then you'll find the inner peace that you seek.

Religious but Not Religious, with Jason E. Smith

"Jung gives me language and Jung provides the model, I think, of wrestling with Christianity. I think so much of Jung's work is his wrestling with Christianity . I think if you want to understand Jung, you need to have some understanding and engagement with Christianity. In understanding Christianity, I think it helps to know Jung, because he gives us some language and some perspectives that can't be had in other disciplines. At the same time, it was also necessary to be able to try to engage Christianity on its own terms, not on Jungian terms, to try to meet it in terms of what it says it is, and not just what Jung says it is. And so, there's a tension in that. In wrestling with Christianity, I'm also wrestling with Jung."

—Jason E. Smith

JL: How did your own journey into Jungian psychology come about?

JS: I came to Jung almost by accident. My original background, my training—what I went to university for—was the theater. So I trained in the theater. I was an actor and so I was living and working as a professional actor for a while, and I was searching for something that would help me to be better at my craft, something that would help me understand how to portray my characters and human beings more fully and more authentically. I didn't want an acting book.

So, I went into a bookstore and I was wandering around and I was looking at all of these books and I didn't know what I was looking for. I had no idea. And I saw this book, which I think was the popular sort of Jungian book, called *The Hero Within: Six Archetypes We Live By*. I think it's Carol Pearson who wrote that book. And I had no idea what an archetype was. I had no idea that archetypes had anything to do with Jung. I had no idea even who Jung was. But I got this feeling immediately that I have to read that book. It was just a very strong sense of, *that's the book I have to read*. And so I pulled it off the shelf and I bought it and I was absolutely captivated by it.

There was this whole experience of something beyond the everyday, these forces and energies beyond the visible world, that just really grabbed me. It didn't help me at all to become a better actor, but it planted this seed that stayed with me. A couple of years later, I was in a play and I was gifted another book, a book about Joseph Campbell. One of my fellow actors gave me the book. And, again, I was totally gripped by it and I started to read everything that I could find by Joseph Campbell. And I just read and read and read, for months, I think. I would spend whole days on the couch reading. And I started reading Jung. And again, I was absolutely captivated and I knew that that was the world that I wanted to be a part of. I knew that there just was this very strong pull. I had this strong feeling of, *this is what I've got to do and there is no way on this earth that I will ever get there.* It's impossible to get from where I am to there. It seemed so remote from who I was and what I was doing. I had no training in psychology. I had no understanding of any of the things that Jung was talking about: mythology, religion, philosophy, alchemy. All of these were so far beyond me. I couldn't see a way there. But eventually I did; I went to train at Pacifica Graduate Institute, which is where I met my wife, and eventually we moved to the east coast—I was living on the west coast—and that's where I decided to enter into training, at the Boston Jung Institute. So I got there, but it was sort of step by step. It feels like it was. With those books and with those experiences, I really feel it as having been a call. I don't know why I had to pull that book off the shelf. But I did. That was the one.

JL: I wanted to sort of fast-forward a bit to the present time and now. I found out about you through the book that you released. It's now two years ago—

2020, yes?—called Religious But Not Religious: Living a Symbolic Life. *Could you start by sharing a little bit about what led you to write the book and maybe something about the title as well?*

JS: So with my coming to Jung, Jung gave me a language for understanding my own religious sensibility. I didn't have a very active religious upbringing at all. But with my engagement with Jungian psychology, I was able to become aware that some of my experiences, my sensitivities, my responses to things had a religious character to them. So that dimension of experience, which maybe in the past might have felt like a dysfunction of some kind, a shyness (or something like that), or a being too sensitive, began to open up as a having another dimension. And so the religious question became very interesting to me.

But over time, the religious experience (in Joseph Campbell, and in Jung, and in Jungian circles, there's this sense that religious symbols are just metaphors for something else, and I don't think this is necessarily Jung's position, but it's something that comes out in Jungian circles in general, this idea that these experiences were—or the images, the symbols—were only metaphors of something else) wasn't enough for me at a certain point, because I was experiencing them as having reality, being very real. And so now I was struggling with this question of, *what was the role of religion in my life?* And what was the role of this sensibility?

And often there can be this sense, in the religious or in the Jungian community, that Jungian psychology is sort of an achievement beyond religion. You transcend religion and you go to something more enlightened. Again, there are traces in Jung that suggest this and then there are traces in Jung that counter this idea, right? So I felt this tension between my Jungian self and my religious self, and I was trying to work out these different aspects. The book is about—in part about—me reconciling these different aspects of my nature: the religious side, but also an appreciation for some of the skepticism around some expressions of religion.

And I was giving talks after my training, when I had become an analyst. I was doing some public talks, and when I would talk on this subject—I had a talk called "Religious but Not Religious"—the response to those talks made it clear that this wasn't just my question, that this was a question that had resonance for people, and that made me realize that it was worthy of a book, in the sense that it wasn't just for me. It was something that could have more general interest. And the title plays off of that idea of *spiritual but not religious*, and that's something that I have some sympathy for, and I would have identified myself in that way at one point. But also, I recognize that there are aspects of the structure of religion, the discipline of religion, the institutions, that have their own value, and that too often a spiritual-but-not-religious sensibility can be just taking what I like about the spiritual aspects that make me feel better and not the more difficult aspects that test you, that challenge you, that make you reexamine your own assumptions, your own experience. And so I wanted to convey something of that nature: that religion is a work. It's a discipline. It's a challenge.

JL: In the introduction of the book, you're also sharing a little bit from your personal journey, and your deep interest in Buddhism and in Taoism. And, also, then how Christianity is coming into your life—or the question that Christianity asks—and that there was at the beginning, also, some resistance, or at least, some wrestling with that. I'm sure there still is. But I was curious because you do share something very personal there: you're sharing a dream.

JS: Right.

JL: And would you be fine with just reading the dream and then we can talk a little bit about it?

JS: I found myself at certain points in my own experience confronted with images, in my dreams and in my experience, that were specifically Christian, and there may have been a part of me that wanted, sort of, generic Jungian archetypes to show up in my dreams. But that's not how it happened. And so this was a kind of fundamental dream, and it went like this:

I found myself going down a river on a boat. The boat came to a spot where the river forked in two directions. Somehow, I knew that to the left was the path of Christianity. I could see that it was a dark, difficult path that led deep into a jungle. It was a hard path with lots of struggles, and I felt afraid at the thought of entering it. To the right stretched the path of Buddhism, a sunny, open, and easy passage. I chose to go to the right. At first, I felt I'd made the wrong choice, but soon I set that feeling aside as I entered into a land filled with giant smiling Buddha statues, hot air balloons, and oddly, several police officers.

JL: Could you share with us also how you first interpreted the dream, and what sort of purpose, sense, it got for you with time, or how it grew on you?

JS: My first response to the dream was to feel very happy about my choice. Right? There's this choice between this dark, difficult path of Christianity and the easy passage to the land of Buddhism. And I felt very happy about it, because I think consciously it was what I would have wanted. Buddhism had more of a kind of cool appeal for me in the circles that I was moving in. Christianity was associated with, kind of, evangelical, fundamentalist Christianity, which I wanted nothing to do with, and so I thought, *oh, here's a dream that just confirms that choice*. But there's this kind of lingering doubt, right? Because there's a moment in the dream where I thought maybe I'd made the wrong choice, and maybe really I knew I'd made the wrong choice. I made an easier choice to stay away from struggle and to go to something easy.

And so there was always this sense that something was missing, that something was left behind. Something wasn't right. And I think that in itself is interesting, that I had that experience. I could have easily just said, great, here's my choice, and left it behind, but the fact was there was something nagging—and it wouldn't let me go. And it wouldn't let me go: it wouldn't let me go in my dreams, it wouldn't let me go in my own reflections. And over time, as I reflected on it, I realized that the move or the choice to go to the land of Buddhism was a choice to go to a place where things were—where I was looking for a happy, easy experience. I was not looking to be tested. I wanted to escape the challenges of life, really.

Religion at its best is a system for confronting and experiencing life as deeply as possible, and we can use it in a way that helps us avoid that. And we can use religion in a way to—and spirituality in a way to—bypass struggle. Or we can use it in a way to wrestle with the angel, to struggle with life, and to let the difficult things in. And so, over time, things like the hot air balloons became clearer to me, right? The hot air balloons are those things that lift off the ground, and it's light and airy, and it didn't have a grounding for me. It wasn't solid.

And the police officers, that strange image of the police officers, led me to think that maybe there was some development that was arrested in going down that road. And I make this point in the book, that this is not about Buddhism. This is not about the relative value of Buddhism, because Buddhism is a—can be a—deep and rigorous path for people, and it can be a powerful system of transformation. For me, it was a path of avoidance. As much as I find value in it, it wasn't going to take me to the places I needed to go, which was that dark jungle, which were my own encounter with suffering, my own encounter even with the difficulties around religion and Christianity, and some of the symbolic imagery in it, some of the way it's expressed. It's much more complicated to go into that tradition—at least for me—and deal with my own ambivalence, and deal with my own doubt, and deal with being drawn to a world that has some pretty dark expressions, has done some damage in the world. It's responsible for great beauty and great pain in places, and that wrestling with all of that has been part of the process.

JL: And was Jung as involved in that part of your process, the wrestling with Christianity? Or has it been a turning more to other sources. Has it been a combination?

JS: Well, yes. One of the things that I realized in my process was that before I could reject Christianity, I had to understand it. I had to engage it, and that meant engage it from inside. And so, going to Christianity was also—on the one hand, it was a kind of challenge to Jung, in the sense that I couldn't just accept what he was saying about his experience with Christianity. I had to encounter it on my own.

I couldn't just decide that things that he said settled the issue. I needed to see where it was living. Jung gives me language and Jung provides the model, I think, of wrestling with Christianity. I think so much of Jung's work is his wrestling with Christianity . I think if you want to understand Jung, you need to have some understanding and engagement with Christianity. You certainly need to read the Bible. In understanding Christianity, I think it helps to know Jung, because he gives us some language and some perspectives that can't be had in other disciplines. So he certainly provides a model. But at the same time that he gives language, it was also necessary to be able to try to engage Christianity on its own terms, not on Jungian terms: to try to meet it in terms of what it says it is, and not just what Jung says it is. And so there's a tension, in that in wrestling with Christianity, I'm also wrestling with Jung.

JL: Religious, but not religious. And the but not religious—could you just clarify further? What is it you don't want to see? What makes you say, no, not?

JS: Yeah. It brings to mind a story about Alan Watts. I think it's told by Joseph Campbell. Apparently, when Alan Watts was asked the question, *do you believe in God*, his response was something like, if you do, I don't. But if you don't, I do. On the one hand, it's a bit sarcastic. On the other hand, I think the intention of that is that we can't get caught too rigidly in the form. There is an element of that that has to stay open, that has to stay unknown.

So, for me, the *not religious* comes around the sense of a very strict Orthodox view—or doctrinal view—something that has to hold to this in a very literal way. Anything that gets too concrete, that gets too literal, starts to close out the transcendent, right? God can't be known.

JL: The Alan Watts story, it's interesting, but it's also, to me personally, problematic. It seems to—maybe this is out of context—but it seems almost also a rejection of the other, or a wanting to differentiate the individual experience, or a putting such an emphasis on that.

JS: I take that point, absolutely. I think there is a need for shared experience, without question. The challenge here, of course, is always that when we're talking about religion, when we're talking about God, we're talking about something that is fundamentally paradoxical. So as soon as you say something about it, you have to kind of recognize that there's something else as well. Without question, we need collective experience. And this is one of the places that I think is one of the deepest challenges of our age, because we live at a time when we don't live in these small communities where we are held within a simple tradition. We live in a global experience, where we are aware of all of these other experiences. We're aware of the Taoist experience and of the Muslim experience and of Buddhism and Hinduism and Native spirituality. We're aware of all of these things, and all of the scriptures are available at a moment's notice. They're not hard to come by. So how do we come to that place of collective experience? I think it's one of the great challenges. It's an absolutely necessary element of religion.

Jung in general doesn't do well with the collective. That's not his strength. His strength is to talk about the individual. He talks about the creed in a very dismissive way, and he talks about, sort of, the merely social aspect of attendance or participation in a religious service. But we are social beings. We are collective beings, and we can't be without some shared process. And so the challenge is holding both a kind of collective—a way of being able to communicate with each other—and also holding the unique individual experience. And making room for both of those, I think, is really—I think it's a great challenge.

JL: Is there a risk of reducing the religious to the individual's individuation?

JS: A quick answer to that, *is there is a risk of reducing the religious to the individual's individuation*, is yes, of course there is a risk of that. There's a risk of making analysis about my experience. There's a risk of making religion about only my experience. We have the capacity to engage things in a narcissistic or solipsistic manner, where it's just about my experience—without question. But I think, personally, that individuation is not in conflict with the larger goals of religion: the sense of the other, the need for the care and concern of our brothers and sisters and those who are suffering and those who are struggling. And I think Jung knows this, frankly. I think Jung understands this.

I think individuation is different than other forms of well-being. I think it's different than wellness. I think it's different even than some of the goals of psychotherapy. A lot of psychotherapy can aim toward healing the self, healing the individual, and there's great value in that, of course, right? But Jung is very clear that analysis is not necessarily about a cure. And analysis does not lead to a state where one is free of difficulties and challenges. And there's one of the things he says about individuation in particular: individuation emphatically includes our fellow man. It is not a course of individualism and it doesn't result, he says, it doesn't result in spiritual aloofness, where you pull yourself out of the collective and you are a law unto yourself. It emphatically includes our fellow men, our fellow beings. And he conceives of it as a vocation, right? And more than a path of well-being, it's a path of—it can be a path of struggle—and it can be a path of pain and suffering, but it's a path of becoming what one is.

Jung has a moment in his own biography, where he has his moment of vocation, where he realizes he's going to become a psychiatrist and that it holds these different threads of value in his life. And at one point there, he says, My life was no longer my own. I had no right to it anymore, for it to be just about myself. So he sees that goal as fulfilling some purpose that has a larger purpose.

I found this letter recently where—it's not in his collection of letters, it's in a private collection and I found it online—where he talks about—someone's written him and asked him about how to live a happy life. And basically his response is don't even try. If you try to live a happy life, you're going to be unhappy. And he says this great quote. He says, You'd better ask where and how you could be useful to whom. So in order to live a fulfilled life, in order to live a happy life, you should ask where and how you should be useful to whom. Where is your place of service? Where is your place where you give yourself to the world?

JL: In the Christian tradition there is a long history of holding contemplation and action (or prayer and work) in the right balance. I've been asking myself at times if we Jungians, Jung included, are sometimes a little bit comfortable, you know? I remember a friend used this term not so positively about Jungians: she said we're "a group of esoteric elitists." And I'm not saying that we all are, or that we all have to be, political. I think there's so much misguided politics. But there is something about Jung and there is something about Jungianism, and there is something—about maybe even the emphasis, always an emphasis, on the symbolic—that I think at times might blind us to what is actually just in front of our face. Because we don't need to go far to see the state of the world. And what I find in Christ and in Christianity and the symbol of Christ: there is something there that I think can also wake us up to reality—the realities we live in, all of us. Not individually, but all of us. The reality that we have been put into, which is a very tragic image—tragic and hopeful at the same time.

JS: I think it's such an important question. And one of the frustrations I've had at times is that there's often the sense that Jungians are talking to themselves, talking amongst themselves. And that there is a way in which we can use anything, whether it's Jungian psychology, whether it's Christianity—any kind of system—we can use it as a means of substitution or we can use it as a means of transformation. And what I mean by that is, Jung says (it's in one of his seminars, he's talking to a group of his students) that some people get a psychological term and they cling to it and say that's it, and they stop. And he says, we always have to remember that psychology is only a stammering stopgap measure in order to be able to talk about life at all. We're not dealing with psychology. It's not about proving that Jungian psychology is right. If Jungian psychology doesn't lead us into life, if it doesn't bring more life, then we're missing the point. And the substitution, right, is that I have a phrase, I have an idea, and now I don't really have to struggle with the consequences of that idea. Or maybe I want to change something out there. Or, now I know why that person needs help or that person is wrong, or something like that. To take it as a means of transformation means something has to change, this has to affect me, this has to open me up in some way.

Without that kind of coming back and bringing things back into the world—and it reminds me too that Jung talks about this as well—he says that individuation has an element of guilt attached to it, that when a person starts to individuate, the process pulls them out of the collective for a time. And for that to not be an immoral act, one must produce new values. So out of the work of individuation, you must come back to the world with something. There must be something that adds to our experience, that alleviates suffering, that frees the prisoners, gives sight to the blind, so to speak, to use some of that Christian language.

JL: There's this dream in Memories, Dreams, Reflections *where Jung's following his father, and when he's going to bow, there's one millimeter between Jung and the ground. But he knows that he's going to be taken to the highest presence. And what is the highest presence? It's the suffering Uriah, the suffering man who was betrayed. That's who—that's what—he meets. That's the highest presence. There is no glory there. There is just a man suffering. So, and then, there's Jung's interpretation of that dream. And there's also Wolfgang Giegerich's critique. I have had a discussion with him around that lately. Yes, somewhere, around there, I cannot walk any longer with him* [Jung].

JS: Hmm. So much to say about that, and I honestly don't know how much I can contribute to that. But there are a couple thoughts and reflections that come up. I was thinking about that dream that you mentioned, Jung and the one millimeter, and there is something there about not being able to put his forehead on the ground, not being able to submit. There's a way in which he holds back. I think about—well, there's a couple of thoughts that come around. One is that idea that psychoanalysis is not the end of the road, as your guest [Sean McGrath] touched on with you. I've experienced that in my own life, that there have been times, there have been experiences, particularly in my own suffering, where Jungian psychology can't help me. It can't save me. There's a limit there. And that's where the religious, where Christianity, has come in, in a powerful way. That there are things that can be met, places at a level of suffering that can be met, that are . . . I couldn't get there, personally, through Jung, as much as I find profound value in his work.

And I wonder how much part of the issue revolves around the question you've also explored a lot in your podcast, around Jung's notion of *I know* versus belief. "I don't believe; I know," right, what he says in the BBC interview. And of course a lot depends on what Jung means by knowing, what that even means, and we could speculate in a lot of directions. But one of the things about knowing, the insistence on knowing, is that it's problematic. My own take on this is that knowledge and faith and belief are not distinct things. There's this interplay between them. They can't be separated ultimately from each other, but knowing insists more on the *I*. *I* have to know. If I don't know, I won't submit. I can't put my head down. And belief or faith has a way of taking a risk and aiming beyond oneself, of aiming toward a horizon that can't be ultimately known, but there's a kind of risk of walking into that. And for me this place of the relational dimension—the relational dimension of knowing or the relational dimension of faith, the relation to Jesus, the relation to God—if you can enter into that space, which is a much more personal one, a much more intimate space, then it opens up avenues of relationship to the rest of the world, to ourselves, to our fellows. To the people closest to us, to people far from us.

So, it's knowing from that other place of *I have to know* that keeps us somewhat safe and protected from life. But the moment you enter into a relationship, whether it's with your friend, your partner, your spouse, or your God, you are vulnerable, and you are open to suffering, because now their experience becomes your experience. And you cannot differentiate between the two. And it feels like that's the kind of place that is so important to be able to risk.

Kierkegaard and C.G. Jung: Learning from a Christian Existentialist , with Amy Cook

"I think what Jungian psychology really needs is a Kierkegaard. I am coming from Kierkegaard as a Socratic figure, somebody who is going to be an absolute nuisance. Kierkegaard understood he was an absolute nuisance. He thought that was his meaning, the whole reason he's here: being a nuisance. But he's, at the same time, he's challenging. So, to my mind, more than anything, I'd love to see analytical psychology find itself a Kierkegaard, someone who's going to shake it up a little bit. Get everyone questioning things. There can be a tendency to always want to defend some pretty big Jungian concepts and always go back to the original writings."

—Amy Cook

JL: Few people have written so lucidly as you have about the unexamined relationship between the minds of Kierkegaard and Jung. How did your interest in researching the two come about?

AC: I've always been really interested in philosophy. I was a history undergraduate, but a terrible one. So I spent all my time reading philosophers. It was Schopenhauer and Nietzsche, Kierkegaard. So, I've always had this fondness for Kierkegaard. I just think, if you're a philosophically-minded teenager, you're probably going to find something of a companion in Kierkegaard: lots of angst. There's a lot of comfort to find in reading—even the most morose philosophy, even Schopenhauer—

there's a comfort there. You're not alone. You're despairing, that's good. You're somewhere along the line of progress.

Really, when I left uni, it was all about studying philosophy. And it was just by chance I returned to where I grew up in Essex, and I think Essex University is one of—I think the only one, actually, in Britain—where you can do Jungian study. I started off with philosophy and psychoanalysis, which I loved. And then, of course, through the master's, I'd become interested in Jung as a figure—again, coming back to this idea of there being this suffering, that you can be suffering, you can be despairing, you can be in despair. But that, see, that's not a bad thing. And that was the real hook for me, and something that I've always been fascinated with.

JL: The people who listen to this podcast—most of them—might have a pretty good idea about Jung and Jung's theory. I was wondering if you could say a little bit about Kierkegaard, with regard to him as a psychologist.

AC: Kierkegaard is a figure who for the most part in philosophy is known to be the father of existentialism. And then, people may have heard of him in terms of his being a very miserable, gloomy, melancholic Dane. Even though existentialism is one of the few philosophies that's really become embedded in our culture, there are very few philosophies that have made that crossover to be really felt. And you have artists and poets and writers all really, massively infused by this philosophy.

But yes, Kierkegaard is a ridiculously good psychologist. I think it's really hard to just talk about Kierkegaard without talking about his personal life. Because his is a lived psychology. And Kierkegaard himself never called himself a philosopher. He really didn't get on with the philosophers of his time; they were on the wrong track. So he's very much a poet, a poet and an author, who—he says this—he says his *raison d'être* is to awaken his reader, to awaken that inner truth in them. So, if you get to take one thing from Kierkegaard, it really is this: this reminder that existence isn't about beliefs, words, thoughts, creeds, systems. It's about you. You must let your life speak for you. It's what we do. It's what we put into action.

Kierkegaard is all about not telling you how to live. He's very silent in that respect. What he does is he uses Socratic irony, and very clever characters in his works that reflect a certain stage of existence. And there's a conflict between them. And so you're reading his work, and what you're seeing is—you find yourself reflected back. And that's what he wants. He wants you to feel unsettled. He wants to awaken something deeper in you. I think we'll talk about Kierkegaard, where he ends up, and it's not a path that I certainly would want to follow. It's full of pain, full of loneliness. But he seems to have found some joy in that place, because, we get to the end of his life, and he is very serene. He's not raging against anything. He diagnoses himself a lot: the thorn in his flesh, the misrelation between his spirit and his body.

JL: In the introduction of your book, you summarize, also, some point of commonalities that you find between C.G. Jung and Kierkegaard. What are the commonalities that one can find in their psychological theory or life-projects?

AC: I think just the very common existentialist themes that run through Jung and Kierkegaard. We've got authenticity, this idea that there is a *true self* and a *false self*. Common to both of them is this understanding that so many of us live in despair of the self that we are, for whatever reasons. And self-deceptions, the resistance of our self-deceptions. We find that a common point in both their work. And I guess the passage to becoming a true self is one that involves suffering, and holding on to that suffering and seeing it through and not relegating it or seeking to medicate it away. And I kind of think, especially in today's world, not only are these ideas completely relevant; I just think there's so much more needed.

JL: Could you help us to elaborate on Jung versus Kierkegaard's view of the self, maybe starting with Kierkegaard, to see how they relate or how they might differ? Their understanding of what it means to become a self?

AC: *The self in becoming*: this is what connects them both. The self is in a state of becoming. It's becoming a self, your true self, your true authentic self, which is going to heal you. You can't develop a religious attitude without this development of self to its full potential. So the self becomes really quite holy, a holy concept.

There's a really difficult argument to make about the relational self, particularly in Kierkegaard. There is a relational self because, of course, Kierkegaard is influenced and can influence others. So there's a relationship, but ultimately, the self has to relate to God. And that God is very much a transcendent God, is very much the Other.

Now Jung—and this, I think, gets quite controversial for theologians, that God that exists somewhere outside of us and is a transcendental being—but Jung sort of puts this God into the Self with a capital S. So the relationship to this God-Self is what matters. And that's a really—you talked about bold ideas—that's bold. That immediately is not cool. It gets people's backs up, doesn't it?

One of the wonderful things about Jung is just how wide his knowledge is of religion. Kierkegaard, we don't see any further than the Christianity that he grows up in; this is the Christianity of Denmark. But Jung's not as closed off as that. So, he talks about: there is not so much the religion, but *the religious,* and that can be commending the figurehead of a God. Or it could be a path to salvation, or—and this is what I really, really love—it can be anything dangerous and beautiful enough to give your life meaning. And I just think that's just the most amazing statement of Jung.

Today, so many people can't find meaning in their religions as institutionalized religions. Because both Kierkegaard and Jung—I've now wandered off from the self, but I think this is an important point—are completely at a loss with institutionalized religion. They both see it lacking something very, very fundamental for the development of the self, where for Jung, this is very much the symbolic that's missing. And for Kierkegaard, you could say, it's the suffering of being a Christian that's eroded. But you could also say that the Danish Church had made being a Christian so easy. That it really had lost the meaning, and it had lost its vitality. Being Christian, for Kierkegaard, isn't sitting in a comfy armchair and becoming very settled. And I think that's the state he thought a lot of his companions were in. They were under the illusion that they were Christian by being born into a Christian society and being baptized. But that's not the end of it. It's your life, it's what you do, it's the essence of your existence.

I suppose I've done—I've done you a disservice, really, by not talking about Kierkegaard's stages of existence. Because it's got three stages. And the first of these stages is *the aesthetic*. And that's probably where most of us will find ourselves. This is really governed by pleasure. We run from anything that fills us with dread; we make no commitments to ourselves or to other people. So, his point is: you have to hurry up and despair, because you will find no happiness until you do. And you can just see it in our modern-day culture. If people feel any kind of anxiety, they have their mobile phone. It's almost like a dummy. You get your mobile phone out, and you're scrolling on Facebook, and you distract yourself. That's the point, in the aesthetic realm: you're always distracting yourself. You just don't want to sit with that restlessness that defines human nature. And I think that's a concept, this restlessness that we see in Kierkegaard and in Jung.

So, to kind of flip this over now to Jung—he would say that this would be—how he says that, I haven't seen a patient over the age of thirty-five whose problem wasn't to do with having lost their religious outlook, or having lost this overall sense of meaning of life's purpose. Pretty much a second-half project of life, isn't it? Not for everybody: some of us make it the first half, and then worry about careers later. You've got this sense of, in this phase, you're even in despair, because you don't know it. And this is absolutely the most basic-level despair, because you're in a state of *spiritlessness*. And you might look at that in Jung and see something like a neurosis. There's something that is missing.

So whereas Jung proposes a process of individuation to come to this meaning, meaningful existence, Kierkegaard has his stages of existence, which are a lot more dramatic: each stage is mediated through a crisis. So, eventually, the idea is that in the aesthetic fear, we simply can't hide from the boredom and the emptiness, and that dread will bubble up. And we'll have to start asking ourselves questions. *What are we going to do in our life? Who are we? Why are we here?* That's where there's a movement over to the *ethical stage*. And the ethical is pretty much that, that second stage of life where you're focused on careers, and families, commitments. It's very much about obligation and finding your place in society.

But Kierkegaard would argue that too: the meaninglessness of that will, to evade and evoke dread. And ultimately, you have to make a leap of faith, that leap of faith to God, to rest transparently in God. I think that's the point for me, where I'm struggling. In Kierkegaard's writing, it becomes very hard to understand, because it's about the absurd. So you have to transcend the ethical in this absurd, paradoxical leap. He talks about Abraham and Isaac, and Abraham sacrificing Isaac as this ultimate act of faith, because it contains this paradox. [Abraham] understands that he's killing Isaac, that he will kill him. But at the same time, he had this faith that God will restore Isaac back to him, which is absurd. It's just not possible. But that's the embodiment of faith.

JL: I think you're leading us into this foundational question, around faith versus knowledge, and Jung and Kierkegaard's respective views on that, and where they base themselves. You write so articulately around that in the book, about the question of faith versus knowledge. And you're also quoting Jung saying in that BBC interview, "I don't believe; I know."

AC: Yes. Jung's faith, I think that's a really tricky thing. Just a full confession: I don't understand. I don't understand where he's coming from. For Jung, he repeats a lot this idea of the original religious experience, this double aspect. He even says something like, *I can only commune with people who have had this experience of God*. And for someone who has never had an experience of God, I struggled to even imagine what it might look like. I've read *The Red Book*. I get the sense that his original experience of God is in there. And I don't understand it. I mean, I won't pretend to.

But yes, so the BBC interview? "I don't believe; I know." And it's a very—I find it a very bizarre statement, particularly when you consider how Jung has this love for the esoteric and for paradox. And in no other scenario does he struggle with belief. It's a therapist's belief and hope that his patient can heal and progress along the stages of individuation. No problem here. But when it comes to God, he's just—he completely just obliterates the idea of a belief. And it's a very strong statement. It's a really strong statement, and I just feel I can't really do a service to understand it because I can't come from a place where I can even conceive what he might be getting at. But in my book, I do make some conclusions about what might be going on. I think it'd be quite well-known to people, Jung's issues with his father. Well, not really his father as much as maybe his father's religious doubts. He kind of kept imploring his—as a child, to give him—he wants to know why he should believe in God. His father would say, *you just believe*. And he starts to see this as quite a hollow, empty faith. He doesn't believe his father has this faith at all: he's just a bit of a lost soul going through the motions. But then, I find it hard not to see that same dogmatic response in his own statement, really.

JL: I have a quote from you from your book here, where you say, "With his statement, 'I do not believe; I know,' Jung is standing patronizingly so outside of his father's religion. Such statements seethe with unconscious doubt and indicate the clear need to quiet an uncertainty by dogmatically defending religious experience. Faith and knowledge through personal experience exists so uncomfortably in Jung's thinking that, to my mind, this really does limit the degree to which we can view Jung as a sensitive and sympathetic spiritual pilgrim."

AC: Yes. It's just so deeply strange, isn't it? Jung, he so brings to life this dialectical process. You have to hold two things in conflict to birth the third. And here we find he can't hold these two things. He can't hold them. It's very much an everything and nothing response. And it's something that is just very intriguing. My conclusion is by no means the only one—at all.

JL: You write in the conclusion of your book, "Although Jung believes himself to have discovered God alive and active within the unconscious, I do not think he managed to recapture his lost faith in God. It would certainly seem that his attempt to heal the split with his father and his father's religion was ultimately unsuccessful."

AC: Gosh, I kind of stand by that, because I think it's so fundamental to—I think any religion—not just Christianity, but any religion: faith has to have doubt. You can't have an enlivened faith without doubt. I think I struggle with, as soon as—I think this is a personal problem—as soon as anybody comes to anything with any certainty, to that strength of certainty, I'd be inclined to take a step back, just instinctively, to just take a step back. But then, at the same time, this could just be Jung's attempt to completely reimagine what Christianity is, because you can be sympathetic to this idea of undergoing the original experience, whatever that is. And, of course, that has to be some sort of confrontation within the unconscious. It doesn't necessarily have to lead to the conclusion that I draw. But I think maybe, if we were to look at it from a Jungian, if we come at it from a Jungian aspect—I think you would find that a troubling statement. There's no dialectical process going on here.

I am straying a little bit farther now—but is there that aspect of analytical psychology that could be said to replace the need for religion? If you look at it as a project, that one finds their self, their purpose, and meaningful existence, individuation encompasses all of that. I don't know—I'm not entirely sure that Jung's wanting to heal Christianity is as pure a motivation as it might seem. I think there is a sense, to my mind, that he does go beyond Christianity and does seek to replace it with something else. But why not? There's nothing wrong with that. There's nothing wrong with that at all.

JL: What would you see is left of Christianity in Jung's project, then? What's left, what is Christian about Jungian psychology, as you understand it?

AC: Very little. I don't know. If you look at Kierkegaard, he doesn't arrive at the faith of his knight of faith. He identifies himself as being a knight of resignation. He hasn't quite made it in terms of faith. But it's still—Kierkegaard you could follow. You can see where he's coming from. There is no sense of, *you have to be certain*. And of course, the religious experience is extremely important to Kierkegaard. But it doesn't supersede belief. It doesn't, because that's the point with Kierkegaard, isn't it? Experience and belief aren't going to get you to that leap of faith that you need to get to. There's something more, there's something that is inexpressible, that you can't reduce to rational thinking. There is just something else; whereas when Jung arrives at this point of talking about faith, that's not there anymore. There isn't any space: it's just, you have the experience . . . . But it just seems so alien: how could you have any kind of experience, and be so utterly sure in that experience, in what have you experienced? Where's the framework around it, to make sense and to contemplate and reflect?

JL: But isn't a part of that related to the idea of individuation, or Jung's rendering of the imitatio Christi? *Isn't that where he speaks of life or faith as something that goes beyond an individual numinous experience?*

AC: You get a very different imitation of Christ in Jung. It's very individual. You carry your own cross. Don't carry Jesus' cross; you must carry your own. It's a completely subjective experience, which—that's probably a good thing. I don't think we want to follow Kierkegaard down his imitation of Christ, which is literally to suffer and suffer, and hate, the stigmata, and suffer some more—and live in complete hostility to everything around you. Does not sound fun.

JL: But you were saying that Kierkegaard found peace in his life.

AC: Yes. But for Kierkegaard, these two things aren't in conflict at all. It's not something that perhaps you or I could live with. To Kierkegaard, he stops going to church. He doesn't have relationships around him. He even stops taking what he refers to as his "people baths"—where he would walk the streets of Copenhagen, and stop and have a natter with people. He stops all that because there was an incident with a magazine there. It's a fight he started, because he decided that because they liked him, he couldn't be terribly important. Because a magazine that took people down—kind of the equivalent of our *Heat* magazine: so he upsets them so that they attack him. And then, of course, everybody else attacks him. And he's absolutely happy now. Because this is to be Christ-like: to be mocked and to be scorned. And if the world's not been hostile to you, you're not really living the life of Christ.

So in Jung, we see a much healthier, I think, imitation of Christ. But there's no conflict here. Because, yes, Kierkegaard, he dies quite peacefully. He's quite serene. He's quite confident in his work. This was his purpose, to lead this body of work that was going to challenge people out of their self-deceptions and into a true life. He's still melancholic. He's still a deeply angsty, anxiety-ridden individual. But that's maybe his truth. And I think—I think for Kierkegaard, he always allows for there being something else.

JL: Would you say that Jung and Kierkegaard can complement each other in some way? The subtitle of your book is Researching a Kindred Spirit in the Shadows.

AC: That's a really good question, really tricky question. Jungian psychology is ripe for existentialism. And I think if you came at it from a—it doesn't have to be a strictly-speaking Kierkegaardian angle—but if you really draw out the existential themes, I think you could have a really interesting infusion. Kierkegaard has a lot to say about self-deception. He has a lot to say about how resilient our self-deceptions are. He has an awful lot to say about authenticity. And I don't think that if you could hold the two together—that can't fail to enliven things, you know? I'm going to be a little bit provocative. But I think what Jungian psychology really needs is a Kierkegaard.

I am coming from Kierkegaard as a Socratic figure, somebody who is going to be an absolute nuisance. Kierkegaard understood he was an absolute nuisance. He thought that was his meaning, that's the whole reason he's here: being a nuisance. But he's, at the same time, challenging. He's challenging us. He's unsettling us. You can't read Kierkegaard and not become profoundly unsettled. To engage with the text is to really engage with your own sense of who you are, of where you are going.

So, to my mind, more than anything, I'd love to see analytical psychology find itself a Kierkegaard, someone who's going to shake it up a little bit. Get everyone questioning things. There can be a tendency to always want to defend some pretty big Jungian concepts and always go back to the original writings. And a little bit of hero worship—Jung is great—I'm not saying he's not great.

JL: Could we speak a bit about Jung's critical reception of Kierkegaard, and Jung's view on Kierkegaard?

AC: Jung's reception of Kierkegaard is profoundly negative. He doesn't seem to see any commonalities between their projects, which is astounding because even if you—just the most basic of concepts in Kierkegaard—it's like Kierkegaard is properly liberating. It's not about what's written down, what theories you're following, what philosophy you feel or think. It's about what you think. This is your truth. Don't live somebody else's life. You can only live yours. It's hard to say how much Jung actually knew Kierkegaard. By the 1920s, Kierkegaard is really very popular. So I can't believe he didn't have a good enough knowledge of Kierkegaard. But Jung reduces him to a religious neurotic, part of the misery institute that has become, not Christianity altogether, but maybe just a certain kind of Protestant religion. I think that's where that misery institute plays in.

JL: You write in the conclusion of your book: "Jung's understanding of the imitatio Christi *carries with it the implication that traditional Christianity has misunderstood both Christ and the incarnation. The incarnation continues in and through the individual, who must understand that his relation to the infinite is to realize the incarnation as an ongoing and continuing process, according to Jung. To exist as an authentic individual requires that we break away from, and go beyond, conventional Christianity in pursuit of a higher religion." So, we land again with that question: is analytical psychology sort of surpassing or replacing Christianity? Or is it to be seen as a sort of reparation or a restoration of some original truth?*

AC: But don't you think the interesting thing is that it can be both? It really just depends how you approach it. If you're somebody with a Christian disposition, you can read that statement (that the change in what it is to imitate Christ) as not a literal imitation. It's the deepest, truest expression of Christ, but through yourself. Comparing that to when Jung is talking about his experience, or religion—I can't follow that, but I can follow this. I can follow where we're departing from conventional Christianity here. I don't think it's that bold. But I can follow it. But in terms of whether it's a process that is about reparation, or a process that's superseding the Christian religion, it's an either–or: I think that's why Jung attracts just such a wide, diverse range of people. And whether, ultimately, he meant it as one or the other, I think it's unanswerable. Jung knows. None of us do. But he does.

Islam and Individuation, with Bernard Sartorius

"Islam, basically, is acceptance... And this acceptance is not exactly identical with Christian faith... This is what interests me very much: in the Islamic perception of the mystery, I would say it is more open to the mystery that God can also destroy. There is no happy end guaranteed."

—Bernard Sartorius

JL: And would you say, based on your theological studies, your research on the deification of man, that individuation is a process of man realizing his or her divine nature?

BS: Yes, divine nature, but not in the sense of something *wholly good*, as we imagine it—no. I mean, this can be also something absolutely horrible—it can be very destructive for mankind, for people. I am personally very suspicious of any kind of idealization of the individuation process, that it would go in some kind of *perfect man* direction. This I am very, very suspicious of. It is not realistic; it is very simple. It is not true. It is an idealization. There is a colleague I will not mention now, but he gave a description of the individuation process that ends with some kind of perfect man. It is completely unrealistic: well-connected to his Self, knowing his shadow well, connected erotically to his *anima*—I do not believe in this anymore.

JL: What's the value, in your mind, of individuation? What value does this theory have for you?

BS: It has the value of something very, very open, absolutely open, in the sense of being basically different between each person—from person to person—and having very much to do with becoming oneself without the possibility of saying, *what is me?* Because this becoming oneself means something different for each person, we cannot make a general definition. I would even not, anymore, give too much value to clinical criteria. That is, some people believe that such would indicate how far the individuation process for somebody has gone. I do not believe in this anymore. I have seen too many illusions in my work and, also, among my colleagues, where this process is concerned.

JL: Too many illusions?

BS: Illusions, yes. Illusions. Hopeful, wishful thinking. And if one looks at reality like this, really, it is phenomenologically far from ideal, it is far from catastrophic. Simply, it is very different from person to person. Everything we think in psychology about ourselves, about somebody, is ultimately hypothesis. Hypothesis. Analytically speaking, we are all hypotheses. No acclamations. I can make hypotheses. It can be helpful, because hypotheses are questions, but open questions. If I give a diagnosis about, let us say, the psychological constellation of somebody, and I make this diagnosis with the sense that *this is it*—this now really *is* the situation of this person—let me take an example, a classic example—a person is repressing his instincts. And he does not see what is in his dreams, in which animals are getting wild—and we might see this as very typical, the repression of instinct, that repression is why this person is dreaming of animals becoming aggressive. Yes, *as a hypothesis*. But when I believe this, that this is now reality, that this *is* the situation of this person, I close something. I lock this person into something—even if I am not expressing it to the person.

JL: In previous conversations, I spoke, for example, to Murray Stein, about what we could learn in the field of analytical psychology from Christianity. It's a very broad question. But he said, "Well, I think we can learn to have faith." And he spoke of the faith in the process; he spoke about faith in the therapeutic room. And I was wondering, because now when you speak, you speak about agnosticism, you speak about keeping the idol relation as holy-we-don't-know.

BS: Yes.

JL: I very much like that, but I'm wondering about the idea of faith. Is that then excluded? Or is that something that you see that we can actually practice as an attitude as analysts?

BS: That is also a very good question. You see, that is maybe where the question comes in, about Islam, because Islam basically is acceptance, and this acceptance is not exactly identical with Christian faith. A Christian faith contains also, I would say, acceptance, to a certain extent, but it is—of course it is not a very sharp distinction, but rather a question of emphasis. In Christianity, the way that I experienced it (at least this is my subjective experience), faith means the outcome will be good. The outcome will be good. Whatever I fantasize when I say good: God is love, God loves me, God has saved me through Jesus Christ. So, doubt cannot be good if I have faith. Faith is the trust in this loving God, and then things either way, or not, will be fine. Some very completist beliefs in miracles, that a miracle will happen, are in the fundamentalist churches: they believe, up to a very highly spiritual way of experiencing this, that ultimately, the individuation process leads in a good direction.

And that connection with the self—or whatever, the so-called self—that Islam has, this is what interests me very much. And the Islamic perception of the mystery, I would say, is more open to the mystery: that God can also destroy; there is no happy end guaranteed, no guarantee that everything is going to be fine. There cannot be an ideal because this abandonment to whatever Allah is—or what most of us have the slightest idea of is—this is really open. It is really open in the fullness . . . So, what image of God is this? It is an image of God that is completely mysterious, in the sense of it does not go into a direction that we can really sympathize with: with our desire, our wish, that things will be fine. And this gives—basically, I would say, though of course in the social world, it is different now (I believe probably many would not accept what I am saying), but in my way of seeing this—it gives an openness to the mystery that ultimately can only be described as agnostic. That is where we have to make the link. We do not know.

JL: So when you speak like this, what I am reminded of is Jesus on the cross. Forsaken at the cross. Don't we find that also there? Or in Islam, it's more integrated?

BS: I would say to a certain extent that it is more integrated. That the wish, when the Muslim says *inshallah*—and here he is mostly belonging to the culture—he would really say, I will arrive—I will take the plane and I will arrive at five o'clock in Berlin, *inshallah*. He means there is a possibility that God brings the plane down. He has somewhere integrated this *inshallah*, because he hopes that the plane will arrive in Berlin safely, but he has integrated the possibility that the plane might crash. So it is really already in the language, as in, *so God willing*. *Inshallah*, so God willing, I will arrive in Berlin at five o'clock. And this is a daily expression that, yes, ultimately, we do not know the will of God, or the will of destiny, or whatever we want to call it.

JL: And you feel sometimes, in Christian faith, that that's lacking?

BS: Yes, I would say this. This familiarity with God through—especially through Jesus Christ, who is our friend and close to us, one of us—and with the same kind of God, the Son of God—this familiarity, one could almost say (from which, by the way, this sequence that you have just reminded me of, what happened on the cross, when Jesus said, *why have you abandoned me*) is very central . . . This is one of the passages that is not very often preached about in the churches, because it is very hard. It does not fit very nicely into the Christian image of God. It is a fact. God has become—let us say, in church Christianity (it is always good to know about which kind of God we are speaking, so I am speaking of the church God)—a nice good, good little friend, who means well for me, and who asks me also to be good with my fellow man. But all this is very nice, and has lost, to a large extent, at least in Protestantism, its real mystery, a sense of mystery.

And it is not enough to say, yes, God is unknown—you see what I mean—I mean, to preach that God is unknown, and to verbalize all this. It is a question of *sensing* it. It is interesting to see this in all the Orthodox Church, we have a possible connection with what we said earlier. There is this sense of mystery, that God is really not just there to fulfill our wishes. But he is really the unknown also. This is much stronger; and in the Russian Orthodox liturgy, we feel it. This Christ figure on the top of the roof of the Orthodox Church is looking, with terrible eyes, down. He is not a nice little—a nice fellow.

JL: After finishing my training in Zürich, I was drawn in to Luther, and the theology of the cross.

BS: Right.

JL: And especially how Luther speaks about how God works. How God does his alien work. He's always hidden in his opposite. In Luther, I think both mystery and the cross, and the paradox of suffering, is very present. There's not this cozy identification with a God. He does not believe in only a good God. There's the question of a surrender to God's will. And there's the breaking of the human will, of the human will, for the sake of God's.

BS: I agree with you. There are many, many overlaps. It is a question of emphasis. I am, of course, I realize—as I am listening to what you are saying—I am very much connected to Christianity the way I experienced it in my parish work, and in my Church work. And, as a Christian in the Church, what I hear in the sermons. I grant you absolutely that if you go deeper, to the Church Fathers, and Thomas Aquinas, and to Luther, and Calvin, you get many more substantial types of perceptions of the mystery of God, and of course of the place of suffering. But still, despite this, my impression was—as I started to have contact with the Islamic world—that they, possibly better than the West, have kept the mystery of God, a sense of the mystery of God, to put it simply.

Of course, the interesting thing is that *Westernized Muslims* are the ones who—how to put this—who are the breeding ground for terrorists. It is very interesting to see that most of the people in ISIS, and the people of 9/11, were educated in a Western way. And they found some kind of perverted connection to the sense of transcendence through their terroristic activities—really death, they are driving themselves into death—but this death-wish, this thought for oneself, is of course connected with transcendence. And when transcendence is not experienced anymore—psychologically, one would say—then it can take this type of pathological shape, where it has to be acted out, for instance . . . . But this is a very small part of the Muslim world.

I just experienced it very strongly in Syria and in Morocco, this sense that the human being is not in the center of the universe; to say this very simply, *it is lived*. It is not a theoretical proposition. While in the West, for a reason that could be interesting to explore, the human being is the Alpha and the Omega of everything—this is very, very strongly maintained, and even has become so more strongly since the diminution of religion. The sense that really God is—that *God* is the center of reality and not *man*—this is not something that you find in the West. Of course, you find it in some pockets, and you find it in some books, but as a general tendency, you find this is really a general tendency in the Muslim world: less anthropocentricity.

JL: Staying with this, when you speak of Islam as acceptance, and the theme around surrendering, I remember when you and I spoke some years ago, and you made me aware of the passage, that dream in Memories, Dreams,

Reflections. *Jung has a dream with his father bowing to touch his head to the floor, and Jung is imitating him.*

BS: It is a very, very interesting passage in this book. They were bowing in front of where the highest presence is, and in the highest presence sits—in the dream, it is in the dream—the general, I think it is Uriah, who has been badly betrayed by David—by King David because King David wanted his wife—and who was sent into battle in a very dangerous situation. He was killed in this battle—what David, in fact, intended, and it was so that he could get his wife, the wife of this general. And this Uriah is, so to speak, the symbolic figure of the highest presence.

My interpretation of this is the following: what happened because David—King David and the Book of Psalms and one of the very important figures in Judaism, Song of Solomon, a king who was very close to *Yahweh*—what happened to this general, Uriah, it was, so to speak, an incredible abuse. This King David wanted to snatch the wife of this general, and thanks to his power—given, by the way, by God, by *Yahweh*—he sends the general to the frontline, so that the general gets killed, so that he, David, can take the wife. *This is just a horrible thing.* The general Uriah was the victim of a *fantastic injustice*, but a fantastic injustice that is difficult to qualify from an ethical point of view, because it was happening by a king *chosen by God*: by David, by King David.

So, we have here a complete paradox. This Uriah for me represents the symbolic figure of someone who is suffering injustice—this is completely unjust—and this unjust suffering seems to be suffering somewhere with the will of God. Not that it happened, at least, but that it happened *through somebody that is okay.* That is the difference between Jung and his father. The father seems to represent symbolically that he is bowing in front of the total mystery of God, including the injustice of God in inducing the suffering of Uriah, in having allowed the suffering of Uriah. Jung's father is in a full attitude of acceptance, because he touches the ground with his forehead. Jung, at this point in the dream, is not able, and he is not able even as he wanted to do it.

In the dream, he says, "I wanted to do it, but I didn't succeed." So, something in him is resisting this total surrender. I am not, for a second, blaming Jung for not having touched . . . the ground, but the self-explanation that he gives in *Memories, Dreams, Reflections*—about why he did not touch it—for me seems to be a little bit constructed. For me, this figure means the freedom of man. He has to save God . . . in front of the almighty God. This is constructed, because in the symbolism of freedom, the theological symbolism of freedom, there is not an opposition between freedom and God. God, the quality of God, gives also freedom to man. It is a reductive understanding of freedom, an almost infantile reduction of freedom, to see God as a father who prevents his little boy from being free. This is another superficial understanding of the connection between determination and freedom.

The paradox is that the closer we are to God, the more we are free. And this closeness to God means also surrender; it includes, of course, surrender. It is very interesting that Jung has this dream in Tunisia where, he mentions in his *Memories, Dreams, Reflections*, he was very much impressed by the call to prayer, which he heard . . . five times a day. Very much impressed, he was. And these prayers are in fact the call to go to pray, but the prayer, the Islamic prayer, is a *prayer of surrender*. It is not a prayer of, *give me this, give me that, save me from that, save my soul*, or whatever. It is an expression of surrender . . . more than the Christian prayer, but there it is very, very precise. So, Jung was impressed by this, and he reacted to this with this dream.

JL: What was lacking in Jung at that time?

BS: He had the dream in the 1920s, and he still had not experienced all of the psychic possibilities. In the BBC interview—one year, I think it was one year before his death—when this journalist asks him, "Do you believe in God?" Jung answers, "I know." There is surrender. There I hear more surrender: "I know."

JL: I previously spoke to Amy Cook, who is a scholar studying Kierkegaard and the relationship to Jungian psychology. She takes this statement of Jung's as representation of his difficulties with faith. Or that he does not—when it comes to faith, she says, he is not open. There are no dynamics; there's no dialectic anymore. There's a knowing, not a believing, so there is no faith.

BS: We have a different perception of this, of the way he is quoted. I have listened to Jung many times, because I was also very intrigued by this "I know." And I just got—every time, since the very beginning, it did not change—the impression that he said it because of an inner experience. And you see this is the fact—I would say it is even more religious than just faith—because in faith, you can, to a certain extent, say, I believe because it is absurd. I believe because it is absurd. There's a Church Father, Tertullian, who said, *Credo quia absurdum*: I believe because it is absurd. The more it is foolish, the more I believe. Okay. But that is maybe the beginning. That is not yet the deepest religious experience.

In Jung's "I know"—this is subjective perception— I can perceive the result of an experience, which you could call mystical, or whatever you name it. But of an experience—not just of one experience. Not just one event. But of a *going into* this perception, which allows him then to say, *I know*. And not "I know" in the sense of, I know that the brain has two halves—for which we can also use the phrase "*I know*," that the brain has two halves. Okay. I know that there are two halves. But the intonation in which he says it is absolutely not the one of this kind—do you see what I mean?—"I know that the brain has two halves."

JL: I think so. And I think many people would agree that there's no doubt that he had these profound experiences that made him understand that there are other powers. That's clear to me as well. One can have many of those experiences, though, but it's not faith. Faith has to do with the end of life, no? With the question of eschatology. It's also a question of, what do we have faith in? What's that highest presence that Jung couldn't bow to? I'm wondering still about this, what he couldn't bow to . . .

BS: You see—I mean, there, I cannot answer that. He did not write anything about that. It is simply there is maybe one little indication that shows Jung's own ambivalence where this question is concerned. I will give a possible answer to this question. When he speaks—I once made a little checker of the passages in which he speaks about the transcendent function. And the famous—when he says, *Deo concedente*, God willing, the individuation process will go like this or that. Or what he wrote over the door of his building: *Vocatus atque non vocatus, Deus aderit*. Called or not called, God will be here.

The transcendent function sometimes is clearly only psychological in some of these expressions. I do not have the quotes now in my head, but I have written them somewhere. But there is a psychological function, and then at one point there is *a third*, which results from the tension between the two, and it is a search, it is a new situation that comes about from the dialectic between the two . . . Then there are passages in Jung's writing that seem quite explicitly metaphysical, and where the God willing, *Deo concedente*, seems to come from the other side, from the metaphysical side. But Jung himself does not clarify this. One just can notice that there are quotes about the transcendent function, which sometimes leans more toward something purely psychic, or purely psychological, and sometimes leans toward something metaphysical in the true sense—that is, pure mystery, not reducible to psychological phenomena.

I cannot say more, so—I have the impression (also in your question) that he was moving in this realm until the end of his life, with probably some more confidence at some point, or surrender. It is interesting, if one looks at *The Red Book*, there are many, many places in which his paintings figure Islamic buildings. Many places. There are about ten buildings. Of course, they are not in the center. They are somewhere in the corner. But they are little buildings with a *cupola* that look like mosques. So, the theme of surrender is helping him from the very beginning. I think he was deeply impressed, somewhere, by the motive of surrender. But at the same time, resisting it.

JL: I hear how you were drawn into your Islamic studies. And I hear the depth and the importance that this has had for you psychologically. And I see, if I go out from my practice and I go a hundred meters, there's a little mosque. Every day, young men coming with their carpets—running, you know—to them. There's a pull, there's an energy. And at the same time, in my little life in Berlin, trying to enter a church. Usually it's closed, or it's rented out for some event . . .

BS: Yes, yes.

JL: Or you come on a Sunday, and you sit down with a group of elderly people—nothing wrong with that—

BS: Yes, I understand.

JL: So, there is something culturally here that we're standing in the middle of.

BS: Yes. You see, I hear you very well. I must say, this speaks to me also, what you feel here. Simply, my impression is this, and it is of course a very personal hypothesis: that this new God—that Jung was trying in his approach as well—was trying to communicate to him, particularly through *The Red Book* or so. And wrestling with Christianity, for sure. But this wrestling with something, with a psychic reality, with a spiritual reality who was still very much alive, to a certain extent, but which was already on its way out. The Islamic reality, as such, with its ethnological aspects, is not necessarily a reality on its way *in*—because in Islam, there is also a lot of reformation that I am sure has shapes for a Westerner that are difficult to follow—it has a lot of anachronisms that do not correspond to our old psyche. It is not easy today to become a Muslim, for a Westerner. But there is something in Islam that I think is highly symbolic of a general movement happening in mankind now.

And a general movement, in regard to which Christianity is outdated. This is to a certain extent outdated. There are a lot of things that are carried on, but in one main point it is outdated. And this is—it is my hypothesis, which I know can be critiqued, but I am deeply convinced that at least there is some truth in it: and this is the anthropocentricity of Christianity. Christianity is based on Judaism, and then Jesus Christ became Christianity, but firstly it was based on Judaism. And Judaism is a religion in which God, *Yahweh*, suddenly takes very seriously the well-being and the destiny of one particular group of human beings. This is amazing. And this God even intervenes in history, in the history of this little group, helping them to get out of Egypt, to go to the promised land, and to fight all the pagans, who are, by the way, nature-God believers who believed that nature is something divine. They were met with all trials . . . in the name of God. So, first a human group was highly valued—the Hebrews. And then mankind as such, humanity as such, was highly valued—*highly* valued. God became man. God did not become an animal, or cosmos, or nature. He became man.

So, there we have, mythologically speaking, a tremendous emphasis upon the value of human being, which, of course, then laid the foundation of a perception of the value of human needs. Human needs. If human being is so valuable, then his needs are of course very valuable. And there we have, then, the American constitution. The fundamental right of freedom, of love, of happiness, and so forth—that humanity and its needs—and then, ultimately, we have also, of course, the consumer society, which at one point, of course, produces perversity (when the natural needs are satisfied, one has to begin to produce some artificial needs to satisfy—you know this better than myself).

So, this anthropocentricity—this is my impression—is coming to an end. And it is coming to an end, not because of some kind of metaphysical reason, but because we see the effect it has had upon the planet. It has for a long time allowed a better life for humanity, but with the industrial revolution and technological explosion (maybe things would be difficult otherwise), it is beginning now to destroy the planet, the very foundations upon which human life is possible. So, this anthropocentricity is showing now its dark side—which means centricity upon human desires and satisfaction—and this, I think, is the beginning of a change of civilization.

And there, of course, Islam, with its *theocentricity*, with God being in the center, the mystery, which is also in the cosmos, which—why not, there might be those extraterrestrial beings landing one of these days, which God is also behind—which is more relevant today than, I think, anthropocentricity, especially for the future. And that is why some people feed this in Islam. They feed it. They are attracted by the theocentricity of Islam. And I must say, I myself, that it is also for this way that I have interest in Islam. I felt, yes, this is not going to solve our human problems, but this is giving again a place—a big place, by the way—to the origin of life and of death and of everything. And giving it an existential way and not just philosophically.

JL: I feel that I need to ask you a very personal question, and you can decide how you'd like and if you'd like to answer to it. Do you believe in God?

BS: I will just say of the various religious expressions, I sense something of *within God*. Or for Buddhism, because they say also, *we are not, we do not believe in God*. But they behave like people who are open to the mystery. That is why I prefer to call it *the mysteries*, because if we have to, by all means, use a word—and I prefer this one.

Jung as a Prophet for the Twenty-First Century , with David Tacey

"I think Jung developed a strong conscience about the way that his work would probably be misused as a purely personal way of attending to your own personal growth, which certainly wasn't his intention . . . .We cannot have a world full of individuated individuals without having also a developed and individuated community. And that's where Christianity, I think, still has a lot to teach everybody, including Jungians."

—David Tacey

JL: Did you grow up religiously?

DT: Oh, yes, I did. Yes. Yes. Strongly Christian background, very strong Christian background, which I took seriously, although my two sisters didn't. They rejected my family's Christianity, but I took it very seriously and sought for a personal relationship with God through Jesus. That was very important to me. And just as important was my contact with indigenous people, because I grew up in a little town in Central Australia, called Alice Springs, which was probably more than half Black: they were from the Aboriginal Indigenous people of Australia. It was their homeland. And White people like myself with European backgrounds, we're almost in the minority. And Aboriginal people have a very strong spiritual life. It's not Christian, or it has some common ground with Christianity, but they have a spirituality that is close to that of the American Indians, for instance, or the shamans in Siberia, in Russia. And those very ancient cultures. They have very strong rites of passage, to go from being a youth to an adult. They have a very strong connection with the earth.

So I got a lot of my feelings for the spirituality of nature, and the spirituality of earth, from the Indigenous people of Central Australia. The Arrernte, the Pintupi, and the Warlpiri people were the three tribes that I interacted with. And then when I studied Jung, of course, this was a wonderful experience for me because Jung explained a great deal about the beliefs of the Indigenous people. Indeed, Jung wrote about the Indigenous people of Australia. In several of his essays, I found Jung not only personally interesting, but culturally, extremely engaging as a way of understanding Indigenous cultures and their symbolic lives.

When I was about thirteen, some of the Aboriginal boys in my classroom would suddenly be absent for, say, three or four weeks. And I'd ask where they were. And the answer was generally they're being taken by elders to engage in what's called *men's business*. And *men's business* is a rite of passage from youth into manhood and involving often a lot of painful activities: deprivations and lacerations over the chest, sometimes knocking out the eyetooth, and also being taught the mysteries of the tribe, and the mysteries of the ancestors.

Their ancestors are what Jung calls archetypes. This is basically the same thing. So they're communing with ancestors during this initiation ceremony, where they're often asked to not eat, not drink—sometimes they're given hallucinatory drugs in order to facilitate some kind of disruption of the normal psychological process. And all that is so terribly understandable in Jungian terms. The ego has to be disrupted in order for the unconscious to be felt—the unconscious that contains archetypes, but in their case, the unconscious is called *the dreaming*, which is an interesting word, because naturally enough, Jungian psychology is based on dreaming, and dreams.

JL: When we wrote some emails back and forth before this conversation, we spoke about James Hillman. And then I shared with you some of the readings I did in the book Lament of the Dead, *where he has a conversation with Sonu Shamdasani. And a lot of that conversation sort of circles back to Christ and the Christ figure, and I just want to share, for the listeners, some quotes where Hillman actually speaks about Christ or Christianity. For example, Shamdasani says, about* The Red Book, *"If there were an index, it would show that the critical feature is Christ." Hillman says, "Where does Christ and Christianity fit into a new psychology?" And Hillman is also saying, "There's a tension in Jung." He doesn't throw it out. He finds a way to remain with Christ." What do you think about Hillman talking about Christ in this way?*

DT: I don't think Hillman would talk about it if Shamdasani hadn't brought it up. But Shamdasani is a pretty shrewd scholar, and very insightful, and I think Shamdasani is absolutely right. So people talk about *The Red Book*, and they talk about this plethora of figures, like Philemon, and all these other figures that Jung encountered through active imagination. But Shamdasani's right: The whole *Red Book* is resonating with Christian images and images of Christ. And Hillman was very enthusiastic about *The Red Book*. I think why Hillman was interested wasn't because of Christ. He was interested because the imagination had burst forth in all this color, and all these astonishing paintings and all this artwork.

What I found contradictory about this *Red Book* is that Jung denounced *The Red Book*, strongly. By the time he wrote *Memories, Dreams, Reflections*, he said he'd been seduced by the *anima* when he was writing *The Red Book* into thinking that he might be an artist (all those artworks, which are, in fact, some of them are very fine works of art). And then he decided at one point to put *The Red Book* behind him, because he needed to focus on the conceptual ideas-based substance of depth psychology, and not just the pretty pictures that he was producing in these states of distress as he was encountering figures from the unconscious.

So, but I think we're very fortunate to have Sonu Shamdasani. And I agree with Sean McGrath that he has singlehandedly made Jungian studies academically respectable. And I think that's absolutely right. We have an enormous debt to Shamdasani. It's interesting that Shamdasani is not an analyst. He's a scholar. Analysts can't quite write with the depth of history and understanding that Shamdasani has, and his training, and everything he has done has been extremely valuable. So I think, as you say, there are echoes of Christ all through *The Red Book*, and Jung clearly valued the Christ figure. But Hillman's right to the extent that we can't necessarily equate the Christ of *The Red Book* with the Christ of Christianity. It's like, we can't equate Jung's God with the God of Christianity, either. Jung's God was seemingly anti-Christian in some ways. One of Jung's first experiences of his contact with his God was that his God let fly a giant turd onto the Basel Cathedral, which of course Freudians read as an Oedipal attack—they refer to it as anal aggressivity. Anal aggressivity against the church of his father.

I don't get too excited by Christians who claim that Jung's work helps Christianity to recover, because clearly Christianity as a tradition is in decline in Europe, and in all European-influenced countries such as my own, Australia, and New Zealand. Christianity, in its public forms, basically, is at the point of collapse. Jung's Christ is a Gnostic figure. I don't think Jung's Christ is in line with orthodox understandings of Jesus at all. But Jung respected the fact that his own soul had historical antecedents and historical background. There was no way that Jung was going to completely reject Christianity.

Although, of course, Christians rejected Jung—many, many of them, especially Father Victor White, but also other Christians who tried to work with Jung found it almost impossible to reconcile Jung's work with Christianity. Jung burned his bridges with Christianity by insisting on *gnosis* about faith. And I think this was the basis of the rift with Christians: that Christians emphasize faith; Jung emphasizes *gnosis* or knowledge. And that's why, in that famous interview, he says, "I don't believe in God; I know." Which is a funny thing to say, in some ways, because it is a very Gnostic thing to say. So, this very much upset, I think, Christians worldwide, when Jung seemed to condemn the idea of belief and the related concept of faith.

JL: But you also told me that Jung can be understood as agnostic, that he counterbalances his Gnosticism with his agnostic scientific persona. Could you say something more about that?

DT: Well, that's right. Yes, he does. Jung's persona, which is what we see throughout *The Collected Works*, except in *Answer to Job*, his so-called scientific persona basically dissolves. And he's writing *Answer to Job* as a very passionate person, and a Gnostic who believes that there is a God, and there is divine significance in the figure of Jesus Christ. But I think these two sides of Jung were often in conflict. I think Jung wasn't really unified in his own personality about Christianity. He certainly couldn't get rid of it. And it had a claim on him, which I think he found almost grew stronger as he got older.

So, as you know, Jung thought that the things that Christians consider to be literally true, like the virgin birth, and physical resurrection, the walking on water, the feeding of thousands with two fish and three loaves, all these for Jung were complete nonsense as historical events. They had to be read symbolically, and taken symbolically as statements of myth. But as soon as you say that to some Christians, they think you're being very heretical and even blaspheming, because we're talking about changing the way the Holy Book is read. But Jung thought that the writers of the gospels were all writing in symbolic ways, in symbolic terms, and that—so Jung reverses the tables. It wasn't that he was reading the Bible incorrectly, but in his view, Christians had *en mass*, in large numbers, read the Bible incorrectly for centuries. And of course, he goes right back. And one of Jung's favorite figures is Origen, who was a strong Christian convert in Alexandria in Egypt. And he—if you read Origen's work—he was, of course, reading the Bible non-literally, reading the texts that were available in his day, including the Gospel of Thomas, reading them non-literally. And Origen said that's the only way we should read. Otherwise, they become documents about impossible events.

So I published a book on that, which was called *Religion as Metaphor*. I published that in America some years ago. And that's my—that was my contribution to this debate. And again, Christians misunderstand my motivation. It wasn't to destroy Christianity at all, because I remain a Christian, but to try and deepen our understanding of Christianity.

JL: You wrote me before this conversation: "I don't think Jung was ultimately a Christian." He was born Christian, educated in the Christian mold, and much of his late work was focused on the analysis of Christian ideas, beliefs, and dogmas. But you say that it seems to you that he outgrew Christianity—and, you say, as soon as he entered young adulthood. And in a way, I hear you, but I'm also hearing you speaking about how Jung throughout his life wrestled and tried and wanted to create a reformation or a revisioning, or a new understanding of the gospel or of Christianity.

DT: So, when I said that Jung is not Christian, I've got my tongue in my cheek, because of course he was obsessed with Christianity all of his life. When I say Jung was not a Christian, I would qualify that statement by saying that Jung was not a Christian as the person down the street in a Christian country would recognize Christianity, the sorts of things that they hold to be true for their faith. For instance, where Paul says in the letters to the Corinthians that if Jesus didn't rise from the dead, then all our faith is in vain.

While Jung just disregards that, and in fact, he wrote an entire essay on the resurrection. It's in volume 18, which is called *The Symbolic Life*. And people who try to reconcile Jung with mainstream Christianity should read that essay on the resurrection before they utter statements like, *Jung is definitely trying to renew or revivify the Christian religion*. Jung, I think, like—very similar to his predecessor Origen—wanted to basically smash Christianity in its present forms, because of its literalism and its supernaturalism, which did not appeal to Jung at all. And if you read *Answer to Job*, particularly his preface to *Answer to Job*, he does say there that the Christianity that we are historically aware of as Christianity will have to disappear in order to give rise to a new understanding of Christianity: all the miracles and wonders and supernatural events, including the physical resurrection, which many Christians say is the foundation of their faith. Well, Jung says that all of that has to be overturned, and we have to rediscover Christianity as a symbolic mythos. The public participation in Christianity in my country is as low as about five or six percent of the population.

JL: I mean, it seems to be happening already that this religion is in a process of, if not dying, mourning or grieving something that was. But I'm also wondering in what way this critique, or this disruption, of Jung's is helpful for dreaming the myth forward? Because still it's the Christian myth, and the dream is still the Christian dream, no? I think sometimes there's also a lot of negativity to relate to in the Jungian field, about Christ and Christianity. Speaking with another scholar, Ann Conrad Lammers, she says that maybe a bridge is not a good metaphor for what one could build between Christianity or Christ and Jungian psychology. It's too, sort of, grand of a building, to try to build a bridge in this way. It's failed, or it broke down. And here we are in a Christian world that is disintegrating . . .

DT: Yeah, the bridge collapsed. Yeah, he tried to build a bridge, but it just collapsed. See, he was only building it from his side. If you ask any engineer or architect, they will tell you that bridges need to be built from both sides of the gap. A bridge can't be built from one side; it would just collapse. It has to be built from the other side. And that's why when the Christians that Jung was working with deserted him, and really that's when the bridge collapsed, there was no bridge. Although, he wanted to build one. And Christians often complain that Jung was replacing religion with psychology. And I think I've heard many Jungians say that. I don't believe that for a minute.

I think Jung was saying, we need an approach to religion. We don't need to replace it. We need to understand it anew from a psychological point of view. That's a statement he makes time and again, in *Psychology and Alchemy*. He keeps saying, *I'm not*—you know, he was accused of psychologism. That was the word religious people used in anger at Jung, as if he was reducing everything to psychology. It simply wasn't the case. If you read him carefully, he was saying that Christian symbols risk being relegated to a "sphere of sacrosanct unintelligibility"—until we unravel all this symbolism and understand its deeper meaning, and then it becomes valid again. So perhaps Jung was the post-doctrinal Christian.

He certainly did not agree with the doctrines of Christianity. He could never read out the Apostles' Creed with any sense of moral conscience. He'd say, *look, this was written in the third century or fourth century.* I think the introduction to *Answer to Job*, which is only about five pages, is the most cogent statement Jung ever wrote about Christianity, and why it had to die in its current form. You see, this is the important thing. Jung felt it had to die in its current form in order to be reborn in a new way. So in a sense, you can see how the Christian myth is operating, even in that statement. You have to die to be born again. In other words, this—what we're going through at the moment—is the crucifixion of Christianity. And the Christians are saying, *help, help! This is not nice. We're on the cross. We want to fast-forward to the resurrection.* You can't fast-forward to the resurrection. You have to experience the agony of the cross. And as I said, I get misread as trying to destroy Christianity, but anyone who tries to change anything is claimed to be a destroyer.

JL: I love your metaphor or image of Christians on the cross at this moment of history. It's a very beautiful, powerful image that you're sharing. I also believe strongly in what you say about the importance of symbolical understanding or reading these stories and myths, mythologically or symbolically, that Christianity is not only about personal salvation. Or maybe some would say it is—but it's also about the world. It's also about community, about the collective. And it's also Christ, which speaks about not only my individuation, but the world's. So, I am wondering about community. This is an aspect that we Jungians are not always so strong on.

DT: That's right. And that's why the Vatican keeps condemning Jung. The Vatican has produced, I think now, three documents condemning

Jung. And one of the reasons they keep condemning him is that they say he's advocating narcissism, individualism, and ignoring the collective. And I'll tell you what, they've got a good point. Because, to some extent, Jungian analysis is about me, my encounter with my unconscious. And that's bizarre because Jung's terms aren't about me and my, they're about the collective unconscious. So why do people suddenly forget that the unconscious is not just my personal possession, but it's part of the collectivity?

And I think that this is the great contribution that Christianity has made, and continues to make, although it's in a very weakened form these days. It's this emphasis on community and this emphasis on shared experience of the Divine rather than my individuation and my personal symbols of the Divine that I've garnered from my dreams. But even that is contradictory, because Jung pointed out that the most important dreams we have are collective dreams. And he, of course, when he was in Africa, the Elgonyi—where was it now, in Kenya and Ethiopia—kept telling him that there's a big difference between little dreams and big dreams. And big dreams are the dreams that affect the whole country, the whole race, the whole nation. And I think some of us continue to have big dreams. But if we just sit on them and think that they're only personal things that have arisen for our personal development or aggrandizement—I do think that Jung started to feel guilty about this individualism toward the end of his career, because don't forget, he constantly tried to correct people. He said, "My work is about individuation, not individualism."

And he would continue to say the individualism is a misreading of individuation. And particularly in that late essay of his called "The Undiscovered Self," that's very much concerned about society, about people in Europe and elsewhere. They can't live, he thought, without an idea of God. Because we have to have something at the center of our lives, which can provide a focus not only for our belief, but also for our development as individuals.

And so I think Jung developed a strong conscience about the way that his work would probably be misused as a purely personal way of attending to your own personal growth, which certainly wasn't his intention. But if you read a lot of Jungians, you would think that was his intention. A lot of the popular books about Jung are exactly rigid in that kind of mode, as if society doesn't exist. And community isn't needed. Well, of course, we cannot have a world full of individuated individuals without having also a developed and individuated community. And that's where Christianity, I think, still has a lot to teach everybody, including Jungians.

JL: You recently wrote a paper entitled "Jung as a Prophet for a New Dispensation." And you argue that Jung actually was a prophet and can only be understood in this light. That Jung is suffering from carrying a prophetic burden. Could you speak a bit about Jung as a prophet?

DT: Well, yes. I know my dear friend and colleague, Sean McGrath, disagrees strongly with me, and I challenge him to a debate, actually, on this. I do think that Jung can only be understood as a prophet. If you read *The Red Book*, the whole book is a book of prophecy. Maybe people like Sean and others are thinking that Jung is not a prophet in the mainstream Judeo- Christian tradition. And I'd certainly agree with that. But that's not the only form of prophecy; you can have all kinds of prophecy concerned with the future.

And of course, that famous discussion Jung had with Max Zeller, from Berlin, when Zeller was leaving Zürich to found the Jung Institute of Los Angeles, in California. Just before he left, he had this dream that people were building this vast temple. And the foundations were already there, but they were building pillars and walls and roofs. And Jung's response to this was very enthusiastic. He'd tap his pipe on his chair, and he'd say, "This is the new temple." And he'd say, "They're building it in India. They're building it in America. They're building it in Russia. They're building it in China." And Max Zeller asked him, "How long will it take to build this church?" And Jung said, "I know." And Zeller said, "Well, how do you know?" And Jung said, "From people's dreams, and from my own dreams. And to build this new temple, this new religion, if you like, will take six hundred years."

That's a long time to wait. So I think what Jung said in his public statements, which he often said, "I'm not a prophet, and I'm not here to found a new religious order. And I'm a psychologist and empiricist and a phenomenologist"—was totally contradicted by what he said privately to Max Zeller. And that can be found in Max Zeller's book, called *The Dream: Visions of the Night*. And I think Jung played a duplicitous game with many of us . He would go to London and give talks to the Guild of Pastoral Psychology, and say that he wasn't a religious leader, he was simply a humble clinician. It's total nonsense. Who's he fooling? He was a prophet. And I think he'll be regarded as such in the future, as a major prophet—not necessarily of some new religion that has nothing to do with his own Christian roots.

Quite the contrary. I do think that Jung wanted to dream the Christian dream onward. And I do think he wanted it to learn a lot of things from Buddhism in particular. They're the two religions that Jung valued most of all: Christianity and Buddhism. He was less keen on Judaism. And he wasn't too keen on Islam either. Nor was he very keen on Hinduism. Although he did borrow from Hinduism. The very idea of the Self comes from Hinduism in its concept of the atman.

But I think Jung thought that the future might be some amalgam of Christianity and Buddhism. And I think he would hope that the new religion or the new faith will maintain Christianity's commitment to community and to social justice, but be incorporated or complemented by the Buddhist emphasis on introspection, contemplation, meditation, and interiority. And as you know, Jung was quite critical of countless Europeans , including many people from his own native Switzerland, who were abandoning Christianity and turning toward Buddhism. And he'd say, *well, you're abandoning the houses that your fathers built, the churches, and you're invading the temples of India and Sri Lanka, and Japan, the Zen Buddhist temples that your fathers didn't build*. So Jung is often criticized for those statements. But what he was saying, in effect, was the soul has history.

We can't forget and ignore the history of the soul. And you cannot take two thousand years of Christian history and just put it in the garbage can. It's not going to work. Christianity has been part of our spiritual and our soulful makeup for a long, long time and a long, long time to come. But that's the good news. The bad news is that it won't survive in its current forms. And its current forms might have to collapse in order to give rise to this sort of fusion of Buddhism and Christianity. So Jung, I think, had a very grand vision. He was a prophet, and too many Jungians try to ignore this dimension of his life and his work when we should not ignore it at all.

Jung is a tragic figure. Shamdasani says this in his book on *The Birth of a New Psychology*, that Jung falls between two stools. He's too religious for the scientists. And he's too scientific for the religious. So Jung, the fate of Jung, is somewhat tragic. He wanted to form a place midway between science and religion. And no one was going to do that, at least not a hundred years ago. They're more likely to do it now, in the age of quantum physics and new biology and new ecology. This is the one of the paradoxes of the whole field. Jung speaks more to the twenty-first century than he does to the twentieth.

And I know I wrote in one of my books somewhere that the twentieth century may have been Freud's, but the twenty-first century, I think, will be Jung's. He will emerge as the dominant figure, not Freud, who will disappear into the background as actually a very minor figure. If you look at contemporary biology, like Rupert Sheldrake, contemporary physics like Paul Davies, and these sorts of people, they're all talking about the numinous dimension of matter. And Thomas Berry, one of the most famous ecologists, whose work of course is based on Pierre Teilhard de Chardin, the French Jesuit who was rejected by his own Catholic Church. All these new building blocks of the new sciences. Look at physics, biology, chemistry, ecology, all the sciences, are moving in a Jungian direction. And maybe we could talk about that in another time.

Participatio Christi: Adolf Keller and C.G. Jung, with Kenneth Kovacs

"I think that individuation should be in service to community. It should lead to one's living within the larger. It's about me bringing my individuality—not my individualism, but the uniqueness of myself—into the community. And in some ways, the community helps me individuate."

—Kenneth Kovacs

JL: I would like to ask you about the correspondence between Jung and Adolf Keller, the Protestant theologian and pastoral psychologist. I know that you have spent time with this correspondence, and I know that you have been to the archives in Zürich. I was wondering if you could start by introducing us to Adolf Keller, and what you found illuminating about the relationship between him and C.G. Jung.

KK: I was very excited about the arrival of the Jung–Keller correspondence. For me, Adolf Keller (1872–1963) was a fascinating human being, and I have to say—maybe I'm projecting a lot onto him—but I really stand in awe of him as a person, as a pastor, as a theologian, as a human being. He was a remarkable soul with an indomitable spirit and drive.

A little bit of historical background: Keller was born in 1872, and he studied theology at the University of Basel, and his interest in the human psyche, in particular, developed while he was a theology student during the two semesters that he spent in Berlin, in 1894 and '95. There he discovered that personal piety needs to be brought into conversation with social engagement and that religion should be a practical concern—an individual concern, but it needs to be a practical concern to the human spirit—such that greater value is placed on human experience, the value of human experience, being attentive to human experience.

When he finished his theological studies, he focused on pastoral work. He was a pastor of the German Protestant Church in Cairo. And while serving in Cairo, he spent one night alone on Mount Sinai and had a profound religious experience that shaped the rest of his life. He was a leader in the Swiss Reformed Church and German Reformed Church circles. He was, we might say, an interstitial person. He was a person who was always making connections and building bridges. He'd socialize regularly with psychiatrists. He was very good friends with Robert Binswanger (1850–1910) at the Bellevue Sanatorium, one of the finest private psychiatric clinics in Germany.

There's this circle of psychologists with religious sensibilities, religious people with psychological sensibilities, who were all engaged in conversations and sharing of ideas at that time. In 1904, Keller became minister of the German Reformed Church in Geneva, and for a time, Keller's pastoral assistant was the young pastor Karl Barth, who then went on to become one of the great theologians of the twentieth century, probably one of the great theologians of the Church, who later was known for his dialectical theology. Théodore Flournoy (1854–1920) and others saw the value of psychology for pastoral care, for pastoral psychology. They thought very early on that psychology has something to offer the work of parish ministry. And then from there, from Geneva, Keller went on to Saint Peter's Church in Zürich, at the time the largest Reformed Church in Switzerland. It was within that context that Jung and Keller—their friendship—really started to solidify.

After the First World War, Keller was instrumental in organizing relief work for suffering congregations throughout Europe. He put an enormous amount of energy into that work. So, he's caring for his congregation, and he's also caring for countless other congregations throughout Europe devastated by the war. He saw the value of ecumenical work, of denominations—Protestant denominations in particular—working together for a common end, for the welfare of humankind. The ecumenical movement emerged in the early part of the twentieth century, after the First World War. And Keller was directly involved in that work, which would later become the World Council of Churches.

Keller saw the value of ecumenical work for Church unity. And even here, you can see Keller as a bridge-builder. He's making these connections. He is trying to maintain connections—he's trying to build bridges, maintain bridges, but he himself, within his own being, he is a bridge. And then, when he found himself in Zürich, within those circles, it was natural for Keller to start building bridges with the psychoanalytic community. Keller was directly involved in the psychoanalytic community—working with psychoanalysts, working with psychologists—and he was not alone. In this growing field of psychology, you see pastors and psychologists working together, crossing boundaries, trying to find places where there's mutual concern. Keller became a very good friend of Jung's. Keller baptized several of Jung's children. Keller's wife Tina was in analysis with Jung and then later became the first woman analyst in Geneva. Keller was often at Jung's home in Küsnacht. So you can just imagine the conversations that took place around the dinner table there. And then, when Jung split with Freud, Keller supported Jung and was there by his side. Keller was a member of the Psychoanalytic Society, which was a forerunner of the Psychology Club. So he's a very important person historically, not only for theological developments, for the history of pastoral theology, of practical theology—which is a new field that emerges in the 1930s and 1940s—but also a very important person for the history of analytical psychology, because he had a huge impact upon Jung and Jung's own ideas.

JL: When you look at that exchange and what's been conserved in those letters, what are the key questions that this correspondence circulates around? And are there questions there that you explore that you feel are relevant also for our time? Can you share something of what touches you?

KK: What touches me is the way, in these letters, that Keller remains consistent. He's always the bridge. He's looking for connections. He's trying to find correlations. He's trying to find a relationship between developments within theology and developments within psychology as psychology develops in the early part of the twentieth century. I'm struck by the fact that analytical psychology develops in late nineteen-teens into 1920, around the same time that dialectical theology is emerging, the theology that's associated with Karl Barth, Rudolf Bultmann, Emil Brunner, and others.

So dialectical theology is emerging—particularly after Barth's commentary on Romans in 1919, all of this theological fervor is happening—at the same time analytical psychology is emerging in Zürich. And Keller sees in some aspects of dialectical theology opportunities for some kind of connection with analytical psychology. Keller struggles with this. He sees opportunities for conversation and for dialogue, and yet he also has some reservations. He sees the tension. He's not trying to blend them together. He's trying to hold them together, maybe in a kind of creative tension, to hopefully wait for something new to emerge. You can see Keller's projections onto Jung. In some ways, they are—this is not a relationship among equals. At the same time, Keller holds his own. He doesn't yield easily to Jung. Keller takes Jung to task where he is theologically going off on detours.

Keller raises important questions to Jung. I think it's striking that there are tensions in the relationship. They had a strong relationship early on. There was a gap in their relationship, and then, later in their lives, they came back together. And the correspondence focuses more on that time when they're coming back together. As the letters show, Jung trusts Keller. Jung gives Keller an early version of *Answer to Job*. Keller's carrying around these documents on his person—he confides in Keller, and Keller then also pushes back and raises critical questions about what Jung is trying to do. Keller is respecting and understanding what's happening or what Jung's trying to say in *Answer to Job*, but also responding with a theological response, a theological critique. So kind of helping him—maybe this is too strong, kind of helping guide Jung a little bit as he himself digests and processes what he's trying to say and do in *Answer to Job*. They are sort of embodying that relationship of psychology and theology, as it were, in the relationship itself, in the flow, in the dialogue, in the dialectic, one to the other. One being open to the other, allowing oneself to be informed by the other, maintaining one's individuality and particularity, but then connecting and relating one to the other and being touched by the other. So, it's almost like a dance you can see in the correspondence, which is what I find fascinating.

JL: Is there, in your mind, change that one can see, then, in either of the two, either in Jung or his psychology that he developed? Was he open to change and changed out of a correspondence like this, and vice versa? You see there were results of this fascinating—and I find, very often moving—exchange between these two remarkable people?

KK: I think there was maybe a change. Maybe a different way of saying it is that Keller was receptive to what Jung had to give him. And he took it in and metabolized it, digested it. Keller was not trying to be Jung, but he was—he was taking in what Jung could offer. He could receive it. He wasn't open to everything that Jung tried to offer. Right? But he took in something; he allowed himself to be touched. And in that movement, Keller was changed. In that movement, it allowed him to—it kind of freed him to be himself. What I'm really stuck by, I was surprised and shocked to learn that Keller gave lectures on dialectical theology at the Psychology Club. That's just extraordinary, I think. And Jung attended these lectures.

Jung wanted to know more about dialectical theology. And in the end, I don't think he fully fathomed what dialectical theology was about and is about; Jung has issues with Barth's theology. And Jung was not afraid to criticize Barth. But you see, there's this questioning, there's this openness, there's a kind of curiosity on Jung's part, that he could take all that in. I don't think Jung was a great theologian. He was interested in theology. I think Keller helped him be a better theological thinker, and perhaps he was open to that. It's very, very touching toward the end of the correspondence—where you see this sensitivity—that he really valued and appreciated his friendship with Keller. He signed the last letter, he signs it, "your old, loyal friend." And there's something very tender and beautiful, I think, about that. So Jung allowed himself to be touched by that relationship.

JL: He allowed himself to be touched on a personal level, but if I hear you right, it didn't make him change his theory or his theorizing much. What is it that makes Jung perhaps not a great theologian?

KK: Formally, he didn't have theological training, but he read theologians. He had access to theology. Jung would pull from a theological idea *here* and then another theological idea from *ther*e, and he kind of pulled them together without spending enough time understanding or dwelling within the theological integrity of a particular theological idea, as it were, and then seeing how it connects with another theological idea. Ann Ulanov says that Jung often pulls theological ideas from here and here and here for what serves his project, serves his purpose. And there's nothing wrong with that. But then don't equate what Jung is then producing as theology. So he pulls from theological ideas, he can quote scripture, he can quote a theologian, but this is often done in service to his own project—they're metabolized or digested, integrated within him, which then yields some kind of theological or psychological statement on Jung's part. But is there a correlation with the intent of that original theological point or writer or text?

JL: That makes me also wonder about, what is it, then, that Jung was serving? What is this project he was pulling things to? There are many speculations and interpretations and different understandings of what analytical psychology is. What was he pulling these things for—developing a psychological theory, or building a new temple?

KK: Yes, that's a great question, too. Ultimately one could say—based upon the *Collected Works* and other texts—he's in service to individuation, the process of individuation, what's involved in individuation, how one helps another to go in and through that process of individuation. In his lecture at the Psychology Club, Keller says that individuation needs to be in service of something larger than itself and that other is fellowship or connection to a kind of a higher connection, as it were. I think personally, when I read Jung as a pastor, as a theologian, someone who's trying to hold all this stuff within me personally, what I sense in Jung—and maybe it's my own projections or the things I hunger for—but what I sense in Jung, and I see it in the letters, is that he wants or he hopes for individuals to have their own life-giving religious experiences that connect them with something larger than the ego or larger than oneself.

Living experience—call it religious if one wants to—but an experience that allows, that connects one to the transcendent, to the Divine, to the holy, something other—Wholly Other, as Barth might say. And to allow the livingness of a living experience with God to touch and enable and enliven the living psyche—to tap into what the New Testament calls *zoe*, meaning life—full life, abundant life—and allow that life to take on life within the individual. Perhaps that's projecting too much onto Jung, but I think there's a case to be made that that's in some ways, what he's trying to do. And I often wonder how that connects to his experience growing up as the son of a Reformed pastor and within the Reformed tradition. Even to this day, within Reformed, that is, Calvinist circles, there is considerable suspicion around religious experience, of paying attention to religious experience, trusting religious experience, trusting one's own interior, inner experience, trusting one's feelings, listening to one's gut, all of these things.

In some religious circles, one finds an emphasis upon the ideas of Christianity, the beliefs of Christianity, that one should be about accepting the beliefs of the tradition and living out the morals of the Church, as it were, or the morals of the teachings of the Church, imitating Christ. There's a place for all of that, but I think Jung saw, perhaps in his own father, and perhaps maybe the weakness within the Reformed tradition, that these ideas and approaches are not necessarily bringing one to life, not allowing something new to be released within one. Some of the numinous experiences that Jung had, the religious experiences that he had, gave greater authority to his own personal experience—and then trusting that experience even if it might be irrational and bizarre, going against the grain, going against the collective, going against what the Church might say. But he's trusting that, and I think that, too, is a place where Keller and Jung connect because, again, Keller had his own religious experience on Mount Sinai.

There are loads of people in churches and outside of churches that have had religious experiences, have been truly touched, and they don't have to be like Paul's Damascus Road experiences of a blinding light. They can be very subtle, moving experiences that change one's life forever. But what do you then do with those experiences? How do you then process them, integrate them, talk with someone about them, dwell within those experiences, and allow those experiences to touch you? What might be trying to come to life through you? All of those dimensions. This is often missing within religious circles. They're there. Those opportunities are there, but you have to go looking for them. Jung made space for these kinds of experiences . And for me, that's a very valuable model, that's very important—just knowing that that's possible—you don't have to agree with everything that Jung says—but he allows this. He creates that container. An analytical experience can create that container.

JL: As you're talking, I'm thinking about the numinosity, and these valuable religious experiences that you share that these people have had and how analytical psychology can offer language and a vessel for that. I absolutely agree. I think that's the beauty of this work—the beauty of analysis, the beauty of this tradition.

But you must also as a pastor come in contact with people who experience the numinous in the most tragic of ways: in losing a family member, in sickness; when life in all its power overwhelms us and throws our life around, there is that side of the numinous, of life experience, that is also terrible.

And we also have saints and others who have had their conversion experiences by facing, for example, the suffering of the world, or facing horrible catastrophes in their life. I'm trying to portray this other side of the numinous that we all have to meet in life. We don't have to be mystics. We all have to meet to the end of things, the tragedy, also, that's a part of this life. This also ties in to Wolfgang Giegerich's critique of Jung as maybe someone who developed a psychology of glory and not a psychology of the cross.

KK: Yes.

JL: I'm taking that from Luther [Martin], *a theology of glory versus a theology of the cross.*

KK: Right, right.

JL: Is there something about it? That God and/or the numinous experience in Jung often has to be this, often portrayed as glorious?

KK: I think that sometimes we overuse the word numinous. I mean, the numinous can be, another word there, sort of a synonym for, a spiritual experience. But I think contained in the numinous is an experience—to cite Rudolf Otto, it's the *mysterium tremendum et fascinans.* It's this mystery that both fascinates and overwhelms. You can see why Barth was attracted to Otto: this sense of the Wholly Other, the numinous. Somewhere, I read that *numen* has a Sanskrit root, which means *to bow, to kneel, to bow.* It's something that is Other that destabilizes me, disorients me. It might even scare and terrorize me. It is something that cannot easily be processed or integrated into one's own experience.

It's truly something uncanny and other. There's a place for the numinous that is truly an experience of glory, right? But there's also the experience of the numinous where one is brought to that place of suffering, where, in the face of suffering, my world, my reality, my understanding of myself and others and God, etc., are all disoriented, are de-centered—we're knocked off-center. And in the presence of those types of experiences, there's a sense of silence and awe and maybe humility before that mystery. So I think there's a place for both. I guess I see what Giegerich is saying. But I don't necessarily see Jung as focusing primarily on a psychology of glory. There's too much suffering in Jung's life and what he sees within human suffering in analysands to make such a strong claim.

JL: Giegerich relates to the dream with the one millimeter and Jung not being able to touch his forehead to the ground: Jung imitating his father, and then being taken to the highest presence, which is not this beautiful palace; but where there's the betrayed, dying god-man Uriah. As I understand Giegerich's critique, there is something odd in Jung's interpretation of that dream. And I've also heard others delivering a similar critique that there's something that Jung has difficulty in facing: a God that is a dying human—or human, a dying man. And of course, it's hard not to associate to Jesus on the cross.

KK: I think it's one thing to say, intellectually, that Jung can't face the dying God-man. One can approach that theologically as a theological idea. Participating in that is something very different. Sure, it's difficult. And maybe it should be difficult, or maybe we should not be too eager to identify too closely with that dying-God image. So that maybe, yes, it's yes, and maybe no. It's about being drawn toward that image but maybe not overidentifying too much with that image.

Maybe this connects to the theme of imitation of Christ. There's a place for imitation, I guess. I don't know. I have seen and experienced a lot of people over the years who were trying to imitate Christ and became martyrs, which was a decision more of their egos than what they were really being called to do by the Spirit. There's a lot of overidentification with that image. I hear in certain Christian circles that to be a Christian, I just need to die, die, die to myself all the time, so that I can be nothing and Christ can be everything in me. I hear that language in many churches. And I understand it and know there are good theological reasons for a statement like that. I'm also kind of cautious and concerned because what does that say psychologically for the individual, where one is completely losing a sense of self or one's own identity and individuality. To live, to identify too much with the image of Christ, identify too much with that pattern, and really lose oneself in that image—and not in a good way—becomes an escape. Life becomes a refusal to enter one's own life. I'm not sure if that resonates or if that makes sense here.

JL: I think it's an interesting perspective and it sounds also like the Jungian analyst in you talking. It makes sense to me on many levels, but, I guess I wonder, do you feel that it would have been a risk for Jung to identify too much with Christ? Because I feel like he's very far from identification. There's a lot in Jung about individual suffering. And there's a lot of suffering in his personal life. But there's not so much in Jung about the suffering of the world, or the poverty in the world. There's not so much in Jung about the poor, let's say. That's not very often raised and that can be fine. But I do think it's important. At least for me in my own wrestling with Christianity, it's been very important to see, how far can I go with Jung? And where I need to depart.

KK: Long before I knew that Jung wrote on the *imitatio Christi*, I had problems with the imitation of Christ idea, just that concept of being like Christ. As a Christian, in my own journey, it's not an image that I gravitate toward. And I—and this might sound heretical, the Church police might come after me—I don't think we're called to imitate Christ but to follow him. And there's a world of difference between the two. They're similar, but they're not exactly the same. And I think this is what pushed me in this direction—personally, in my own analysis, in my own journey, but also in my experience as a pastor. I have seen (countless people have told me) that this prospect or ideal of imitating Christ, of being like him in every way, of denying myself and kind of taking up my cross—there are countless people that I know for whom this became a recipe for spiritual and psychological disaster. Years ago, I read that Kierkegaard says comparison kills. There's a place for comparison, right? But comparison can also kill: to compare oneself with Christ can set one up for failure. Right? It sets one up for enormous disappointment. For how could one ever fully realize that goal of that projection, that perfection? And then people have said, well, I can't live up to that. I can't be like him. I can't be a Christian if it means all these things. Then that leads to enormous amounts of self-recrimination, self-loathing, judgment, internal punishment, of never ever measuring up, and failure. And I just—this is my experience as a pastor—I feel that that's a terrible burden to bear. And then I have to ask, well, where then is the joy? Where is the good news in all this? Where is the gospel in all this?

And I know countless people who have left the church or Christianity altogether because they were taught that following Christ was about perfectly living up to this particular ethical, moral standard—and because they could not reach it, because they could not do it, they left the church. They left the faith. They left it because they felt it was destroying their souls to stay in that environment where there's an enormous amount of judgment for failing to live up to a particular ideal.

So, I think a turning point for me was years ago. There's a verse in Matthew's Gospel where Jesus says, "Be perfect, therefore, even as your heavenly father is perfect" (5:48). And that verse never really sat with me, and that comes out of my own perfectionism, the kind of complexes that I personally deal with. But *be perfect, even as your heavenly father is perfect*, that word *perfect* is a loaded word for us today. And it's not the best translation of the text. It's not incorrect. But it carries a completely different valence in Matthew's Gospel. Instead of perfection, it really has to do more with wholeness, completeness, and integrity. Or another way of putting it: of living out one's end or purpose, one's *telos*, the same way God lives out and is faithful to God's own end or purpose or *telos*. So, live out your end—live out your *telos* appropriately. That's a very, very different understanding and is far more freeing and liberating, I think.

And I wanted to say that I think this is a really important bridge for theology and psychology here because if one is a disciple or a student of Jesus, then that means following *after*, in other words, learning the way or the style of the teacher, following the teacher. This is particularly important—in John's Gospel, for example, it's all about the relationship. It's relational, and that relationship is ongoing. It's about a living relationship with Christ in the Spirit, in the life of community, that a Christian, then, is called to.

What I found myself moving toward is that instead of an *imitatio Christi*, the Christian life is about *participatio Christi.* Participation. Participating *now* within the life of Christ, increasingly conscious of what God in Christ is bringing to life in us as we discover what is trying to come alive or what is trying to be born within the individuality of the person and of the soul. This notion is directly related to developments in Pauline scholarship over the last ten years, scholarship that now views *participation* as incredibly important in Paul's theology. For example, Paul himself says, *I, yet not I, but Christ*. That's the formula in Galatians 2:20, *I, yet, not I, but Christ*. It's about holding that tension, always, and not losing the *I* in Christ. *I, yet not I, but Christ.* And there are a couple of places where Jung himself makes that point. He pulls from that, from that understanding of Paul. So that's how I would respond to the question—there's a place for the *imitatio*, but it's—where is the *participatio*? Or where is that living experience coming alive within us?

JL: There's also the other side of it. Wholeness can be a very dangerous idea, I believe, if you start to look for wholeness. As I see the image of Christ, it very much speaks to me of participation, that we're already participating in his life. And seeing him on the cross. This is the highest presence. I think this connects to Keller and that lecture that you were referring to that he delivered at the Psychological Club back in 1918, entitled "The Gospel and Christianity." And you quoted a part of that earlier, when you said that the ultimate goal is higher fellowship, and I just want to read that full passage:

> *The natural man is in bondage. When we speak in analytical psychology of complexes, these are the same bondages expressed by the Gospel. The dominion of the flesh of the law of sin. Liberation from this is accomplished for the Christian, as it were, in an analogy of the life of Jesus. Through repentance, through sacrifice, through taking up the cross, and in the resurrection, to a new life.*
>
> *The same dying and becoming is achieved that made the life impetus of Jesus into the illuminating pattern it is. Every outworking of this life emanating from Jesus urges man to save his soul. For, what has a man profited if he should gain the whole world, and lose his own soul? But the discovery of the infinite value of the soul is not the end. The value of the completely liberated individual is complemented by the value of highest fellowship, finding its universal expression in the idea of the kingdom of God. Jesus leads man to both: to individuation, and at the same time, to the highest fellowship.*

KK: I find that absolutely beautiful, and I resonate deeply with it. And I think of the liberation from those things that bind us, that hold us, that weigh us down, that hinder the new life from beginning and emerging, being within us. I think that is, in many ways, the Christian life. What I think of as wholeness—I think of wholeness as including all of that, taking in all this. It also includes the suffering, taking in all that; integrating, not rejecting, the dominion of the flesh, which doesn't mean sexuality, but that which is against life or against God. And it's the liberation of those things that—so that a greater integration or connection can take place, so that transformation can take place. Or, maybe a better word—*transformation* is a pretty good theological, religious word, but maybe a better theological word in this context is *reconciliation*. When I read Etty Hillesum, that's what I hear. It's that she's not afraid to see all the reality and all its horror and all of its brutality. But there's something about how she then holds all that within herself because she trusts in something underneath it all. She trusts that something is there underneath it all that kind of holds it. That holds us.

And so there's that last line there: "Jesus leads humanity to both individuation and, at the same time, to the highest fellowship." I think that individuation should be in service to community. It should lead to one's living within something larger. From a theological perspective, it is about *koinonía*, right? It's about community. It's about me bringing my individuality—my uniqueness—into the community. And in some ways, the community helps me individuate. And the image of the kingdom of God that Keller's talking about here—countless times, Jesus talks about the kingdom of God as a feast. We are gathered around a table. We are living in community. There's a kind of dance in that community. There's the power of the relationships found within the community, where individuals are bringing their individuality into the community without losing their individuality in the community. And that's a risk sometimes. Religious communities and congregations are not good at fostering one's development. They often hinder one's individuation and one's personal growth. Sometimes, religious communities say you need to deny your personal experience. You need to deny what you're feeling right now. You need to set those feelings, those experiences, aside.

But what Keller's talking about here is individuation, a person who is aware of how those complexes, as it were, are at work within oneself, having a new relationship vis-à-vis those complexes, and then bringing one's fuller humanity into relationship with others and into the community.

Jesus was the First Psychoanalyst: Superego, Conscience, and the Voice of God, with Donald Carveth

"Jesus was the first psychoanalyst, the most brilliant psychoanalyst of all time. The whole theory of projection is right there. 'Why do you complain about a mote in your neighbor's eye, when there's a beam in your eye?' So much of psychoanalytic insight is there in the New Testament, especially in the words of Jesus and in St. Paul, so I became increasingly struck by these parallels."

—Donald Carveth

JL: I would like us to spend some time talking about the book that you wrote in 2013, published through Karnac, The Still Small Voice: Psychoanalytic Reflections on Guilt and Conscience. *In this book, you argue that we need to help people, our patients: We are their guilt. And you make some important distinctions between the reparatory guilt that is needed in individuals (for the development of civilization), versus persecutory guilt. You write that "the essential ingredient of the conscientious practice of psychoanalysis involves knowing the difference between the conscience and the superego," and that you had come to the conclusion that the only way out of persecution by the sadistic superego is through reconciliation with conscience. Could you speak about this important differentiation, and maybe also about the book, how it came to you to write this?*

DC: As a young man, I did not want to have to be good. I wanted to be bad. Well, I didn't want to be bad, exactly, but I wanted what I wanted. I did not want to say no to myself. I wanted self-gratification, and I sought it, and in seeking self-gratification, I was very selfish. I hurt people. Ultimately, I hurt myself, and I guess that's the point. I learned that, as smart as I am, I'm not smart enough—no one is smart enough—to be able to get away with it.

I decided that ultimately nobody, nobody gets away with anything. Even Donald Trump. I mean, it looks like he does. But if you put a person's life under the microscope—if they came and lay on your couch four or five times a week—you would see that they are not getting away with anything. I realized I was paying too high a price for my ongoing effort to have my cake and eat it too.

I did not want to lead a life of having to sacrifice impulses because they were wrong, or out of loyalty to someone, or whatever. I did not want to *go straight*, as they say. I didn't want to go straight. But I finally realized, *I'm sorry, I have to go straight and I don't have to go straight because God says so, no, or the Church says so, no.* I have to go straight simply because anything else will end up hurting too much. You could say that I became a very enlightened hedonist. The only way to ultimately find—and I don't like the word *happiness*, I much prefer inner peace—the only way I'm going to find peace is by becoming a good man in my own eyes, not anyone else's. One of the wise things my father said to me when I was a kid was, *Son, there's only one person you have to live with 24/7. And that's yourself.* Boy, was he right about that.

I realized that I have to start doing right so that I can see myself as a good man, and then I'll be able to sleep at night, and then I'll be able to have peace sitting in the garden in the sunshine. So, I decided, the lesson there is: you must reconcile with conscience. Otherwise, your superego—which is pseudo-moral (it isn't really moral, it's cloaked in morality, but really it's a Satanic attacker and will go on persecuting)—will make your life a living hell. I think of the superego as the devil, basically. It's demonic. It cloaks itself in a moral disguise, but it is out to destroy us. It's our enemy. And it will.

That's the way I understand heaven and hell. These are states of the soul *now*. I'm not talking about a future. But I have been in hell. And

I have experienced heavenly moments of grace. And the way to escape from hell and access heavenly moments is by turning away from what's wrong and doing what's right. So it's personal—I feel driven by personal experience into this position.

And then clinically, I certainly see it with patients. I see it with my patients: They have to stop. I don't moralize with them. I don't tell them that cheating on their wife is wrong. I don't tell them that going to prostitutes is wrong. I don't tell them that stealing from the company is wrong. I wait, sitting back in the bushes, until I see what the consequences are of cheating on the wife or stealing from the company. I watch what happens. Every time you do that, the migraines come. Every time you do that, the ulcers kick up. And I play a little naïve: *seems like there is a connection between your being unfaithful to your wife and these terrible attacks of migraine headaches*. The patient gradually begins to come to understand that the wages of sin are death or pain or sickness or mistakes that lead to great losses. Whatever. That's what I point out.

JL: What led you to write the book?

DC: I was always a peer-reviewed-journal article writer. As an academic, I never wrote a book. I was in my late sixties when I wrote that book. I had progressed through the ranks. I'd become a full professor because I'd published a fair amount, at least one or two big articles a year. But I had an inhibition—I never published my doctoral thesis. The idea of publishing a book intimidated me. And then a very strange thing happened in around 2011.

I was teaching. I had this book by Eli Sagan on my bookshelf for many years. You know, you buy books. They've got great titles. They look good. You put them on the shelf or you don't get around to reading them. One day, for whatever reason—if I want to move into the paranoid schizoid position, I would say that God led me to take that book off the shelf (I usually don't think that way or talk that way, but sometimes)—I took the book down. I read it. It blew my socks off because Sagan had answered, addressed and answered, many of the things that had puzzled me about Freudian theory, bothered me for many years, especially the superego issues. And I started teaching his book to my students and one day a student said, *so, who is this guy saying it, anyway?* And I was embarrassed. I didn't know who he was, really. So I went and did a search on the internet and I could find out nothing about him. He seemed to have no digital footprint at all. But finally, I came up with an address in New Jersey. So, I wrote him a letter and then a week or so later, I'm sitting in my office and the phone rings. And this squeaky, "Hello Carveth, this is Eli Sagan." And we started talking. Every second Sunday, we had a phone call for a couple of hours.

I read through all of his big books, and we talked about all of that and then he was reading my stuff. Next thing, I'm writing a book. I needed some unfinished business with a father. My father was a family doctor. He was a self-taught kind of intellectual guy, but he wasn't the real deal. Sagan was the real deal. Very impressive intellect. He'd written all of these big books. Suddenly, I'm writing a book. I needed that identification. I needed his blessing. And boy, did he ever give me his blessing. We started to disagree. He made the distinction between superego and conscience. Essentially, he threw the ball. I caught the ball, and I'm running with it.

Okay, I'm running with it, and he's saying, *slow down, slow down, you're going too far, you're going too far with this distinction*. And he wasn't a trained analyst. He was an intellectual, but he was not a psychoanalyst. And I'm taking his distinction into psychoanalytic quarters, and he's thinking, *no*. And then suddenly, about three or four weeks before he died, I was up north, like barely had a cell signal, but he got a message through to me. He told me to read a particular chapter in Pelican's *History of Christian Theology*. He had come across St. Paul. St. Paul's distinction between the law and the gospel. And he had recognized that his own distinction between conscience and superego was echoing that. And he realized that I was running with this because I had a Christian background as well as a psychoanalytic background. Somehow, my reading of the New Testament had set me up to be ready to make that distinction. And then reading Pelican and so on had reinforced it. So that's how I came to write the book. Eli started me off, and then at the end, he gave me another push.

JL: Staying a little bit with law versus gospel and superego versus conscience. Could you help us unpack this?

DC: My understanding of Jesus is precisely that he is an attacker of religion. He did a savage attack on the religion of his time, which happened to be Judaism and the temple. "Man is not made for the Sabbath. The Sabbath is made for man." He was constantly violating the Jewish law for humane purposes. He was a critic of the superego, the law. "Let him who is without sin cast the first stone," he says to the mob who are stoning a woman caught in adultery. So Jesus is conscience rebelling against law. But for a time, I went overboard, and I joined Freud, Ferenczi, and Alexander, who said that the psychoanalytic cure is the complete elimination of the superego for a while. I went for that, but then I came back to the gospel, because Jesus says, "Think not that I come to abolish the law and the prophets. I come to fulfill them," which I then interpret as, *our goal is to subordinate the superego to the conscience*. The superego must be disciplined by the conscience. We still need a superego. We need a book of rules. We need to know the law, but the law has to be subordinated to the conscience.

JL: In your practice and with your patients, or within yourself, the differentiation between the two (conscience and superego), is there anything you can offer as a technique, as a sort of help on the way for people?

DC: I think the simplest way to think about it is that conscience is governed by love. And it speaks in the language of love. And there is a bite to conscience. But at the same time as conscience is saying, *Don, you're on the wrong path*, I'm not sleeping well, because my conscience is uneasy. *You're on the wrong path, Don*. But that voice is also my father who will welcome me home and kill the fatted calf, and there will be a celebration because I heard him and I turned back onto the right path. So this is a loving conscience.

When he reproaches me for being on the wrong path, there are tears in his eyes because he doesn't like reproaching the son he loves. It makes him very sad to have to see that his son has gone off, and he is delighted to welcome me back.

The superego is a sadist. One of my greatest personal images of the superego is from the great film, *Fanny and Alexander*. Who's the filmmaker? The famous filmmaker.

JL: Bergman. Ingmar Bergman.

DC: Ingmar Bergman's *Fanny and Alexander*. And so, the two children, the boy and the girl, their father dies and their mother marries this stuffy Lutheran pastor of some kind, of the kind that, you know, *spare the rod and spoil the child*, and he likes beating the children. And I wish that Ingmar Bergman had done a close-up on him when he's beating the children to reveal that he's got an erection. Because he's getting off on beating the children, 'cause he's a sadist. That's my model of the superego: it speaks this moral language, but it really is fueled by the id. This is pure Freud. Freud said the superego is id aggression turned back against the ego. That's the first layer of the superego, id hostility turned back on me. Second layer: internalization of the culture via the parental superegos. But what Freud fails to point out is that the culture that's internalized is racist, sexist, heterosexist, classist, etc. Freud gives us no critique of the contents of the superego, but it's basically ideological crap that fills the superego. Not entirely. Look, some people go to church and what do they hear in church? They hear, *do onto others as you would have them do unto you*. Every once in a while, the superego says something coincident with conscience, and some people who are particularly healthy people, they have a superego that is almost entirely indistinguishable from conscience. That's a great situation to be in. You're hearing the right message from both superego and conscience, because they coincide, never perfectly. With humans, nothing is ever perfect, obviously. But yes, when you hear the hate in the voice, the moral voice, when you hear the cruelty, you know you're dealing with superego.

I think, and I've said, too, the patients depend on us to have a conscience. We mustn't moralize. We mustn't be superego-ish with patients. My classical colleagues, they may disapprove of my Christianity, but they know that—they know that I know that I must not be superego-ish with my patients. But the error that they fall into is they've lost the distinction between superego and conscience. They've not—they're not able to recognize that while we mustn't be superego-ish, we do need, at times, to be the voice of conscience. We need to have a conscience, and every once in a while, we need to voice it.

JL: I think that's maybe where Jungians use the concept and the experience of the Self. Jung also said that he saw Christ as a symbol of the Self.

DC: But I have to say that I agree with your interviewee Sean McGrath. I was very impressed with him. He's saying that Jesus is not an archetype. I think—oh, you asked why I chose from Jung back to Freud. I think I forgot to say that even back then, I read Martin Buber's essay on Jung. And Martin Buber, as a religious Jew, he put his finger right on the same thing that McGrath put his finger on. That Jung is a Gnostic, and Gnosticism is a heresy for both Judaism and for Christianity. And when you relocate God in the unconscious, you're relocating God in part of the Self, and I wish I could quote it exactly. But one of my favorite passages of all time is from G.K. Chesterton. And he's writing about what he calls the God within. He says, "Of all possible Gods, save me from the God within." He says, "You all know how it works. Anyone who knows anyone from the Higher Thoughts Center will know how it works. When Jones comes to worship the God within, what that means is that Jones comes to worship Jones." He says, *Christianity came to get us to worship the God without, not the God within*.

JL: I agree with you, there's a lot one can critique. But I also believe that it's important to differentiate, because Jung didn't ever say that there's a God within , he said there's an image, an imago Dei. *There's an image of God within. So, there's that. But then, of course, taking Jungianism literally and many of those ideas become, yes, they become problematic. There is something about psychologizing religion and turning it into navel-gazing that can happen. But I must say, in my experience, in my practice, I think that Jungian analysis, done right, helps people at times to find back and deepen their faith.*

DC: Ah, okay. But you're quite right. I respect what you're saying. You're absolutely right. And the same thing can be said about the Freudian tradition. People take Freud literally. I'm not a Lacanian, but one thing I appreciate about Lacan is that he metaphorizes psychoanalysis. It's not about that stupid little piece of flesh called the penis. It's about the phallus, which is a very important symbol. So he metaphorizes psychoanalysis and that's very important. Once having read Lacan, your understanding of Freud is quite different. So I see the same would apply to Jung. You can take it literally or you can treat it more metaphorically and symbolically.

JL: Moving forward to recent times, in 2020. And you published a paper, "Psychoanalysis is Spirituality." And in that paper, you write that, "While others fail to practice what they preach, we, psychoanalysts, refuse to preach what we practice. We disguise our ethic of love. It needs a medical façade." And further you write that "we lie to ourselves and others and call it mental health when it really amounts to salvation."

DC: Yes. Yes.

JL And you write—you describe it as a conversion.

DC: Well, I was asked just recently to speak to the Ottawa Psychoanalytic Society. And I've been thinking about the topic. And the title that I've come up with so far is "Transformation: Clinical Psychoanalysis as

Deconstruction and Conversion." That's the title of the paper. Two things. In deconstruction and conversion. Well, let me start with the conversion, because that's what you're asking. I think that in a deep psychoanalysis—and I think this is the difference between psychoanalytic psychotherapy and psychoanalysis: in psychoanalytic psychotherapy, we do a lot of things to help people cope with their anxiety, to relieve their depression, and so on and so forth, but it's more like repairing a house rather than gutting it and rebuilding it from the inside out. I think of a deep psychoanalysis as something like gutting an old house and rebuilding it from inside out. So we're talking about a radical transformation from—if I want to speak in religious terms—from Adam to Christ. Old Adam, the old sinner, to Christ. That's a conversion. I think there's a perfect correspondence here between that and trying to help a person, as Freud says, transcend narcissism in favor of object love.

All these people who think they're in love, but the person they're in love with simply stands for the self they were, like the old guy who falls in love with a young woman. She just represents his lost youth. He doesn't even know who she is, except her body is smooth instead of wrinkly. The self that I am or the self I would one day like to be. Why is she involved with him? Because to help a person move out of that field of narcissism into recognizing that other people are actually real, and beginning to actually care about their welfare, that's a conversion. That's a radical personality transformation, to help a person move out of the paranoid schizoid state, where life is a jungle and it's kill or be killed. That amazing show *Succession*. That show is about life in the paranoid schizoid position. Also life in late-stage capitalism. It's like rolling over a rock. That is a sinful—that's what sin looks like. That's what hell looks like. We're trying to help save people from these hellish states, and they will continue to send themselves to hell, unless they decide to convert and be good.

And we're trying to help them achieve that. Not by sermonizing, not by wagging our fingers, not by reproaching, but by closely analyzing the consequences for them of their own choices, their own paths, that they're choosing. We help them see how they're putting themselves in hell, which opens up for them the option to stop putting themselves in hell. So, yes, I think we are out to convert our patients. But in a very subtle and respectful and patient way.

JL: Hmm. I think when we use that word, many people associate it also with religious conversion. And I'm thinking maybe, at least myself, I'm thinking of something very radical, and it can be a conversion. But our work is so slow, and it takes such a long time, but conversion is still—that's the word you would use for it. Somehow it's a slow conversion—

DC: It's a slow conversion, a gradual conversion. But I think it deserves, still—it's not a sudden conversion, which is unlike Paul on the road to Damascus. But it ends up being—I think it can be—so profound. It deserves the word. Because when you switch from an entirely self-interested approach to life to grab—grasping the need for sacrifice, to actually being able to sacrifice your self-interest out of loyalty and commitment to others, to say no to yourself—the ability to say no to yourself, which is the ability to be a good father to yourself or a good mother to yourself: *no, I'm not going to let myself have that pleasure or gratification, because I have loyalty and commitment over here*—you're a very different person now.

JL: Well, a few months ago, I very much enjoyed the podcast interview or conversation that you had on Psychoanalysis On and Off the Couch *with Harvey Schwartz, and at the end of that, he tries to summarize some of your insights and he uses the words, "Okay, if I understand you right," he says, "an advanced civilization requires each of us to care about each other and care about our impact on each other." And then you say, as a response, "I would make it more challenging than that by saying that the advance of civilization depends on finally coming to understand what was meant in the Judeo-Christian doctrine of the Fall of Man." You also emphasize the importance of us needing to know how sinful we are as human beings.*

DC: I meant what I said. I agree with him, of course. He's right that we do need to develop a capacity to actually transcend narcissism and begin to care about the welfare of others, the welfare of the society, and so on. But I do believe that we need to be able to acknowledge our sinfulness. I always laugh because many years ago, I found a letter to the editor in the Toronto *Globe and Mail* and I clipped it out and I put it in a file folder in the library for my students to read. It's a woman and she lost any religious interest she'd had as a teen, but now she's a mother of two young girls and she's not happy with the level of moral education that her daughters are receiving in the public school system. So, to supplement that, she's been taking the girls around to various churches, looking for a church that has a nice nursery school that would teach the kids.

Okay, but wherever she goes, the pastor or the minister or the priest and their service are all telling her she's a sinner and she isn't. But, and I'm thinking, *Here's a woman who's convinced she's not a sinner. I can't get through two seconds without knowing I'm a sinner.* I'm always sinning one way or another. Fortunately, as I've gotten older, the sins are diminishing in significance, but I'm still a sinner. I'm not just a sinner. But I am a sinner. That is what it is to be human—is to be a sinner. But in today's society, this culture of narcissism, people can't stand it. They get enraged at the idea that they should have to acknowledge. I think it's because of splitting, frankly. I think that especially very narcissistic and borderline-y kinds of people, they can't acknowledge any sin because everything becomes totalized. If they acknowledge a little bit of sin, pretty soon it's going to go like ink in the water, and they're going to be all bad, and then they'll have to kill themselves. So they can't admit a little bit of badness because it will be totalized. So that's what I meant. I think the ability to move into that space where you have a very jaundiced view of yourself, a very suspicious view of yourself—I hear what I say, and then I think a part of me...And my wife has even more of a jaundiced view of me than I do, and so she helps with this: *really, Don? You just said that—really? Come on.* You have to be suspicious of yourself. Because we're liars.

We are liars, and we're selfish. And we can make great progress, but never total progress. The devil is always whispering in our ear.

JL: The importance to realize that we are sinners, but I'm also reminded of what you just shared about the patient of yours who feels he is a bad person, he's a bad—

DC: He's totalized it, right? That's the different solution. *Yeah, let's avoid that.* That's another split. Look, some people are very bothered by an excessive sense of sinfulness. Certain psychotic patients. A guy was found living in a cardboard box in a ravine here in Toronto, he'd gone off his meds, and he believed he stank. He was a stinker. He had to retreat from human society because he gave off such a foul smell. Now, living in a cardboard box for months, he probably did start to smell. But that's a psychotic delusion of foulness, right? The patient I mentioned is not nearly that severe. It's a mild neurotic-level delusion of having been a disappointment or being rotten at the core. It's not on the psychotic level, but it's all just a matter of degree. So no, I don't want, when I say we have to admit that we are sinners, I don't want us walking around beating on ourselves. I want us to have a forgiving attitude toward ourselves. I want us to have an ironic attitude. Irony toward oneself: being able to laugh at ourselves and see the ridiculousness of all of our stances and self- images and whatever, our theories of ourselves. It's a more forgiving, ironic, humorous, Of course I'm still tempted, et cetera. Yeah.

JL: Mmmm. I'm also thinking about this, to be a sinner without belief. Or you're a sinner without God. It's also helping people [move] *to a pretty empty space for some people, yes? To realize this sinful nature, but to move from there to the more forgiving one.*

DC: Oh, absolutely, you don't want people facing their sinfulness unless at the same time, they see the clear possibility, the love of a father welcoming them home like the prodigal son. Yes, you're sinning, but you could be good. You could love yourself. You could be loved by the people you care about. Why don't you avail yourself of this available love? No, I would never want to point someone's sinfulness out to them if they don't have an image of another light of being lovable to themselves and to others, of course. I don't frame it as God. I don't have any supernatural sense of a God. If someone asks me nowadays, *Don, do you believe in God or don't you?* I say, *yes, I do. And no, I don't.* And then they say, *you can't have it both ways.* I say to them: you haven't understood Freud. The Freudian Revolution is that we are all split. We are all contradictory and, of course, in saying that, he's in touch with the New Testament because the New Testament says we're all split between old Adam and Christ. So here again, Christianity and Freudianism completely correspond. There is no unitary stuff. Freud was embarrassed about this. He was ashamed of his interest in numerology. And he of course projected his own—those kinds of mystical [sensibilities]—onto Jung. And then he got rid of Jung because he couldn't own that as a part of himself.

So, I have a paranoid schizoid position. I visit it frequently. And when I went for surgery, I was praying before the surgery, and I woke up and there was a Muslim family and of course—the grandparents, the aunts, the—like, there must have been fifteen people in the space next to me in the recovery room—and I'm coming out of morphine and they're all praying in Arabic and I'm thinking, *oh God, I'm so glad they're there.* It was like I was praying with them, and I felt the presence of God , but I don't believe in God, but apparently, I do believe in—okay? I do and I don't. That's the only honest position on this, it seems to me.

Jung's *Answer to Job*: Yahweh on the Couch, with Paul Bishop

"The six-million-dollar question is, What is this God that Jung is talking about? What is *Yahweh*? In effect, he's putting *Yahweh* on the couch. That perhaps the entire genius of what Jung is doing is putting God on the couch. As also, if one were to look at it from a faith perspective, that's the entire problem. It's that you don't put God on the couch."

— Paul Bishop

JL: I thought we should address what Jung called "the great whale." Jung did write in a letter to Aniela Jaffé from Bollingen: "I finally landed a great whale," and he was referring to Answer to Job. *A podcast about Jungian psychology and Christianity is not worthy without really addressing this whale, and this great work of Jung, but also this greatly criticized, and maybe also greatly misunderstood, work of Jung. Let's see. I know, Paul, that you are probably one of the people in this world who has spent the most time really digging into the book. I would like to start by asking you, how would you describe this book of Jung's, and what type of book is it?*

PB: I think it's a very good question. Of course, it's the question we can also ask now about *The Red Book, Black Books*, which weren't available when I was writing the commentary on *Answer to Job*. Obviously, what sort of a book is this, is a very good starting point. And in the case of *Answer to Job*, I think the first thing is to think about what's there in that title in German. Because I think it loses something in translation. And the German title is, as you'll know, *Antwort auf Hiob*. And the *antwort auf* is just so much more dynamic than *answer to,* because it's both an answer to, but it's also in the sense of a response and a reaction. It's a much more dynamic kind of interaction. And I think that's typical of other aspects of Jung's thought, which get lost in translation, as it were, simply to do with the paths of these fine points of language. I think, for example, of the phrase *confrontation with the unconscious*, which loses that interactivity that is there in the German, *auseinandersetzung mit dem unbewuss. Auseinandersetzung*, as in the sense of a dialogue, an engagement, a working with. *Confrontation with the unconscious* is as if you've sort of gone around a corner too quickly and suddenly bumped into it.

Auseinandersetzung is a much richer kind of term and I think it's there—with *Antwort auf Hiob*, there is this sense of it's a response to Job. It's not simply an answer. It's a response to—well, if it's an answer, what's the question? I suppose. What is it that Jung is responding to in that work? And I think that then raises the question about its genre. What kind of work is this? Is this a work of, to put it in its most banal terms, is this a work of psychology? Is it a work of philosophy? Is it a work of theology? And, of course, again, that's a typically Jungian kind of mixture of all of those things moving around, and on my reading of it, and going back, looking at what I had written in 2002, I both kind of agree and disagree with myself in relation to it.

It seems to me that it shows Jung doing this trick that he has, of moving from one stepping stone to another, that when somebody says, *well, that's not right theologically*, he says, *well, I'm doing psychology*. And when somebody says, *well, that's not right psychologically*, he says, *well, that's because I'm doing theolo—*. So he's constantly moving around there, and that makes *Answer to Job* such a fascinating, such a kind of tricky book as well, because it's interstitial work—it's between these areas. It's interdisciplinary, in a preeminent sense, it's intercultural as well. It really is just a fantastic piece of writing, and I think that's one of the things, which Jung doesn't always get the credit for: he is a great writer in this particular work. He's produced a fascinating text, and it's a very, very clever piece of writing. And I think that's kind of fed into some of the discussion that's been there around it: that what Jung wanted to do with it is to get *our* response to what he's talking about in Job.

JL: Where should one fit this in, in Jung's own life? Where did this come from? Do you have any information on that biographically?

PB: It's 1952, I think, when he works on it. I think one of the things that we can see now is that it fits into a continuity of the project of analytical psychology that begins with *The Red Book*. And there are points of contact between what's going on in *The Red Book*—if, anyway, I understood it correctly—and what he's doing all these decades later in *Answer to Job*. That's not to say they're saying exactly the same kind of thing. Only that *The Red Book* is a personal work, in a different sense from *Answer to Job*, because *Answer to Job* situates itself in the biblical tradition in a very clear and obvious fashion. And at the same time, of course, it's also situating itself in a very German cultural context as well, because the opening scene in the biblical Book of Job, where Satan and *Yahweh*, Satan and God, are talking to each other, is the basis for the prologue in heaven at the start of Goethe's *Faust*. And I think we can see there how Jung's perception of Goethe, Jung's engagement with theology, are different aspects of a similar problem that he's working through, and that goes all the way back, if we're to believe *Memories, Dreams, Reflections*, to some of his earliest experiences as a young child as well.

JL: So, God as sending the devil as a temptation—or there's a tempting aspect of—or God also as someone that can tempt you into development?

PB: That's right. The basic premise of the opening of the Book of Job is this conversation that takes place, this kind of divine wager, as a thing that would be presented in Goethe's *Faust*, between God—and one of the sons of God—who is a tempter, or who is an adversary. So who is not tempting so much in the sense that we might think about it, but as someone who is there to provoke, who's going to test, *prufen*, as one might say, scrutinize, if you like that translation.

And that really sets up the theological context for the work, which is to answer the question, *where does evil come from?* And that's, I think, the purpose of the biblical book—which is part of the wisdom literature in the Hebrew Bible, in what Christians like to call the Old Testament, and therefore as a piece of wisdom literature—it is trying to reason, it is trying to reflect, on the nature of wisdom itself. That's to say, also God—because, with God is wisdom, or wisdom is an aspect of God—and it's answering the question, or trying to answer the question, or explaining why you can't answer the question, *why is there evil?* Why do bad things happen? Of course, such a timeless question, and founded then and valid now, *why do bad things happen to innocent people?*

So it's a genuine problem there, and it's one that, again, if you were to believe *Memories, Dreams, Reflections,* Jung says, at a very early stage—and he relates it again to his reading of *Faust*—which is, *why is there evil, why is there Mephistopheles, why does Faust have to go to the mothers, and in what sense is good dependent on evil?* And I think it's a very tricky formulation, it's a very difficult idea that Jung's trying to engage with there, and a problematic one, a dangerous one, in some ways. We might have to come back and reflect on it there. But it's fitting into this biblical tradition of wisdom literature. To use a philosophical term, it's an act of what Leibniz would call *theodicy*, the justification of God.

JL: And what would be Jung's attempt at answering that question, then? Why is there evil, and if this is a working through of that question, is it possible, and what would be Jung's reply?

PB: I think the answer has to do with the dynamic that's worked through in the case of the Book of Job. There is a psychological dynamic that Jung wants to trace in that work, which is part of an overarching dynamic, which he sees across the biblical text, the biblical period as a whole. And one of the first things that I wanted to do in the commentary was just to try and sort out some of the chronology, because the way that the work is structured—it's structured in a very clever way—almost starts *in medias res*, with the Book of Job, and then launches back to look at earlier biblical texts, and then forward, to look at the New Testament, and in particular the apocalyptic tradition of the New Testament. And so what Jung is trying to do is to track the psychological development that goes on in the Book of Job, and place that within the terms of a larger development, as he sees it, as he describes it in this configuration that is called *Yahweh*.

And that's why the six-million-dollar question is, *what is this God that Jung is talking about?* What is *Yahweh*? In effect, he's putting *Yahweh* on the couch. And that seems to me, if you think about it in that way, the entire genius of what Jung's doing—putting God on the couch—as also, if one were to look at it from a faith perspective, that's the entire problem. It's that you don't put God on the couch. It's just not what you do (laughs). You're not able to do it.

In a sense, it's what Job tries to do as well, or Job and his friends. It's to put God on the couch, it's to try and think their way through, and in turn, make their own accusations of God, until the turning point comes where God speaks out of the whirlwind and puts Job back in his place. But Jung, I think, rightly draws attention to this pivotal moment, this shift that he thinks has taken place, both in the way that Job views *Yahweh*, and in the way that *Yahweh* views Job. Because even if you can't put God on the couch, you can try to do that. Even if you can't accuse God, you can try and do it. Even if you can't understand God, you can try and work out rationally what is happening. That's often the whole point about Scholasticism, that's the whole point about the Judeo-Christian theological tradition, isn't it, that you can bring *ratio* to the theological table, as it were? And so in that sense, Jung makes the point that God himself changes by being put—by being tested morally—within this narrative framework.

There is something that changes not only in Job, and in the way that Job sees God, but in the way that God sees man as well. And that then looks forward to the way that Jung wants to provide an analytical-psychological understanding of the incarnation, of Christianity, of God becoming man, and the sense in which God becomes man in a way that is common to the Western mystical tradition: that we can all have God born within us. Thinking about "My Sermon on Christmas Day," which Jung refers to in several places—the sense that God is born in various ways: historically, in the incarnation; liturgically, on Christmas Day; and mystically, within the soul of the believer.

JL: In what way does God change, from Jung's point of view, in the Book of Job?

PB: I think the change is that God realizes that he has a thinking creature, and a creature that's able to ask moral questions as well, like, *where does evil come from?* Of course, that question only makes sense in terms of the narrative that one has in the Book of Job, or in terms of the theological tradition of Judeo-Christianity. In other religious traditions, I don't think the idea of good and evil is necessarily as polarized, as opposite, as one finds—it's a different question to ask about evil in Hinduism, evil in Buddhism, evil in Shinto. It's a very Judeo-Christian problem. So to ask the question about where does evil come from is immediately to situate oneself within a particular intellectual-historical tradition—which is, to be fair, the major dominant one in the West. That's the tradition that Jung, for the most part, sees himself as working in.

Let me give you a point of comparison that might help. I think we can see that what Jung's trying to do in *Answer to Job* is very close to what Hegel tries to do in his writings on religion, and his writings on Christianity. And if we go to the lectures that Hegel gives on the philosophy of religion, on the philosophy of history, Hegel wants to present Christianity as representing a significant shift in human consciousness, a significant shift in the way that the spirit, as he would say, manifests itself. And without wanting to get caught up in the technicalities of Hegel's argument, what Hegel seems to be arguing is that, in Christianity, there is an approximation of the Divine and the human in a way that he thinks is not reflected in Judaism.

Now, people of Jewish faith may want to take issue with Hegel around that, but I think that's the kind of argument that we can see in Jung, in an entirely non-Hegelian—and as we know, Jung doesn't have a lot of time for Hegel, and has some rather negative comments to make about him. And I don't think he takes his argument from Hegel. But one can see that he's offering something that is in line with what Hegel is trying to do.

And remember, what Hegel is trying to do is—what I think he's trying to do—is to save religion. It's that he's trying to intellectualize—in a demythologized way, in a kind of turbo-charged philosophical way—what is happening in this great Christian tradition that he's received but that is for various reasons in the eighteenth and nineteenth century simply seen as not working anymore. And partly that's to do with changes in church authority, it's partly to do with the work that's done by the Tübingen School of theology, and understanding how the Bible has come into being, as well as the historical moment: that you can't in the nineteenth century have a medieval view of Christianity, simply because we're no longer medieval human beings.

It seems to me that Jung is saying something that is structurally similar to it, which is to say, in the twentieth century, and in the context of all the evils that have happened in the twentieth century—even though Jung doesn't actually have an awful lot to say about them, and doesn't specifically refer to them—given all the evil that's happened in the twentieth century, can we still believe in God? It's a bit like, to paraphrase Adorno's remarks about how you can't write poetry after Auschwitz, it's you can't do theology after Auschwitz. Significant, of course, that Jung never talks about Auschwitz.

JL: Sonu Shamdasani writes in Lament of the Dead*: "It's reincorporating evil into the Godhead. It's the great theme of Answer to Job." And he writes in the foreword to Answer to Job that, "it was in* Answer to Job *that the theology first articulated in the* Liber Novus—the necessity for "Christification," and the replacement of the one-sided Christian God-image with one that encompassed evil within it—found its definitive expression and elaboration."

PB: I think Sonu's right in his encapsulation of Jung's endeavor. In this way, the argument that's put forth in *The Red Book*, and which is then explored in *Answer to Job*, about incorporating evil into the godhead, is a very strange idea, but I think that's the kind of phraseology that we find from Jung.

So what is he doing there with it? In part I think it's tied up with Jung's obsession with this question of the third and the fourth. And we notice that—and maybe that's another topic that we can pursue on another occasion, but he's insistent in several writings, including in the *Collected Works* and *Psychology of Religion*—the idea that the Trinity is somehow incomplete, and that it needs to be completed by being turned into a four, into a quaternity, by reintegrating, or integrating for the first time, something that has been excluded or shut out or ignored or repressed, I suppose you could say, in the trinitarian—in the formulation of things in terms of three. So, if we map that onto the Christian tradition, well, it's very obvious what the Trinity is. There, it is God: Father, Son, and Holy Spirit . . . So what is that fourth going to be? And it seems to me that Jung has various goes at proposing what's going to turn that trinity into a quaternity. And one of those repressed things is, well—if all of these three terms are masculine, then that fourth occluded term is going to be the feminine. If the three terms are good, then the fourth term is going to be evil. If the three terms are light, then it's going to be dark. And so that's what I think Sonu is trying to draw attention to there.

But of course, that seems to me a highly problematic set of things that are occluded, on Jung's account, not least by saying, *well, on one account, what's missing from the Trinity is something feminine*, that is to say, the feminine is the fourth element. But it also seems to be very strange if you're saying, on another way of looking at it, what's occluded is evil. So does that mean that the feminine is the evil? And that seems to me to be one of the curious questions that arises in *Answer to Job*.

JL: Would you agree that this is the book where you most clearly can see Jung's theology being expressed in Answer to Job?

PB: Well, I think a very good question is, *is it really, in the stricter sense of the term, a theology at all?* And remember that there's an occasion, and when people say, *well, you can't say that about God*. Jung says, *well, I'm not saying it about God; I'm saying it about the God-image, I'm saying it about the God-archetype*. If all we have is God-archetype or God-image, then you might as well be saying it's the human understanding of God. Thinking about it in a Hegelian way, or a Feuerbachian way, to say that God really is only an idea that you have, and so, if you talk about God, then theology is essentially psychology, or theology is essentially philosophy. I think the lines that Feuerbach and Hegel would put would be very, very similar to what Jung does when he says, *well, if it's not theology, then it's going to be psychology*. But it's the psychology that uses an awful lot of theological language, and also, of course, reflects a lot of theological understanding as well.

It's clear that Jung has reflected, meditated, on the Book of Job, and as we know, in that text and in the *Collected Works*, is immensely learned, immensely erudite. So he brings the full force of his learning, the full force of his emotional responses, to this text, with its provocative question, *well, if God is good, where does evil come from?* And Jung's even more provocative answer, which is that, *well, evil has in some way to be incorporated into God*. Again, I think I'd want to ask, in what sense is that actually a valid notion of God, or in what sense is that a valid Christian or Judeo-Christian understanding of God?

I think, for example, Augustine says in his *Confessions*, he says, in Book VII, he says, "I surveilled the things below you," he says, speaking to God, "and I saw that they do not wholly exist, nor wholly not exist. They exist, being from you, but they do not exist, not being you." But this Augustinian conception of God would preclude evil—he expressly says it precludes evil. That's why he can talk about God as a thing of perfect beauty. Augustine says—again, in Book VII of the *Confessions*—"There is simply no evil in you," he says. "Not only for you, but for the world of all creation. For nothing is able to break in from the outside and wreck the order you have set in place."

Now, that's the Christian conception, let's say. Let's equate Augustine's view with the Christian tradition, and you can see Jung certainly disagrees with that. If we're talking about integrating evil into God, it's simply not playing the same ball game. I think there are Hegelian and Feuerbachian elements that would say that it is. Or is it a psychological game, and again, Jung himself says—that's the kind of response that he makes to Victor White, doesn't he? He says, *well, I'm explaining what I go through with my patients, with my clients. I'm explaining what I went through myself.* He'll say in other ways as well, and we can see that that's true of what's going on in *The Red Book*. But for me that question is, if we're talking about incorporating evil into God, does that in any way make sense from a Christian point of view, bearing in mind what Augustine clearly and expressly says—I think we can take him as speaking *pars pro toto* for the Christian tradition as a whole—does it make sense to talk about integrating evil into God? Or, in that sense, does it make sense to talk about integrating the feminine into God? In a way, the feminine is already there: through the Holy Spirit, who is said to have feminine characteristics; the idea of Sophia, divine wisdom, associated with the Holy Spirit, associated with *logos*, with the Son of God, therefore with Christ as well.

JL: I'm still curious about this: what did you imagine Jung's reply to be to that question, why is there evil?

PB: I think it's because Jung frames it in relation to this almost obsessional question that he has about the opposites, and the problem of the opposites. And of course Jung would say in relation to those passages that I was talking about from Augustine, he would say, *well, look, there we go, this is precisely my whole point, it's why putting emphasis on the goodness of God, the lightness, the light quality, the positive, the creative aspects of God, where does that leave those other opposites, destruction, evil, and darkness?*

And of course, Augustine's question to that is to say, really, those things don't exist. They exist only inasmuch as they are, in this famous doctrine of *privatio boni*, merely a privation of goodness. And I think it's a difficult argument for us to understand today, but I think you can see why Augustine would get very upset if he were to read *Answer to Job*, because he would say, *no, the whole point is that those dark elements are going to be redeemed in the sense of falling away. They're not going to be redeemed in the sense of being integrated.* I don't think from an Augustinian or a more general Christian point of view it makes sense to talk about incorporating evil into the godhead. And that's why I think this shifting that Jung does between the theological and the psychological is partly an argumentational tactic. I think it's also partly being honest about it as well, and he'll say, *well, I'm talking about God, the image that we have, the image of the totality or perfection, so what does that say about the evil that's in our own life, or what does it say about the evil aspects of ourselves?*

Or, to use another term, he talks about the inferior functions, the inferior side of the selves, but what does that say about, to use the other Jungian term, where does that leave us in terms of the *ressentiment* that we might feel, and also then, where does that leave, to use the term that theology does, where does that leave us in relation to evil? The evil that is within us? And I think that, on this point, we have to salute Jung for raising this question, in the twentieth century, raising this question of evil, even though, as I say, he seems to be curiously reluctant to point to what would be very obvious examples of evil in his own time. And it strikes me as strange, possibly problematic in some ways, that in the works that Jung writes after the 1940s—so, in the '50s—he approaches the question of evil, he approaches the question of darkness, he approaches the question of negativity, but increasingly and exclusively through alchemy.

Where it seems to me that the problem is, okay, it's there, but it's less critical than if you'd think about it in terms of the Second World War, in terms of the Holocaust, in terms of the concentration camps. And Jung seems reluctant to want to point to those as evidence of the urgency, that he's saying, *well, it's human beings that did these things. How do we explain that human beings can carry out such monstrous and barbaric acts?* And I think that's his question. The theological question is, *why does God allow that to happen?* And I think that's just another way of asking this question, which is, *why does a good God allow evil to happen?* Which can be retranslated as, *why do good people do bad things?* And of course that's one of the most shocking things about the Holocaust: tales of guard camps, quite happily going into work to these places where people are systematically brutalized, dehumanized, and murdered, and then going home for supper and putting on some Beethoven and listening to the record player.

JL: I'm reminded of Etty Hillesum. I'm not sure if you're aware of her.

PB: Oh yes.

JL: Yes. Etty Hillesum, who died in Auschwitz but who wrote her famous diaries at the Westerbork Camp in Holland in 1941, around there. And she was also inspired by Jung through her analyst Julius Spear. And she says somewhere, and I'm not going to quote it, unfortunately, perfectly, There is no savior God. She knew where she was going. She knew her whole family was going to Auschwitz. She knew exactly what was there: there's no saving God. There's no savior God. But what we can do is to cultivate a place inside of us, to hold; we have to carry God, we have to carry him inside of us. That's our work for this time.

It also brings to my mind: Jung's statement that to be unconscious is evil. But he's saying, if I understand it right, that God is unconscious in the story of Job. That God becomes conscious through the interaction with the human, through Job, so the work of incarnation now has to be done by individuals, or by humans. Humans have to do the work of God. The work is not only about evil, no? It's also about a new type of responsibility for the individual to carry God forward.

PB: Well, I think you have given a very good summary, if I may say so, of Jung's argument in the work, and I just want to say that—but that's fine as an argument—to me, that sounds so much more like a Hegelian–Feuerbachian approach than one from any existing theological tradition with which I'm familiar. Again, we go back to Augustine: *no, it's God who's the creator and we are the creatures*. Pretty clear line management there, we might say. Jung absolutely confuses that, you're quite right. He inverts it by saying that not only has Job changed throughout this encounter, but crucially, *Yahweh* has changed as well. And I think that's the point that Murray Stein makes as well, that when Murray is talking about God, he says, there is a new relationship that comes between God and his creation.

Now, I suppose that theologically, one would say that Christianity sees a new relationship existing between God and his creation. In fact, that's expressly there in the Gospel of John, when Christ says to his disciples, *look, I'm now going to talk to you as friends, as brothers*, and he talks of them as brethren, so there's a greater approximation between the divine and the human. But of course, as I understand it in standard Christian theology, that comes about through God's initiative. It is through God becoming man, in line with, thinking of Paul's letter, I think it's to the Ephesians, where he talks about God having this plan, which he's worked out in advance, that he's going to send the Son to earth, and save us. So that comes out of God's initiative rather than the human initiative.

But it seems to me that's the crucial difference between, *is this something philosophical or theological*—is there some thing philosophical or psychological, or is there something theological? It's the question of initiative, because, it seems to me, from a theological perspective, what the incarnation shows is God's initiative in saving humankind, rather than the human one. Sure, it calls upon us, going back to Meister Eckhart, that we allow him to be reborn within us, or that we ask that he be reborn within us. But, of course (*chuckles*), Meister Eckhart, famously accused of being a heretic. One might say it's a kind of heretic Christianity, or maybe a kind of Gnostic Christianity, which Jung's wanting to propose in this text. But I don't think it's anything that Augustine, at any rate, would recognize.

JL: But I think that also Jung in Memories, Dreams, Reflections *writes that the problem with Job was foreshadowed by this dream he had about his father. And that is the dream in the temple, and the question that we discussed before, where Jung's father is kneeling and touching his forehead against the floor, and Jung is imitating, but he cannot. There is one millimeter between his forehead and the ground—something that also Wolfgang Giegerich has discussed—Jung cannot surrender, so he imitates his dream father, and he gets to understand—he doesn't see it—but he gets to understand that there's another level here, where the higher presence is, and that's where you see Uriah.*

After that dream, there's also Jung's interpretation about the creature versus the creator, and Jung writes that the creature has to sometimes overwin or go further than the creator. There's almost a competition, it seems like, between the creature and the creator, in Jung's mind. Somehow, his interpretation of that dream seems somehow to play into his theology in Answer to Job.

PB: Yeah, no, I think that's very helpful. To my mind, it certainly indicates that Jung takes these problems very seriously. And even though there is a kind of, a certain kind of, playfulness in *Answer to Job*, and I think there are flashes of humor, there are flashes of sarcasm. It's a very emotional kind of text as well, as well as one that operates at a high intellectual level. There are flashes of a dark kind of humor, sort of sarcastic outbursts, which are in there as well. But it's actually taking these problems seriously. And I think that that's something that—even if the relation between Victor White and Jung came to grief—it's something that one respects, and can see the significance of Jung today, which is: taking these theological questions about evil seriously, and trying to, within terms of the system that he is developing, just in the same way that Hegel and Feuerbach do, and formulate some kind of a response to it.

So we're very far away from the kind of popular expression of religion, of everybody clapping hands and singing *kumbaya*, and everything's going to be fine, and God loves us all, and that kind of banal

Christianity. And Jung, you can clearly see, has no time for that, that he's wanting to actually understand what's going on in this religious dynamic, and he thinks he has, again, like Hegel, like Feuerbach, *oh, I've got a very handy intellectual system that I've just been working out, that we can translate that into, and that can give us answers as to what we're meant to do next, or point to what we're meant to do next*. And again, I think, maybe we can see in Jung the same kind of question arising that one would find with Hegel and Feuerbach, which is to say: *you've translated Christianity into your German-idealist terms, but then what does that then look like in terms of religious practice, what does it look like in terms of liturgy, what does it look like in terms of praxis?*

Same thing one would answer to Feuerbach, in the essence of mankind, of humankind, *okay, well, where does that now take us?* And of course it's significant that the German Idealist tradition that one finds in Hegel and in Feuerbach, actually then shifts into, as we know, Marxism, and it takes us into a very materialist dimension—actually then, in the case of Marxism, I suppose it would be fair to say, a kind of atheist tradition. With Jung, it doesn't go that way, not only because I think Jung, kind of as a rather bourgeois individual , doesn't like leftwing politics and doesn't like communist politics and Marxism, but also because he's much happier talking with notions of *Geist* and spirit and archetype and keeping things working at the spiritual- psychological level in a way that, it turns out, that isn't the way that it went with Hegel and Feuerbach.

JL: Well, that's a great difference, no? Jung also developed techniques, analysis, dreamwork, active imagination, and he was also delivering the tools for people to go on a path similar to his—their own path, but still. Although Jung always says he was not a theologian, and although he's often criticized for not being a great theologian, in a way he is delivering a theology, and that theology is implicitly underlying the Jungian corpus. And there are so many believers. There are many people, not praying, but doing active imagination and such. This is also part of the critique from Martin Buber—and I would like to discuss that with you—Buber's critique of this work as a Gnostic work.

PB: Yes, that's right. Just to briefly pick up on something you were saying at the beginning. I suppose it would be fair to say that there are many very different Jungs as well. And that there is one that is a lot closer to the aspect of a church—I'm hesitating to use the word *cult* for obvious reasons—which offers a kind of spiritual exercise (let's talk about it that way), or spiritual exercises, in the sense that he talks about it, so, those kind of tools of active imagination that you were referring to. But that Jung's system could also be used—and still also, I understand, is used, because of his writing on typology—as tools, not for self-discovery but of management—I'm thinking of Myers-Briggs and this very different kind of way that Jung could be received as well. So he's a multifaceted figure. I'm not too keen on the Myers-Briggs kind of aspect, I have to say. But nevertheless, there it is, and it's obviously going to stand as party to that tradition as well.

In regard to the reception of the work, there is this remark that I think Anthony Starr quotes as well, from Jung, where he says, "What I've produced is pure poison. But I owe it to my people." It's a great quote, and it has the kind of ring of truth about it, and it's the kind of thing Jung would say. Because in a way, it is pure poison, certainly it would have been pure poison for Victor White, on the Roman Catholic side, because, from the Catholic perspective, you just can't talk about God like that. It doesn't make sense to talk about it. And I think it's very poignant of the relationship that was there between Victor White and Jung, where they start off and they think they're talking about the same thing, and then it becomes clear, as the conversation goes on, that they're really talking about completely different things. That's leaving aside the whole question of the *soror mystica* and all that aspect of a very strange kind of friendship that goes on.

But that sense of, *but we're really playing a different kind of game*, I think is there in relation to Buber and his critique of Jung, and Jung's response, which, at first sight, is rather surprising, isn't it, because Buber accuses Jung, or Buber describes—I shouldn't say accuse—Buber doesn't think of it so much as an accusation. It's a description. Buber thinks, *well I've seen this before, and what Jung is talking about looks to me very much like Gnosticism*. And that was a very fair description, because after all, Jung does quote lots of Gnostic writings and you've got the Jung codexes kind of floating around, people are buying him Gnostic scriptures and launching the Jung Institute and so on, so it doesn't seem such a strange accusation or description to make, and yet Jung immediately goes into reverse gear, by saying, *no, no, absolutely, Gnosticism has nothing to do with me; I am the last person that you could describe as a Gnostic*, even though he has this Gnostic ring on, that he used to keep on his finger and so on. And I suppose in some ways that seems a bit of a surprising response. Except perhaps it isn't, and it's a very Gnostic response, which is to hide and to disguise and to refuse to fall into line with the interpretive schemas that are offered to one.

Perhaps it's not so surprising that Jung would say, *well, no I'm not, because I'm not going to allow myself to be categorized by somebody else*. He feels the description of himself as a Gnostic is a kind of categorization, but also, that he might say, *well, look, no, again, you've misunderstood me. Just as I'm not trying to offer a Christian theological response that is in line with what the Vatican is going to teach, or in line with what the Tubingen-Stift is going to teach in terms of Protestantism, just as I'm not going to fall in line with what those organizations are saying, nor am I going to allow myself to be told, well, this is what Basilides says, so it must be true, or this is what Valentinus says, so it must be true*. In other words, he wants to use Gnosticism in the way that he uses all those other intellectual sources, sometimes mystical—Meister Eckhart, Angelus Silesius—sometimes philosophers—preeminently Nietzsche.

I don't think Jung would be happy to be described as a Nietzschean, though he is spending years and years commenting on *Zarathustra* in great detail. So it's a rejection of this description of him by saying, *yeah, you're simply lining up with what these other folk are doing*. In a way, I think it's Jung trying to say, *no, I'm trying to work out my own answer, and I'm Jungian, thank you very much; I am sui generis*. But even then, as we know, at one point, he says, *well, thank goodness I'm not a Jungian*. Because he doesn't like the way that he sees his system as being systematized, or presented in a popularizing systemic way, and he thinks that's missing the authentic—prophetic, I think we can say—aspect of what he's trying to do. So I think if we see it in terms of, any time somebody comes up with a label for Jung and tries to put it on him, he says, *no, I'm not that, thank you very much*. And that applies to Gnosticism, too.

JL: But what I find so remarkable in Jung's response to Buber is that he disowns Seven Sermons to the Dead. *He says it's the sin from earlier in his life. It's also the question about, what did Jung try to build, with his psychological project? A theology or a new belief system of sorts? Shamdasani also in his statement* [quoted earlier] *shows there is a clear lineage between Jung's early experiences and works until* Answer to Job. *He had the experience and he wanted to convey that into psychological and conceptual language. And he used theological language to speak of God as needing to be completed . . . Do you have something to say about this, Jung owning his experiences,* Seven Sermons to the Dead, *in his reply to Buber*?

PB: Yeah, no, I think that's a good point. I suppose we ought to remember, oughtn't we, that Jung had no idea, did he, that his *Red Book* was ever going to be published. He originally published the *Seven Sermons*, and it was given to a very small number of people, and I suppose that if he regards it as something that is intensely private, and intensely personal, only for sharing with a few people: if that's true of the *The Seven Sermons*, it's true of *The Red Book* as well, isn't it? It was shown to a very select number of people. That he's going to say, *well, hang on, Mr. Buber, this is not for you*. Or, *this is for myself, primarily, and for the few people that I choose to share it with*. And I suppose describing it as *Jugendsuende*, a sort of sin of his youth, is, in a way, a kind of collective gesture. It's that he's anticipating some of the critique that would be made if *The Red Book* were to be published, or that indeed, has indeed, taken place subsequent to the publication of *The Red Book*. And whilst I'm delighted the *The Red Book* has been published, I would be more delighted if I understood what was going on in it, I think. At the same time, it is intensely personal, intensely private. I think it was when I was first reading *The Red Book* that I did have the sense of, *ought I to be here? Ought I to be looking at this? Tread softly if you tread on my dreams*, and so on, *tread softly if you tread on my visions.* And that might seem a bit rich from someone who's published on *The Red Book*, and talked about *The Red Book*, but there are moments when I suddenly have a twinge of conscience and think, *well, actually, I don't know, should we be doing this?* At the end of the day—well, one, it's out there now, so it's too late. And I think it actually bolsters Jung, it supports Jung. I think the worst position would be the one that we were in for many years, where we knew there was *The Red Book*, but we didn't know what was in it. I don't think that that's going to be a sustainable position, but I wonder if that response to *The Seven Sermons* is to say, *look, I can see that I'm going to be profoundly misunderstood if all of this stuff gets out there*, and bear in mind, some of the comments that people have made about *The Red Book*—well, maybe Jung was right. Maybe he could foresee some of the criticism that was going to come his way if the *The Seven Sermons of the Dead*, or indeed *The Red Book* itself, were to be published.

JL: Why do you think it was so difficult for Jung to be called a Gnostic? Why was he fighting that so hard?

PB: Well, I think part of it is that Jung presents himself in various ways, depending on the audience that he has and depending on the kind of mode of self-presentation that he's in at particular times, and again I think it's—Peter Kingsley is quite good about bringing this out in his book *Catafalque*—Kingsley's view is that Jung was a prophet, and that Jung saw himself as a prophet. But one of the things that prophets do is not simply to go around prophesying all the time, it's that Isaiah or Jeremiah or some of the other prophets do prophetic things that have to be understood, so they play with a clay pot, or they do things that we wouldn't say, *that's prophetic*, we would probably say, *that's pathological*. And so there's that whole fear of being misunderstood, which is part of prophecy, or built into prophecy. It's actually core to it. And that, I think, is this line in Isaiah, which Christ himself quotes, where the disciples ask, *why do you go around talking to everybody in parables?* He says, quoting Isaiah, *so that they may look, but not see, that they might hear, but not understand.* And so this whole question about, *how do you transmit the message* is built into that prophetic tradition.

JL: But isn't there also something in his reaction that has to do with the view of God that he's presenting in Answer to Job? *This is a God that has the dualism integrated, so to speak. It has both sides. While, I guess, Gnosticism is also the idea of good and bad forces fighting over the human soul, or there's some creator that goes beyond the all-loving God. Isn't that a part of this argument, that God is double-sided, that God has these two sides, and that's—true monotheism is to see that God holds, also, the evil aspect. Otherwise, according to Jung, we're splitting things into God is all good, and evil is all bad.*

PB: Yep. I think that's right. One of the responses that Jung could have made to Buber, would be, *well, what kind of a Gnostic do you think I am?* Because it is a very broad label, isn't it? And Jung might have wanted to go back to Buber and say, *well is it Basilidian or Valentinian? What particular school do you think I belong to?* And I think you're right, that there is this—I'm thinking of the fact that the Vatican produced this document, "Jesus Christ, the Bearer of the Water of Life: A Christian Reflection on the New Age" and it's, I suppose, the moment when the Vatican engages with Jung and accuses Jung, not so much of being a Gnostic, but of being New Age.

So. And I think that one can sympathize with the Vatican's response, inasmuch as it's saying, *look, what these people are doing is not what we're doing. And there is a problem for us, potentially a problem for us both, if people get mixed up and confused about what our respective projects are, and what they're meant to be, and what they're meant to be doing.* And I think that Jung himself would resist having the label *New Age* applied to him, just as he objects to the label *Gnostic* being put on him, just as he objects to the label *Jungian* being put on him. Because in all cases, that's people trying to circumscribe what he's doing, control him, contain him, pop him in this neat little box, rather than allow his texts, his techniques, his ideas, to work on one. And I'm thinking of that remark that he makes about how each of us should have our own *Red Book,* should have our own cathedral for the soul, have our own kind of projects of existential authenticity.

Of course, that's at the heart of the problem. I suppose it's there in Nietzsche very, very clearly when Zarathustra says, "the way" is something that doesn't exist—*Den Weg gibt es nicht*—there isn't the one way, and you can't present a gospel of existential authenticity as something where you have to present this, that, and the other. If you're going to be authentic you've got to go and do it for yourself. Thinking of the moment in the Monty Python film where they all say, "Yes, we're all individuals." Well, that's precisely undermining what the idea of an individual is. I think that's why Jung, as a strategic move, doesn't want to have labels applied to him, because that will simply get in the way of what he wants to do, which is evoke a response from us, either, I suppose, in a therapeutic mode, as patients—as patients or clients—or, in the way that a lot of people, including myself, have come to—which is true—the effect of his texts, the effect of the *Collected Works,* and now the experience of reading *The Red Book* as well. And that, when one reads *The Red Book,* it seems to me that it is profoundly useful as a text, you can be sure of that, but it's not going to be a work that will leave you alone, which you will remain neutral to. So if Jung is trying to produce an answer to Job, we are all trying to produce our answer to *The Red Book.*

JL:. You ask yourself in the conclusion of your book, "Does Answer to Job *tell us how Jung finally ceased to be a Christian and became instead a believer in a different religion, perhaps the first Jungian?" I was curious how now, twenty years later, how would you answer that question yourself?*

PB: Well, I think I wouldn't have formulated it in those terms in the first place, twenty years on. I suppose it's worth reflecting that what I really wanted to do in the commentary was to kind of help [*Answer to Job*] on in that way. Obviously what I didn't know was what was going to be in *Red*

Book. And I think that *The Red Book*—I don't think I would necessarily take away anything that I wrote about in the commentary, but I'd want to add a kind of third part, I think, which is about situating *Answer to Job*, not only in terms of preceding books, like *Aion*, perhaps. Some of the writings on alchemy—but say, look, we've got this amazing thing with Jung, that he begins, if you like, with *The Red Book*. *The Red Book* comes after all the work that he's done in *Transformation and Symbols of the Libido*. That's another kind of discussion*: what's the relationship between those two books?* But if we take *The Red Book* as representing some kind of a starting point, or a second starting point, after *Transformations and Symbols of the Libido*, the concern that we have there, again (which is a kind of repost to Nietzsche): *God is not dead; he is as alive as ever*. That's an inversion of Nietzsche. The whole question of Izdubar and turning God into an egg. What does Jung say? *It's not about if God can save us, it's if we can save God.*

So we've got an extraordinary inversion of theological tradition there. It's all about how Jung, or humankind, can redeem God. That's the big thing that is in the work, isn't it? We get that at the beginning. But then, I think, passed a new light on what's happening, at the end, if you like. Not quite the end, but one of the late works in *Answer to Job,* where he reworks through this issue we've touched upon at various points in our conversation, the notion of salvation, the question of evil, the problem of the opposites. If in *The Red Book* everything is reflected inwardly, because it's to do with his vision, then in the question of the *Answer to Job*, it's reflected outwardly by engaging with the biblical texts of the discussions and indeed the visions, the encounter that takes place between Job and *Yahweh* in that biblical text.

And I suppose that what I would want to do, if I was able to write the book again, would be to try and bring out and tease out what defines the difference between the Christian reading and the Jungian reading. And I think I'd try to formulate it in this way and say that: on a Christian reading of the Book of Job, what really matters is that Job comes to understand Christ as being wisdom, as being *logos*. This moment, this famous moment, where he says, "I know that my redeemer liveth," a beautiful manuscript inflection where you can see Job seeing this kind of figure. And on a Christian reading, I think the reason why this book is important is that Job understands that his redeemer is going to come, that Job is there as a witness to the *logos*, as a witness to Sophia or wisdom.

But I think the Jungian view of Job is significantly different, that on the Jungian reading, why Job is significant is that he is a kind of prefiguration of the suffering Christ. Not that he sees Christ, but that in his sufferings, he is a prefiguration of the suffering that has been described as the redemptive act of Christianity in the New Testament.

JL: So when you make this distinction between the Jungian reading and the Christian reading, and also you say in this question that maybe you wouldn't formulate it the same way twenty years later. I'm still curious about, do you view Jung as a Christian? Or being a Jungian is not being a Christian? Or how do you understand it?

PB: Well, I know there are lots of Christians who are Jungians.

JL: I'm thinking Jung.

PB: And Jungians who are Christian. So they are compatible in that way. As a matter of fact, I think I would have a hard job reconciling them. Just because it seems to me that ultimately the game of theology and the game of psychology, you have crucial points of categorical difference between them. I think it certainly shows that Jung is someone who takes religion seriously. And perhaps that is, at this particular moment, the greatest resource and the greatest help you can do with religion, either religion in general or with Christianity in particular: is to take it seriously, engage with it, is to present it at a time, at a historical moment, when knowledge of the Bible, knowledge of traditions, knowledge of what biblical symbols mean, seems to be disappearing very, very fast.

There's a moment, talking to the Guild of Analytical Psychology in London, where Jung says with great pathos, he says, "you know, I want to believe all these things, but I'm just unable to do them anymore." And I think he's talking there in the [19]50s. That, really, in my mind, anticipates the loss of the symbol that we have at the moment. Bread and wine aren't automatically seen as eucharistic symbols, but more kind of like picnic items. But the image of somebody suffering on a cross, suffering on a cross—we have these debates about whether British Airways stewardesses are allowed to wear crucifixes around their neck and so on. That is such a trivialization of, how do we understand the suffering God?

And it seems to me that Jung is an immensely useful figure for our time and an immensely uncomfortable one as well, because he keeps reminding us of this question of suffering. And that, I think, is part and parcel, it's tied up with, the problem of evil, isn't it? The problem of evil is putting a theological gloss on this question of something that can be very, very visceral. Why is there suffering? Either one's own personal suffering, or it might be even worse, seeing the suffering of other people and being unable to help them. So it is in our very, very happy sterilizing kind of world, which wants to look away from things that are very difficult:

I think one of the ways that I can see Jung, at any rate, being reconciled with theology, is through this insistence on the problem of suffering and the meaning of suffering, if it can be said to have a meaning. I think that if you think about any pain that you're in, talking about pain having a meaning becomes a very, very difficult idea. But that seems to me central to the theology of Christianity, and its image of the crucified Christ. And it's central to Jung as well in *The Red Book*, which does talk about suffering, loss, the sense of immense isolation, and being bereft, and yet fighting one's way through to some kind of reconciliation with that shadowy figure that he meets in the garden at the end of the *Scrutinies*.

What is the Role of Conscience in Psychoanalysis? Sean J. McGrath and Donald Carveth Discuss

"Somewhere Jung says that the only evil is unconsciousness. And this, I think, touches on your work, Don, that this growth in consciousness that psychoanalysis aims toward has to be understood as a moral drive toward the good."

—Sean J. McGrath

JL: It could be appropriate to start this discussion on conscience with Martin Luther. Luther has been accompanying me through and after my psychoanalytic training. And he has a lot to say also on the theme of conscience. A starting point could be the Reformation movement at the Diet of Worms back in 1521, when Martin Luther, standing before the emperor and pope's representative, said the following:

> *Since then your serene majesty and your lordships seek a simple answer, I will give it in this manner, neither horned nor toothed: Unless I am convinced by the testimony of the Scriptures or by clear reason . . . I am bound by the Scriptures I have quoted and my conscience is captive to the Word of God. I cannot and will not retract anything, since it is neither safe nor right to go against conscience.*
>
> *And supposedly the secretary to the Archbishop of Trier disregarded Luther's appeal by shouting: "Lay aside your*

> *conscience, Martin. You must lay it aside because it is in error."*

Luther's appealing here to conscience, and the assertion of freedom of the human conscience against the power of the church and state. And this is seen as the start of the Reformation process, but it also shows that complexity separating conscience from other inner voices of authority. When can one be sure that conscience actually speaks the voice of good or the voice of truth or the voice of God, and—or—when is it the devil in disguise, or perhaps one of our parents, or other authority that we grew up with, our superego speaking to us?

Sean, to see where you would go with this, could you share your reflections on this moment, but perhaps also to give a little bit of a theological framing of conscience?

SM: Well, Luther, in this moment, is in fact being a good Scholastic. There is something in this moment that veers away from the tradition, but it's not what you think. So Luther insisting that he stands by his conscience is in fact completely compatible with the tradition, the medieval tradition, that he's trained in. And his critics, accusing him of having an erring conscience, are also compatible, because conscience in this medieval tradition—very much like in the Jung article ("A Psychological View of Conscience")—conscience is not identical to knowledge. It's compatible with ignorance. Conscience means *co-scientia*. It's a double knowledge or a knowledge that accompanies knowledge, and so there's a kind of ambiguity of conscience, and it seems to me that that's what's coming to the fore in this exchange.

What Luther does in this moment that's actually *against*—that violates the Catholic tradition—is he says, "I will stand by scripture and reason and conscience," and he excludes tradition. So that's the Reformation moment. The Reformation is not that Luther insists on standing by his conscience over and against the Church that encourages him to violate his conscience. That's kind of a pop version. The real thing going on here is that he's cut tradition out of theology. But if we go back to the business of conscience, it's a medieval principle that *every conscience binds*, even an erring one. Thomas Aquinas argues that one should never go against one's conscience, and if you think about it, it's pretty clear what he means there. What would it mean to go against your conscience? It means to do something that you believe to be wrong. That's always, always a sin.

Now, that said, conscience—this is what I like about the Jung piece—the conscience is not innate knowledge of the good. It's not enough to just kind of spontaneously follow your conscience, because your conscience can be in error. And this is what Luther's critics are saying: "Your conscience is in error." So the question is whether Luther's conscience is informed enough, whether his conscience has become—if you want to speak psychoanalytically—conscious enough to be trusted. Because conscience is not simply innate knowledge of the good. It's a kind of innate capacity for the good, or it's an innate tendency toward the good, which requires knowledge—that's how the Scholastics would put it—or requires consciousness.

And so there's this idea that one has to be responsible to one's conscience. One has to inform it. One has to read. One has to think. One has to listen to authorities. And one has to discern whether there is any doubt whether what one regards as the conscience of the good, and if there's a bit of doubt there, then one has to actually pause, expand the judgment, and inform oneself. And what Luther is saying here, which is perfectly in accordance with the Catholic tradition, is that there is no doubt in my conscience, and therefore I need to do what I'm doing. That is a fully Orthodox position.

JL: And what about the conscience as standing for the consciousness of sin? Can you say something about that link between the two?

SM: Well that's what's so interesting here. So, this is a complicated story that goes all the way back to Plato. And it's the connection between knowledge and virtue. So out of Plato you get this idea that knowledge is virtue, that one cannot know the good and not do the good; and one cannot do the good and not know the good. And sometimes that's been spun as a kind of determinism, but it's actually an extremely deep point. And I think it's the very root of this idea of the duality between conscience and consciousness. It's that they're not the same thing. And that is that a conscience that has become fully conscious, you could say, is a knowledge of the good.

And at that point, everything is in place. It's a complete and entire participation in what ought to be done. But anything short of that is going to have trouble. So this idea that comes from Socrates, who says that no man can do wrong knowingly, that is, you can't look into the face of the good and choose evil, that is, we all desire the good on some basic level, even if it's just the good for ourselves. Even a suicide, even a masochist, in a certain way, is preferring death and pain to life and pleasure, and saying, *this is my good*. And so there's a kind of inborn—and this is the tradition out of which Luther is speaking—there's this inborn drive toward the good, which is incompatible with voluntarily doing the bad.

But that said, the good has to be brought to consciousness. That is, there has to be a growth from this unconscious—it's very interesting—but conscience in the tradition is an unconscious inclination toward the good. Left on its own, it is not enough. It has to be raised up to consciousness. And with this elevation of conscience to consciousness, we have, then, all that's required for the moral act. Now of course it has to be done freely. So this is not a mechanistic thing. So, one's will is involved. And so this leads to certain kinds of paradoxes.

How do we accuse somebody of being guilty of sin, that is, of knowingly doing what's wrong? And Aquinas, who's a very subtle thinker, said, *well, what's going on there is disavowed*—he doesn't use the word—but basically when you see evil, culpable evil, what you see is culpable ignorance. Somebody is refusing to elevate this unconscious inclination toward the good that we call conscience to the level of consciousness so that it could be a fully moral act. Instead, they're at a kind of certain—and this is a very puzzling moment—they're saying, no, I *will* not to know. It's what Žižek calls ideology. Now I will *not* to know. I do not know. I will not know what

I need to know in order to trust my instinct, you could say, my spontaneous inclination. And at that point you have something problematic. But nevertheless the principle remains. Every conscience binds. Even an erring one. And that rich paradox at the center of the medieval tradition is coming right to the fore in this dialogue that you quote here.

JL: Don, do you have any spontaneous reactions to what's been shared?

DC: Well, the idea of the need for conscience or for the voice of conscience to become conscious: my thoughts immediately go to the Jung paper ["A Psychological View of Conscience"] and the superb example he gives of the man who has the dream of both arms covered in black dirt. So this is a man who, before his discussion of his dream with Jung, has been having an unconscious conscience, an unconscious reaction of conscience. He has not been conscious of what his conscience is aware of and is saying. Through the analysis of the dream, he becomes aware of, conscious of it. So, our capacity to blind ourselves to conscience is profound. It's all over the place. I think much of my practice involves the kind of thing that Jung is describing in that dream.

SM: And what I think Jung is so superbly pointing out there is that this voice of God, conscience, is not enough. Sometimes it's just the voice of the community, sometimes it's some buried instinct for what's right, and sometimes it's actually something that should actually be resisted. In other words, the spontaneity of the voice, the fact that the voice is direct and instinctive, is not enough. It has to be brought to this other level. And I think this is very strong in Jung. Somewhere Jung says that the only evil is unconsciousness.

And this I think touches on your work, Don. That this growth in consciousness, which psychoanalysis aims toward, has to be understood as a moral drive toward the good, or as an ethical drive—this is the way Jung would prefer it, because he sees this distinction between morality and ethics. And I think your work has brought this out. What I understand

Don to be doing is he's giving the lie to a kind of classical Freudianism that understood the psychoanalytical tradition to be kind of amoral in a certain way, or indifferent. It's amoral, and then I guess metaphysical and religious questions, because they all tend to go together, Freud saw pretty clearly. And once you start talking about morality, religion and philosophy's around the corner. Freud didn't want to go around that corner.

But it seems to me that what Don has done in this book is he's argued that you've already turned that corner, insofar as the conscious, a growth in consciousness, is always a good thing. And a resistance to consciousness is always a bad thing. And that seems to me to be something that's actually a medieval principle.

DC: So, I have a problem with a part of what you said earlier, Sean. And it's a problem, I think, in a lot of the literature. I think also in Jung. Part of the problem is the failure to distinguish conscience from superego. The word conscience is being used too indiscriminately here. I think we really need a radical distinction between conscience and superego. Both conscience and superego appear as voices in our heads. Both conscience and superego can show up in dreams, as in the dream offered by Jung. But they're very different principles. And it very much confuses our thinking to use the word conscience to describe both. Because I think conscience is of God. And I think it's a lot of the time not nearly as hard as people think to discriminate between these voices in our heads.

Well, I suppose, my favorite passage from the New Testament is 1 John 4:7–12:[48] "Beloved, let us love one another because love is of God.

[48] McGrath quotes verse 7. Following is the full passage, from the King James Version: "Beloved, let us love one another: for love is of God; and every one that loveth is born of God, and knoweth God.[7] He that loveth not knoweth not God; for God is love.[8] In this was manifested the love of God toward us, because that God sent his only begotten Son into the world, that we might live through him.[9] Herein is love, not that we loved God, but that he loved us, and sent his Son to be the propitiation for our sins.[10] Beloved, if God so loved us, we ought also to love one another.[11] No man hath seen God at any time. If we love one another, God dwelleth in us, and his love is perfected in us.[12]"

Everyone who loves is begotten by God and knows God. Whoever is without love does not know God, for God is love." Okay, the conscience is the voice of God, because the conscience is a principle of love. The superego is a principle of hate. So when these voices speak hatefully, cruelly, sadistically, mockingly, attackingly—that we're dealing with superego there. When the voice is loving, however sad and aggrieved it may be because the child is off the path and the father who's calling him back to the path has tears in his eyes, that father with tears in his eyes speaks in a very different way than the superego does. So I think a lot of what—well, let me just leave it at that. I think that this distinction is crucial to our discussion.

SM: And it strikes me that while both remain unconscious, the distinction between them cannot be made. That is, superego and conscience become confused precisely because they're left in the basement.

DC: Exactly.

SM: This connection between conscience and knowledge, they're not the same thing. And even in the quote, the passage from 1 John that you just cited, there's this play on loving God and knowing God, and he who loves, knows God, and he who does not love does not know God. There's always this reference, there's always this connection to knowledge that's coming forward here. And the connection is there because we need to recognize that it's not enough, for example, to have a spontaneous drive toward something. It also has to be, in a certain way, illuminated by knowledge. So like John could have said, *he who loves is of God*. But he adds that loving God and knowing God are actually one. And if you do not know God then you're not loving in the right way. It seems to me that's the implication.

This strikes me as important in our day and age, because we are still neo-Romantics, we're so fascinated by spontaneous and instinctive behavior, we're inclined to trust it. I trust my heart, I have to do it, I cannot do otherwise. Kind of doing a Luther in our post-post-modern moment. The spontaneity and the directness of an action is not enough to validate it ethically. There needs to be this second moment and this is what I think is coming out of the medieval tradition and that Jung is kind of brilliantly touching on. The second moment, where conscience becomes conscious, and I think—Don, you correct me—at that point the distinction between that voice, which is just an introjected parental voice of repression, the superego, and the voice of God, they can be distinguished. They can only be distinguished at the level of consciousness—not on some kind of spontaneous unconscious level.

DC: Right, I agree. The whole psychoanalytic project is trying to make that which is unconscious conscious, and to promote the development of self-knowledge. So I completely agree with that point. But in terms of the critique of spontaneity, I hesitate a little bit there, because one of the things I learned from the Jung essay: I finally found a way that I could agree with his idea of the archetype. Because—to me—the archetype has always seemed like a very fuzzy, woolly concept of sort of innate ideas or mythical patterns that come from *where*, I don't know, what are they grounded in? But suddenly I realize that part of what he's trying to do with the concept of the archetype is to say he's referring to nature, he's referring to elements of our being that are natural, that are unlearned, that do not come from culture. And of course he's saying that conscience is such a natural thing.

And he's referring to archetypal patterns—unlearned, given, built in—and I think that conscience is grounded in our mammalian and primate inheritance. I think part of the problem in our discussion again is—then here I go Freudian—we need the distinctions, we need the id, as well as the ego, the superego. We also need the conscience and the ego ideal. We need five structures. But for Freud the id is grounded in our animal inheritance. Jung seems to be sort of saying that—he makes me think that conscience is part of the id, because conscience is grounded biologically. So, the id would contain natural urges like aggression; urges that could lead to evil and destructiveness are part of the dark side, but the id, I would argue, also contains our light side. The id contains conscience as well as aggression. I think Jung is pointing to this with his idea of the archetypal basis of conscience.

So just a word in favor of the spontaneity, the built in, the natural. There is something there that is very important that I think Jung is pointing to and that I'm pointing to by trying to ground conscience in attachment. Bowlby points to our primate inheritance. This is where our attachment, our tendency toward attachment, is grounded. It's instinctual in that sense. It's innate, unlearned. So this is a big important thing and it's enabled me to connect with Jung in a way that I never was able to connect to before.

SM: I hear the point. And it strikes me that, the id, right—*das es*—that's the German—is really just a word for the it, it's a term to name the impersonal dimension of the psyche.

DC: Yes.

SM: At least formally speaking. And it seems to me, what you're touching on here is how differentiated Jung's sense of the impersonal stratum truly is.

DC: Yes.

SM: So the impersonal is not just violence and excess and animal, but it's also, you could say, angelic, in a certain way.

DC: Yes! Yes.

SM: Our demons and our angels, they're also transpersonal or sub-personal or something like that.

DC: Yes. Yes, but here, grounding the angelic in the id, I think we get around a problem that I don't think Jung got around. He's stuck on—he's such a profoundly dualistic thinker, and he has such a profound insight into the dualities of our nature—and he's stuck on this dualistic concept of God, which I find utterly unacceptable. God is not both the dark and the light. God is the light. God is love. And when he points to the Lord's Prayer, "Lead us not into temptation," this is an image of God as leading us into temptation, putting us into danger. And to me, all I can say is that is either a flaw in the Lord's Prayer that needs to be revised, or I want you to tell me there's a translation problem somewhere if we go back to the Greek or if we go back, we'll find that that sentence, *lead us not into temptation*—but of course, the Bible is full of images of a destructive God, a punishing God. But to me, this is not God. God is the *Summum Bonum*, God is love. This other stuff comes from elsewhere, okay? What's your reaction to all of that, Sean?

SM: Okay, so, yes, Don, you said a couple of things there that are really important, at least to my mind. Jung's dualism, on the one hand, and the question of spontaneity on the other. And the question of spontaneity I find an easier one to deal with than the dualism.

DC: Yes.

SM: With regard to the spontaneity, there seems to me two problems here. One is that we can repress our spontaneous self to such a degree that we become what Schelling calls a *Verständnis Mensch,* a person of just empty understanding, a rationalist automaton. Someone with no life in them. And clearly psychoanalysis is dealing with that kind of illness all the time, we might call it a predominant form of neurosis. Someone who's sort of cut off from their instinctive life, whether it's their animal life or their moral life. Or even just their personal being in the world. That's a certain kind of evil.

DC: Yes.

SM: But there's another kind of evil, of course, which is that one has so surrendered oneself to nature, you could say, that reflection and moral discernment and responsibility have become negated.

DC: Yes.

SM: And this is the Deleuzean problematic, because Deleuze has such difficulties with reflection, that at the end of the day he just wants people to spontaneously produce themselves without any kind of moral discernment, and ultimately that leads to a denial of the distinction between good and evil, the distinction that you just quite clearly articulated in response to Jung. So I, for me, and my guide here is Schelling, who in a very famous passage says, there's two kinds of madness. One madness is the madness that suppresses the spontaneous self by the understanding. And in that kind of person, there is no life. Nothing comes from them. They're kind of a walking dead.

And there's another kind of madness, of course, in which this spontaneous natural self has completely eclipsed consciousness and knowledge and culture. You know, some kind of psychosis. So there's a kind of delicate balancing act required here, and I think that's what we're trying to get at.

DC: Yes.

SM: And that's what Jung is getting at quite articulately in this essay, in the best parts of his essay. But let's talk about the bad parts of his essay.

DC: (*chuckles*) Yeah.

SM: For me, Jung is a complete theoretical mess. You know? This is why he's so interesting. Because he's just—he produces one insight after the other insight and they're full of genius and possibility, but the thing never gets knitted together in any kind of satisfying way, and he'll say one thing that one could develop, but then follow it up with something else, which completely confuses matters.

DC: Exactly, it's exasperating to read for that very reason.

SM: Entirely confused. And with regard to this question that God—the dark side of God, and God has this shadow side and God is beyond God and evil, and he's neither good nor evil, and so we end up with some kind of, I don't know what to say, some kind of monistic idea out of Asia, rather than the moral discernment between good and evil that you were discussing earlier. Those are two very different ideas. And they do not fit together in Jung's world at all.

So for example, if we follow the dark side of God theme, which many Jungians are very attached to, the logical consequence of that is that we should do whatever it is that we want to do. We should be like Alistair Crowley—my will is the only law. Because I want it, it should be. And any kind of judgment about that is something to be abjured. There is no good and evil. There's just really power and the expression of it. And I think a thinker like Deleuze, who is very influenced by Jung, he actually brought, he actually filled out that sentence, and brought it to its conclusion, where he says, *actually, no, there's neither good nor evil, there's just power and its expression, and its failed expressions*. Kind of a Nietzschean, Spinozistic amoralism.

But this Nietzschean Spinozistic amoralism is entirely at odds with the other element in Jung, which is this strong sense that there is a kind of moral responsibility, an ethical responsibility of the individual to develop their consciousness and to discern. For example, with regard to the archetypes—domination by an archetype is also the source of the worst things in all the world. That was Jung's analysis of the National Socialist movement.

DC: Right.

SM: We're not to surrender ourselves to the collective, the archetypal, the impersonal. On the contrary, we are to build a bridge to it, what Jung calls the transcendent function. So to maintain this kind of ego pole, which is in constant lifegiving dialogue with the impersonal archetypal dimension, neither surrendering to it nor repressing it.

DC: Right.

SM: And that for me is the moral, the ethical axis of Jung's thought, and I think you're right, it's for me incompatible with this Asiatic monism that he tends to fall into when he tries to be a metaphysician, which is always a bad idea for Jung.

DC: Yes. Yes. That's helpful. I agree with everything you've just said there. But can I bring you back to his point about the Lord's prayer? A God who leads us into temptation?

SM: Remind me of what he says on that?

DC: Well, he's saying that we can't just trust conscience as the *vox Dei*, the voice of God, because this is a God who can lead us into temptation.

JL: Let me just come in with actually quoting that. Because I think it could be really helpful. So this is the quote from the Jung paper ["A Psychological View of Conscience"], *where he speaks about the Lord's Prayer:*

> *But if the voice of conscience is the voice of God, this voice must possess an incomparably higher authority than traditional morality. Anyone, therefore, who allows conscience this status should, for better or worse, put his trust in divine guidance and follow his conscience rather than give heed to conventional morality. If the believer had absolute confidence in his definition of God as the Summum Bonum,*

> *it would be easy for him to obey the inner voice, for he could be sure of never being led astray. But since, in the Lord's Prayer, we still beseech God not to lead us into temptation, this undermines the very trust the believer should have if, in the darkness of a conflict of duty, he is to obey the voice of conscience without regard to the "world" and, very possibly, act against the precepts of the moral code by "obeying God rather than men" (Acts 5: 29).*

SM: Yes, lead us not into temptation. This is a God—well, Jung is right, that God in the Lord's Prayer is identified as one who could lead us into temptation, or at least surrender us, leave us. I think the point of the Lord's Prayer is that the only reason we are not led into temptation is that God protects us from such temptation. And should God withdraw that protective power, we will fall into temptation. I think that's the point of the prayer, not that God leads us into temptation, but God preserves us from temptation, and should God for a moment withdraw his hand, we will fall into temptation. That I think is being said.

With regard to a God who can let us fall into temptation, are we therefore to conclude that this is a God who is neither God nor evil but he needs to be transcended or something? So there are stages of correction happening. So first you have *Yaweh*, who's obviously capable of wrathful acts, violent acts, and so on, a God of wrath. And then you have the Christian correction of this, which is to, in the mythic language, appease the wrathful God with the sacrifice of the good son. And then you have—but Jung is not happy to leave it there—he says now there's a third correction required because of the one-sidedness to the Christian correction: namely that it has excluded the dark, rather than integrated it, and this third correction apparently is happening at the level of psychoanalysis.

So when I hear Jung speaking about Christianity, he seems always to be thinking of something that needs to be corrected and transcended psychoanalytically. Now on the one hand, I think that's an interesting point, because we can't just leave the tradition where it is. The tradition dies if it's not constantly being appropriated, adapted, even expanded. And so I'm all on board with the idea that the psychological age needs to be an age of the Church, in a certain way, and that the revelation, the religious tradition, of at least part of the world, has to be somehow critically appropriated and corrected in certain ways. Who wouldn't agree with that? But where I have difficulty is with the kind of correction that Jung thinks is required. Because there it becomes incoherent. There we suddenly say that actually we're going to go back now, and we're going to correct the Christian correction by integrating the dark side of God into the light. And at that point the whole thing falls to pieces, because now we have even worse than *Yahweh*. We're in something that's pre-*Yahwehic*, something that is really deeply undifferentiated—

DC: Believe me, I know. I was a creature of the 1960s, which started out with peace and love and sweetness and non-violence, and wound up at the Altamont Festival with Hell's Angels killing people while the Rolling Stones sang "Sympathy for the Devil." And that youth counterculture got entirely into this *two faces of God*, including worship of the Dark Lord, and there are elements of this in Jung, which frankly really frighten me.

SM: Yes, and unfortunately, in my experience it's what is most predominant in Jungian circles, where Jung's psychology of religion is discussed. I rarely hear the criticism. I hear rather the repetition of this. It's entirely inadequate, what we're getting at here—so one of the ways that I've dealt with this theoretically is to say, *listen: good and evil are not opposites*. And that's very New Testament. They're not opposites. Good is not in conflict with evil. That's the theology of George Lucas. That is not the theology of the New Testament.

Goodness is transcendent of evil. Evil is only permitted a space of time for the sake of some inscrutable ends that God has willed. And we're told, in Revelation, in the end, Revelation 20, that evil will be entirely cast out and rendered nothing.

DC: The devil is always already defeated.

SM: Exactly. Or the light shines in the darkness and the darkness does not comprehend it. So we're not talking about two countervailing powers here that have to be held in balance in the interest of some third. That is not the image of goodness. We're talking about something quite different, which is, you could say, more hierarchical. And that's a bad word today, but nevertheless. The good is infinitely, qualitatively transcendent of anything that we might call evil. And whatever is evil only is insofar as it's permitted a space of operation, for whatever reason, and reasons that we can't comprehend. And that's what I hear Christ saying in the Lord's Prayer, when he says, "Lead us not into temptation," he's saying temptation, the devil, the dark that we deal with, the sin that we are so vulnerable to, all of this really is something that God could wipe away in an instant, but he has not, for reasons that we do not comprehend. And so we are therefore vulnerable, and we need to depend entirely on the mercy of God to protect us from this. It's not a question of a duality here at all. It's a question of absolute dependence, to quote Schleiermacher.

JL: But Sean, on a theoretical level this all makes sense to me. But as we also know, Jung was not a theologian. He was foremost a clinician. He was foremost developing his theory out of his experience with himself and his patients. And good and evil, you say, is not in conflict. I agree theoretically.

SM: No, I didn't say they're not in conflict. That's not what I said. I said that they're not counter poles. They're not opposing forces.

JL: They're not opposing forces. But in man, they are.

SM: Yes.

JL: And that's what Jung is speaking of. He doesn't try to develop a theology here. He's speaking of, in the human nature, they absolutely are in opposition and conflict all the time. And in the story of Job, God sends the devil to tempt Job. God is the man behind the temptation in that story. And Luther also says, "sometimes God sends the devil." But we have to see how we should work with that devilish element in us. You said, Don, in our last conversation, we cannot sort of get away with the superego. We need to have it working for us. The devil needs to cut the grapes.

DC: Yes.

JL: Referring to Luther.

DC: So, I'll leave it to Sean to address that part of it, God sending the devil to tempt Job. But let me just say that in terms of the battle between good impulses and evil impulses in human nature, here is where I think we need the Freudian concept of the id. Because it's pretty clear to me that we can trust our conscience. We have to distinguish it from the superego. We have to distinguish the voice of conscience from all of these other voices. But the voice of conscience is the *vox Dei.* It's guided by the principle of love. It can be trusted. It is quite distinct from other id contents that can be absolutely destructive and demonic.

SM: And as you said earlier, the discernment of spirits here is a work of consciousness.

DC: Yes.

SM: Yes. That's crucial.

JL: And I think Jung would agree with this. And I think the dualism of Jung speaks about the duality in the human heart, and the struggle on a human level, not—he doesn't form a theology out of this.

SM: And this is where, Jakob, I'm completely sensitive to the idea that Jung wants to speak as a clinician. And if he only spoke as a clinician, I'd be all on board. He's constantly transgressing this limitation. And he loves to play amateur theologian. He even loves to play amateur metaphysician, with the psychoid, the objective psyche and this kind of stuff. So I've just never taken it seriously, that Jungian psychology has obeyed these strict boundaries between clinical work and more theoretical speculative work, whether it's the theology or the philosophy. I just don't believe it. I don't believe it in Freud and I don't believe it in Jung.

That is why I think Don's work is so important. He's kind of saying, listen, we're already transgressing these boundaries. We're already in the domain of the ethical. We can't pretend that we aren't.

JL: I agree with you, Sean, that Jung is moving between positions. But my point is that I think he speaks about the human heart and the struggle that people have, and that's a very dualistic struggle at times.

SM: I agree. But if Jung is happily transgressing the boundaries, why doesn't he invite the others in? Now he does on occasion—Victor White was invited in. But generally speaking there's a lot of hesitation and even a kind of naïve critique of the theological or philosophical voice in Jungian circles, you know? They're speaking—even some-one who is as speculatively adept as [Wolfgang] Giegerich has this kind of epoché. I remember once asking Giegerich, shouldn't we talk about metaphysics? And do you know what he said to me? He said, that's a temptation. He said we cannot go there.

So "absolute psychology" so fills the space that there is no room for any other voice. There's no plurality there. There's no voice, there's no room for the theological voice, or the philosophical voice, coming from whatever tradition. And consequently what happens is a kind of amateur theology tends to kind of colonize the space. And we have all these confusions perpetuated.

JL: I can agree with you that there's a lot of confusion within the Jungian field and discourse, and I wouldn't protect the Jungians per se. But I would also say that it's interesting, no, that we're discussing this paper that Jung wrote, one of his last papers, in 1958, "The Psychology of Conscience," and we still get so many insights from it.

DC: It's a magnificent paper. The Freudian tradition never got there, to this distinction that Jung sees very clearly, in certain aspects. I have a problem with your mentioning the concept of the heart earlier, Jakob. Like the division, the conflict-within-the-heart-of-man kind of thing. I have trouble with that because I think the heart is closely allied with the conscience. And I think that the demonic does not come from the heart. It comes from other aspects of our nature.

JL: But it gets into the heart.

DC: The heart is pretty reliable.

JL: But I think the demonic comes into the heart, that that's the part of the work. When you're in sin, I mean, it goes to the heart of man.

SM: That's actually Christ's—Jesus does say that himself, right? So the heart is a metaphor. I love the metaphor. But as a metaphor, it's got a lack of precision, right? So, when we say the heart, we mean what? The core, the innermost, right? The ground, if you like?

DC: Well I see it as the seat of love. The heart is the seat of love. And therefore it is not the seat of evil.

SM: But wouldn't you say, Don, that evil is—only one with a heart is capable of evil?

DC: Yes.

SM: So in a certain way, you could say that out of the heart spring all evil thoughts, which is a paraphrase of what Jesus himself says. Not that the heart is evil. But only one with a heart can so misuse themselves as to be productive of evil.

DC: Well that I would agree with. But that's not saying that the evil comes from the heart. That's only saying that only someone with a heart could be drawn into evil.

SM: So that's why I find the heart a rather imprecise way to speak. I would prefer to speak about the ground or the core of freedom out of which personality grows. There's a certain kind of perversion that only human persons are capable of.

DC: Yes.

SM: And this is why I think it's a mistake to speak about goodness and evil in the non-human world. In a certain way we admire plants and animals and the universe precisely because it is so confirmed in its being, but there's a kind of vacillation at the core of the human being. We don't have to say it's the heart, if you don't like. But at the ground of the human being there's this vacillation.

And Schelling says that out of the ground emerges a decision, a decision for good or for evil. What Schelling means by that is not that we *choose*—he says decision. *Entscheidung*. We actually divide at this point. It's not as though we choose preexisting possibilities: Jakob chooses his good Jakob over evil Jakob. Rather, that in the decision, personal ground produces something that has never been before. And it's either a form of evil that was never before, or it's a form of goodness that was never before. But in any case it's produced out of this ground of freedom.

DC: Yes, yes. Out of the ground of freedom for sure. This is why I love my dog. My dog is incapable of evil.

SM Exactly. But I hate to say it, Don. It also means that the dog's incapable of good.

DM: Oh, absolutely. That's true too.

SM: So we misuse the term when we go, *good dog*.

DC: (*laughing*) That's true.

JL: Sean, I just want to hear if you have any comments about the temptation . . .

SM: God sending the devil. Well, that's exactly true, that God sends the devil. That's exactly true, we certainly know that's biblical, that's New Testament.

JL: But in the Lord's Prayer you had an issue with that?

SM: No, I didn't. I was actually speaking precisely. If the devil's on the scene, it's only because God has allowed the devil to be on the scene. So that's the terrible insecurity, the situation of insecurity in which we stand. We do not command this terrain. We're not the master of this house, if you want to speak in the Freudian phrase. So that means there's a kind of dependency on the mercy of God, to protect us from these things. And the truth is that we shall be protected.

The whole story of Christ is, here's the best man who ever lived, if you want, or the *logos* incarnate, more accurately, and he is constantly subject to the power of the devil. If you take his first appearance to be at the baptism at the Jordan, as he appears in Mark, without the infancy narratives, which are very likely, well they are constructed, they're constructed after the fact. I think Jesus enters history as a thirty-year-old man being baptized by John the Baptist in the Jordan. What happens immediately afterwards? At this moment of initiation, where he is actually being called the Son of God, he is led into the desert where the devil has his way with him. Or at least tries to have his way with him. And he withstands that, and then the devil departs until the appointed hour, which is the moment of his greatest trial, which is the passion. The point being that this, the best man, is not the man who is never subject, or is never tormented, by evil, but the one who is constantly, constantly subject to the power of evil, and nevertheless holds fast, or is held fast.

JL: A question that I'm sitting with is the question of conscience in the analytical space. You, Don, with your theoretical work, have done a great service, and Eli Sagan as well and others, in dealing with and working on these matters, and showing the importance of differentiating between the superego and the conscience. Then we have this comment from you, Sean, that Jungians are sort of, as a whole, a little bit immoral, or there's sometimes a lack of ethical compass. I wanted to hear about you, Don, first, what you think about this. Is psychoanalytic practice today a practice without conscience? Or is it actually there?

DC: Well, I think conscience to some extent is built into standard psychoanalytic practice. But, Freud lied about it and Freudians have been lying about it ever since. They hide it behind this medical façade, they talk about mental health. Rather than try to convert people from badness to goodness, they won't admit what they're doing. But nevertheless, the value system is there. They could do so much better if they raised it to consciousness. If they got honest about what it is they are about, they could do it much better. They're embarrassed about the ethical nature of their practice.

There's also, they're not going to get paid in Ontario by OHIP for trying to turn people from badness to goodness. Or even from narcissism to object love, which is the way Freud put it in 1914 when he momentarily slipped up and forgot his disguise. He stopped talking that way and it shifted to the language of mental health. So it's there in the tradition, but the tradition has really suffered from not being fully conscious, not being fully honest about itself, major failures of conscience, unconscientious elements within the psychoanalytic tradition, which I think might have been avoided if we had been able to be honest about the ethic that undergirds the whole enterprise.

Just on the question of working in the clinical room, much of my work follows the line of the example that Jung gave us. My patients are doing all kinds of immoral and unethical things, and they're lying to themselves, but they produce dreams in which their hands are dirty. Or they're doing things like stealing and cheating. And I'm not going to be superego-ish and reproach them for this. But I am going to be alert to, *what do they do with the dirty money?* Mostly, they lose it. Or they get it stolen from them. Or they get hit by a car. Or they develop migraine headaches. And I am always pointing out, *look what happens whenever you cheat on your wife. You get the headaches. Or you get that rash all over your body.* Whatever. So I'm confronting them with the consequences of their actions. Thus trying to lead them to face the fact that they have a conscience, and they have a superego. They're busy blocking both superego and conscience. That's how I work.

SM: Well, there's so much on the table here. I don't know where to begin. So I'm going to start with the first thing that I remember and bring it back to the very interesting thing that Don just said. So first thing that you said, Jakob, was that Jungians are immoral, that I—actually, I can't think of a single Jungian I met that I would call immoral. On the contrary. I think that they just don't understand the ethical thrust of their practice and they're misnaming it, and that Jung has not helped them with his monistic idea of a good–evil God. That was my claim. Not that they're immoral but that their theory is inadequate to the ethical thrust of what they're doing, which is more or less what I think Don is saying about the Freudian tradition.

DC: Yes.

SM: And with regard to the Church, what does *church* mean? There are two words in the tradition. *Ecclesia,* and *circe. Ecclesia* is the one I'd like to best, because *ecclesia* really just means a gathering of concerned citizens. So it's a gathering of people, and in the New Testament context it means those people who have gathered around the Christ. And if we wanted to secularize this, which I think we should because as I've said many times before, Christianity is self-secularizing: it's the gathering of those called to love. It's the community of those called to love. That's the Church. So what if it happens in your consulting room, in their cathedral down the road from me, that is of no moment, really. Wherever it's happening, the Church is active, and I'm convinced that the Church is alive and well wherever it's regarded in this much bigger sense, this ontological sense. And stop identifying it, like certain transitory institutions that are passing away, that weren't always part of it, and that won't always be part of it.

But what I wanted to come back to, though, is this embarrassment about the ethical. I thought this was so interesting, Don. So, you use the word *lie* multiple times. They're lying about what they're doing. They're promoting health. I immediately thought of the etymological relationship between the word *health* and *whole* and *holy*. There's a kind of reductionistic refusal of that etymological and I think ontological relationship between *health*, *holiness*, *wholeness*. And it occurred to me as I heard you speak that I can well imagine many situations in which the right thing to do is to lie, but I can't imagine a single situation in which the right thing to do is to lie to yourself.

DC: Mm-hmmm.

SM: It seems to me there we have the thing that cannot be forgiven. Not because there's a judgmental God who's punishing us for us, but because we put ourselves into a place in which we cannot possibly—

DC: Well, and here's the thing of the psychoanalytical tradition opposing self-deception, while ongoingly deceiving itself.

SM: Yes, and what I wanted to ask you is, what do you think the root of that embarrassment is? It's obviously not an accidental thing. It's kind of a structural feature of the Freudian tradition, I think.

DC: Well, I think it has to do with the Enlightenment. Enlightenment rationalism and materialism, and so many—Freud himself—and so many people are steeped in their respect for and their identification with Enlightenment rationalism and science, and they can't bear to see themselves as people who are committed to love, and to kindness over cruelty, and they see this as sentimental, and non-rational, non-scientific. And they find it all very embarrassing.

SM: Yes, I would have thought—my own take on Freud and, to a lesser degree on Jung, is that there is this attachment to what in philosophy we call the positivist tradition.

DC: Yes, positivism.

SM: Yes, what's real is a thing that can be measured in space and time, that's localizable. There's an interesting passage in the *Interpretation of Dreams*, where Freud says, the psyche has its own laws and it should be understood on its own terms and not explained in terms of something else.

DC: Yes.

SM: But then he adds, and with time we'll find out that those are the same laws that pertain to physical things. Right?

DC: Ultimately mind will be reduced to brain.

SM: That's right.

DC: And so many of my colleagues have lost touch with psycho-analysis altogether. They're into what they're calling neuro-psychoanalysis. And it's all about the brain and it's a total waste of time. Not for brain scientists, but for psychoanalysts it's a waste of time.

SM: Oh it's—we're in a far more deeply positivistic age than Freud was in 1900 when he wrote the *Interpretation of Dreams*.

DC: Right.

SM: And neuroscience has—it's just dominating our understanding of ourselves. What gets me is how—there's a kind of paradox there—people seem to be—here's the difference: Back in the end of the nineteenth century, when positivism 1.0 was destroying our cultural institutions and our ethics, people were horrified. Think of the characters in Dostoyevsky's novels, who carry the positivism all the way through and go and butcher their landlady or something. There was this horror that it's all just actually meaningless matter in motion. But now, when we have this seemingly more sophisticated scientific demonstration that it's all just meaningless matter in motion, we're all relieved, we're all delighted. It's like we've found the God molecule. We've found the little part of your brain that if I tickle it with electricity, it'll cause you to feel oceanic bliss. And people are relieved by this, they're happy about it. I don't understand it.

DC: Well, I guess one, it saves us from freedom. It saves us from guilt. It saves us from humanity.

SM: I think we're in a deep, deep, dark positivist age. I think this is why psychoanalysis has become so out of mode. When I talk to philosophers of mind, they can't believe that I have anything to do with something as wrong as psychoanalysis.

DC: Uh-ha. Well, because you're also involved in something as wrong as Christianity. It's odd. People don't understand that it was psychoanalysis that brought me back to Christianity. So, psychoanalysis is profoundly involved with the soul. Maybe I should forgive my medical colleagues and leave them alone and let them continue to hide behind their medical disguise. Because they're doing soul work. And maybe it's—maybe they need a shield in this age of positivism.

SM: Yes. (*Silence.*)

I do think that something is coming, and it's going to be neither the Christianity that we are familiar with, nor the psychoanalysis that we have, more or less, worked through to the end. Neither of these things are finished. So, in that regard—I do —I very much like Jung when he plays his prophetic note and he looks toward this future integration or this new stage of whatever it is that's working its way through time in at least the European tradition. I think that's the proper attitude. These things are not dead but they're actually changing into something new.

JL: I think there's something prophetic in Jung, but I also think there is something very reformative. The way I understand Jung is that he could have been the greatest of reformers of Christianity if he would have taken a stand, if he wouldn't have hidden behind his persona as a psychiatrist. It's also something in Jung, I mean, he's envisioning the future, he's prophetic, but he's always rooted in tradition.

SM: What would it mean, Jakob, for him to take a stand?

JL: A stand would I guess mean, first of all, that he would have to touch his forehead to the floor. It seems he never did that [referring to Jung's dream as told in *Memories, Dreams, Reflections*]. *He was until then, as I understand it, ambivalent, in some sort of opposition, so therefore that wasn't his life. But his theories are alive, and we can work with them. And we can do what we're doing here on our small turf. And what you've done, Don, with your work, bringing conscience back into psychoanalysis and into Jungian psychoanalysis.*

SM: I wonder about religion. You say he should have touched the floor with his head. Are you saying we want a religious psychoanalysis? I imagine Don isn't quite ready to go there.

JL: No. No, no! I think we should see that psychoanalysis is, as Don says in one of his latest papers, it's spirituality. It's bringing us back to seeing life more truthfully. It takes away the blindfolds. I'm not saying that we should develop a Christian psychoanalysis, but done right, it can help us to see reality.

DC: Yes, it's a spiritual practice, I believe, and always has been, but in disguise.

SM: What does it mean, exactly, to say that it's a spiritual practice?

DC: Well, I think, first of all, I think psychoanalytic practice is a form of meditation. Everyone is so preoccupied with mindfulness mediation. I think that psychoanalysis is a type of that that goes on toward what I call heartfulness meditation. The patient is free-associating and the analyst is enjoined to have freely hovering attention. So both the patient and I are sitting there in a meditative state, and we're watching what comes up in the dialogue and what comes up in the dreams. So the whole thing seems to me to be a daily meditative practice. For patients who are on the couch maybe four, five days a week, it's a deep meditation, among other things.

And to the extent that it clarifies conscience and distinguishes it from superego, and helps the patient sort out these voices in his head, and helps him—oh that last question you mentioned in your list, Jakob. Murray Stein is talking about how we not only have responsibilities to others, but we have responsibilities to the Self. I think of Winnicott's true self. I think true self is often ignored and abandoned, and I think a conscientious person owes others but also owes his true self.

And terrible conflicts, obviously, would emerge. Sometimes to do justice to my true self, I may have to break a covenant with another. So this is just a lifelong ethical struggle. I think conscience is linked to the true self and I think creativity is linked to the true self. So I think in analysis we're trying to help people make contact with their true selves by helping them make contact with their emotions. And their dreams. And we're trying to bring them closer—I think that psychoanalysis involves self-realization and self-actualization. And the end result is a more conscientious person. So I think psychoanalysis is a spiritual practice.

Healing Fire:
Orthodox Christianity and Analytical Psychology, with Pia Chaudhari

"I think *Eros* is often confused with lust in our world. And it's not that. It's a deeper, more powerful, broader, richer vein of desire that can unify and can unite, without confusion, different aspects, both of ourselves and of the cosmos. It has to be real. Otherwise, it's not *Eros*. It can't just be a kind of lip service to kindness."

—Pia Sophia Chaudhari

JL: Welcome to the podcast, Pia Chaudhari. Today we're going to discuss your book, Dynamis of Healing: Patristic Theology and the Psyche, *which was published in 2019 by Fordham University Press. It took some time to read through the book, but I would just want to say that it's a beautiful book and very thoroughly written. What you're doing is tying links between the tradition and practice of Orthodox Christianity and patristic theology, with a view to depth psychology, and specifically more of a focus on analytical psychology. So, we're going to talk about the book and we're going to talk about your findings in all this research. But before diving into the book, I was wondering if you could tell me a little bit about yourself, and maybe what led up to you writing this book.*

PC: Thank you so much for the opportunity to be here. It's really wonderful to have a second conversation with you now and to explore some of these topics. It's not a book I ever imagined myself writing. It's not something I set out to do a long time ago, but it was a kind of culmination of many years of wonderings. I care deeply about healing. I always have. And at a certain point in my journey, I became Christian, which was also an unexpected move for me. And Christianity is a religion that—and we don't always hear this emphasis—in fact, is very focused on healing. The Church is a hospital, and even the early understanding of the word *salvation*—the early Church used the word *therapia*—there was a therapy of the world taking place. So there is this idea that something was actually being healed and restored, and, not just in an abstract way, saved. My father was a scientist, I grew up in a scientific world, and I tried to hold these two areas together for a long time. There's science, there's psychiatry, there's psychology, and then there's religion and there's faith, and there's apparently now, what I was coming to understand in my own journey, this whole area of healing in the Church as well. So I think for quite some time I held, I just wondered, without doing much about it, how do these areas relate? Do they relate? Can God cure depression? How does this work? And eventually I found myself in seminary and had the chance to work in a really fantastic program that was run at the time by Ann Ulanov, and at the time it was called the Department of Psychiatry and Religion.

And this just seemed like a place to really wrestle out a lot of these questions working with the primary sources from Freud, from Jung, Winnicott, Fairbairn. It was really a deep dive. And at the same time, I was studying early Church history with Father John McGuckin, who was an Orthodox theologian, a Church historian. And so in a way, the holding of the two areas was coming closer together. At least I had everything in one school now and was able to go from office to office rather than from medical school to religious school. And so the worlds were coming closer. And yes, I began to see and feel and trust that there were really—what I call in the book—*meeting places*, that there's some kind of sense of integration, which is in fact something that both Eastern Orthodox theology and depth psychology emphasize. And it made sense to me after a while that of course there would have to be, because we are one creature. So for our psyches not to be split between the Divine and the natural, it would have to be integrated in us in some way. And I think that's where I began to find that, no, it's not as simplistic as, *oh, God will just cure your depression if you pray hard enough*. That, I think, is a very dangerous place to go sometimes. But it is true that it's all connected in some way and that there are places of shared understanding between Orthodox theology and depth psychology.

JL: How come you were drawn to or started to go into Orthodox Christianity, of the different orthodoxies? Can you say something about Orthodox—

PC: Right. Again, one more path I never imagined myself on. I wasn't raised with any connection, although my beloved's second family is Serbian Orthodox. I had a little bit of exposure as a child growing up, but that was it. I think what happened is I got to seminary, and I was studying with Father John McGuckin in early Church history because I had had some experiences that led me toward Christianity. I wanted to explore them. I wanted to explore them in my own way. I think a lot of young people who arrive in seminary and aren't necessarily on an ordination track have questions, and I had questions. And I wanted to get back as close in time to the original event, the *Christic event*, as they call it, and then go from there to see what I was going to make of Christianity. I didn't want 2,000 years of accretions on top of it in my understanding.

And so I spent some time in what I later came to understand as early Church history, and then also early Church theology, and I found it captivating. And in large part because there was a very strong emphasis on experience—that people, that the Church Fathers, were writing out of an experience that they'd had, that this was experiential. It wasn't abstract or cerebral, as heady as they can be. There was a real sense of connectedness to lived life, and that they had experienced something that led them to then change their lives, to write, to reflect, to sacrifice themselves in many cases as well. So I was drawn to that . . . As I got further along the theological journey and was able to ask more involved or sophisticated questions of the theology than I had been previously, I had concerns about atonement theory and understandings of Christ's sacrifice, and whether, wouldn't that, in fact, lead us to some kind of setup within ourselves of, *are humans bad?* And God had to sacrifice himself to save us? And doesn't that kind of clash with the therapeutic understanding that we're not bad and that we have to work to heal?

And so, I had these kinds of questions, and I found that within the Orthodox Church, every time I would ask these questions, they would be answered in a way that made sense to me. Yes, there is a sacrificial aspect, but we also have to focus on the incarnation, and we also have to understand that this was a question, much like in therapy—it was almost like a rescue mission rather than the penal substitution of, "God had to die Himself to satisfy God's own honor," the kind of legalistic understandings that came later or were emphasized later. I don't know if that addresses what you're saying, but I think I found space in the Church for understandings that did not contraindicate or contradict what I was also learning in my study of depth psychology, and in my own therapeutic journey.

JL: And could you say something short about also that, the therapeutic journey and Jung and analytical psychology, how you got involved in that and also then practiced as a therapist?

PC: I had the great good fortune to study with really wonderful teachers, Ann Ulanov, Harry Fogarty, both of whom are Jungian and in the Department of Psychiatry and Religion. And I found that there was a capaciousness there, for all kinds of experience. And I don't know how much the listeners will be interested to know the differences between, say, Jung and Freud; one of the main differences as I experienced it is that there isn't just the emphasis on the reductive in Jung, this idea that we have to go back in time to find the origin of the wound or the trauma and then kind of wrestle through it. But there's also the prospective. The question is, *where is the person going?* Where is the symptom *taking them*, and not just where does it originate? What is the *telos* of their journey?

And I found that very enlivening because it's a very, very hopeful paradigm for healing to have. Someone could come in and say, *oh, well, I've got this depression, or I've got this crazy fantasy that keeps coming up, or I've got this kind of compulsion*. And one of my dear colleagues in my former training institute is working right now on a whole paper and book on compulsion and the role it plays in moving us forward if we can understand it properly. So this idea of symptom as symbol, and not just symptom as pathology or issue to be removed, was very, very powerful. And—again, just to link it back—it's this kind of almost allegorical way of thinking, which was really a big part of early Church theology. Even Origen and others used allegory all the time to understand scripture and to understand theology.

JL: So for people like myself who are not well versed in Orthodox Christianity or patristic theology, I wonder if it would be possible to give some context, or to define some key fundaments, of Orthodox teaching—that can be helpful as we're exploring these, what you call, meeting places, between the field of Orthodox Christianity and analytical psychology?

PC: It's a vast question. It might be that along the way it's easier to flesh out a few things, but the first thing to know, that comes to mind to me, is that Orthodox Christianity is a sacramental Christianity. So there's a heavy emphasis on the sacraments, which are in fact considered meeting places between the human and the Divine. And in the twelfth century, St. Gregory of Palamas wrote extensively on the difference between the Divine energies of God, the uncreated energies of God, and the created energies of creation. It brings a few things in—the first is that the belief in God can be experienced directly in the sacraments. It's not a cerebral experiencing, it's not a moral experiencing. I was just reading, earlier, a wonderful quote by St. Maximus about that, which I can bring up later. But it's a direct experience of the uncreated energies of the Divine. We are created and we're on this side of creation, along with all of creation. We are created; we're not the Creator. And so the sacrament is the meeting place between the uncreated and the created. And the second you bring experience in, you can now reflect on it. And the second you're reflecting on experience, you're already in the realm of depth psychology to some degree. So that's sort of how that got set up. It's also a very sensuous experience of the Church. There are the icons, and the incense, and the flames, and the smell of the bees' wax, and the chanting, and the paintings on the wall. There's the prostrations, and there's fasting, and there's feasting—so it's very embodied, which also gave me a place from which to engage with the psychology.

JL: The second chapter in the book, you've given the title "That Which is Not Assumed is Not Healed," which is, as I understand, the core maxim of patristic theology. And I think the quote was from St. Gregory of Nazianzus. And with that quote, that which is not assumed is not healed, you start to draw links to depth psychology and the valuing of the shadowy parts of the human psyche, and the integration of parts or complexes that we might not want to face.

PC: This is really core. I think you've gone right to the heart of the matter, because I think many people confuse religion with morality, and, as such, have a kind of (understandably so) fidelity to a certain, not even moral stance, but moral self-understanding. One of the things that Jung struggled with on his own (as I'm sure many of your listeners know, Jung was the son of a pastor and grew up at a certain time in Protestant history)—when you read his writings, he's obviously struggling to find the meaning in the symbols of the Church. So Jung goes on his own journey when he writes about the shadow and the need to encounter the shadow. I think over time he really developed his thinking on the shadow, but I think initially there was just some sense of, oh, hey, look, you've got to really confront who you *really* are, not who you think you ought to be from a moral standpoint. Kind of like the Pharisee and the Publican, it's like, well, thank God I'm not someone who's envious or spiteful or greedy or jealous. And then of course, you go into analysis and you find out you're all those things. I think he was sort of reckoning with the shadow in a way that the Church actually encourages people to do as well, through confession. But of course in the Protestant Church, you didn't have confession. So that's sort of one difference there.

But I think that this idea that we would split away from the parts of ourselves that don't meet our own moral standards or our own sense of who we are or want to be: that's sort of depth psychology 101. But the danger then in bringing religion into that is the danger of putting a God complex (I would say, rather than God) on the throne that says: well, don't go there into that part of yourself. Don't look at the porn addiction. Don't look at the cheating or the lying or the stealing or any of that, because God hates that about you (and you can maybe take it to confession, and hopefully you are), but it's nothing to be explored or understood in any particular way. Whereas Jung would say, oh, let's go right there and see what's going on. I think '"that which is not assumed is not healed" ' just rang so clearly in my head through the centuries. My goodness, if that's what they were saying, and they were saying it with regard to many things—it was also, as Maximus picked it up later, to do with the human will—it was a basic understanding of, if we are being saved by Christ, then Christ must have within himself all of who we are. Because if there's any part of us that is not in his human experience, it cannot be saved by him. Does that make sense? But if he knows suffering, then suffering can be healed. If he knows grief, then grief can be healed. But the temptation then, of course, is to say, yes, but of course Christ never did steal, and he never did kill, and he didn't do all these terrible things that we do. But he has to have had the ability to do it, or else our will can't be healed. His will was free. He has to have had a free human will. And I kind of elaborated on that to say, so we're also talking about the psyche then, that *all* of the psyche has to have been assumed into this project of *therapia*, of salvation. Otherwise, there are just parts of our psyche hanging out that can't be healed. And that's surely not what the Fathers were saying.

So that means even our porn addiction, even our envy, even our murder, has to have some place in it where healing can happen. Some place where redemption can happen, and not just in a juridical sense of, you're absolved and you can still have a shot at heaven someday. It's more: can it be reached and can it be integrated and can it be pulled back? And I've found such a depth of wisdom in the patristics around, again—it's tricky because you don't want to be anachronistic in the language—Pseudo-Dionysius talks about how everything has to participate to some degree, however minute, in the good, because if it didn't, it wouldn't exist, because God is the good and God is being. And so even someone—who has a light filled with what you might call sin or complexes or whatever—is still attached, is still participating in light, and so therefore is still connected to the good. And that's the starting point. And then I think where Jung took it further was then to say—sort of circling back to what we were talking about earlier—okay, but even this point of sin now, does it have a purpose? Does it have a meaning? What is behind—I'll just use again the pornography addiction online, it's so rampant—is there a search for intimacy here? Is there a desire for communion here? It may be distorted, quote unquote, but is something trying to happen here? So rather than writing it off as a sin, why don't you explore it and see what it's trying to pull the person toward? And it seemed to me that when you do that, you will often find one of the goods of life behind that, pulling the person toward *Eros* and communion and desire and all of those things that are embedded in it for them. So I think it's a very important understanding that God's grace is so beyond what we think it is when we set ourselves up as God, and that it all is assumed in some way, it has to be, all of the human experience. Not to say that God in Christ—if you're Christian—assumed all of the sins, but that *all of the psyche was there*. And it's the psyche that it's all rooted in.

JL: As you speak, I got curious about if the Orthodox Church and sacraments—if you would say that they hold the therapeutic process alive? If there are things there that it would learn from or benefit from in depth psychology, or if it already has a depth psychology sort of integrated into it?

PC: Some years ago, with some colleagues, we started something called the Analytical Psychology and Orthodox Christianity Consultation. It's called APOCC. And we started putting together some gatherings to try to address exactly some of these questions. So we would invite Orthodox priests and speakers, and we would invite Jungian analysts, and we would try and get a conversation going, just across the border, as it were. And I think it's a tricky thing to say—it's both a tricky thing to say that neither one can learn from the other, and it's a tricky thing to say that they can learn from each other, because they're not operating with the same set of assumptions and the same set of values. So I think you always have to be very careful to respect: these are two very different animals meeting each other, if I may use that image. And not to expect them to act like each other or to appreciate or want or desire the same things necessarily. This is also why I wanted to find out whether there were any meeting places. And mainly (because otherwise we risk being very split as persons), I'll just say this, that one of the areas of conversation that was lively was around the issue of fantasy, for example. The Orthodox world does have a certain kind of depth psychology in my experience. It certainly runs very deep. And of course, many, many priests and spiritual fathers and mothers now are also psychologically informed. It's sort of hard to say, to just tease out—it's as if they've never influenced each other, but of course they have. There's always a concern about fantasy and what can come in, is one thing that I've experienced.

So when you're in the clinical room and a client comes in and has a dream about a demon—a nightmare with a demon or something—we tend to not immediately assume it's an actual demon. But rather what's going on, what's the psyche, what's the dream ego saying, etc. You interpret it and analyze it. I think images like that, and others like sexual images or violent images, have had a different meaning in the Orthodox Church, as, if not overtly demonic, a symptom of passions or sins that are in need of tending. And they can be tended to with compassion, but they're still seen maybe less—I could be wrong, but I would propose—less symbolically than as in in-depth psychology. The idea that there might be something else behind this image that's just trying to happen as a psychological event is not as focused on, understandably, because the focus of the interior life in the Orthodox Church is the union with God through prayer. So it's a different emphasis. And in that life, you can have a lot of images come up that they will look at more as temptations or as something to be prayed through, perhaps, whereas we might in the Jungian world tend to look at them more as, oh, look, here's a fantasy. Let's work with the image. So it's a different emphasis.

JL: And on that note, I wanted to ask as well about dreams, like historically, is that something that has been valued or emphasized in the tradition? Or is it more a skepticism? Or is there something you can say about that on dreams?

PC: I'm not really an expert on that. So I haven't studied dreams very much in the Church tradition. But it is striking that they do show up in scripture. And it says, *warned in a dream*, and *an angel appeared in a dream*. So there's a kind of openness to dreams. But again, I think where you will (as I'm thinking out loud right now) run into trouble is that—and this is a question of method—the Orthodox (and let me lay this out without saying that I'm agreeing or disagreeing with one side or the other, but this is my experience of each one)—in the Orthodox Church, you are talking about the ultimate, right? You're talking about God and there are truth claims that are made about God.

In the Jungian world, Jung himself says, no one can know what the ultimate things are. So, I'm going to talk about psyche and that's all I can talk about. And then, of course, he talks about God endlessly. But you're supposed to have caught that first caveat he makes where he's saying, I'm not speaking as a theologian; I'm speaking as a psychologist. The danger, I think, on the Orthodox side is that when you make truth claims about God, you are making claims about the ultimate. And so people who don't share those are not going to understand or agree. But that is the nature of religion, and that's the nature of the Church, to make these claims.

I think the danger on the Jungian side can be that it becomes that the psyche is all-encapsulating, that everything is psyche, and you can't ever have an experience of God, because even that's a psychological experience that's generated by psyche. And I think that's the danger on the Jungian side. But if you respect that each is coming from one of those two places, and you understand that then there's going to be a limitation on how much you can agree on, then okay—but you can still have a conversation. It's still an interesting conversation to have. You just have to understand that these are two very different places that we're speaking from.

JL: Well, I would say, just that kind of warning, I feel, about depth psychology making everything into psyche: It reminds me of Sean McGrath (who has been a guest on the show, and we also did a podcast together called Secular Christ). He speaks about psychological absolutism (and the dangers of it), and the limits of psychology and of understanding them better. But I was also thinking as we ambulated around, and as you helped to unpack this beautiful quote—"that which is not assumed is not healed"—I was thinking about a book that came out a few years ago.

I don't know if you saw it, but it became very popular. It's called No Bad Parts, *by Richard Schwartz, who developed a therapeutic system or technique called the Internal Family System, which is becoming very, very popular. And it basically works much like active imagination: you get in contact with different parts and start dialogues, but it's a little bit more, I would say, maybe a bit more concrete, and a little more systematized. But it's just something with that title,* No Bad Parts, *because it connects to the idea that it's all there for some sort of reason, and that we have to be open to examine it, and to look at it, and as you act, to see it.*

PC: I think one of the things that I think is important to say—and obviously there are many different types of schools of depth psychology, and many analysts out there, and so there's a whole wide range—but Jung talked about how you can only be morally responsible for that of which you're conscious, right? And so I do want to clarify that it's not in my understanding, at least, that if everything is assumed and there are no bad parts, then that therefore everything goes—anything, you can do whatever you want, it doesn't matter. I don't think that Jung himself was disavowing any kind of moral stance toward ourselves or the community around us.

But simply saying that, first of all, you can't be morally responsible for what you're not in control of, and you're not in control of the unconscious, and you're not in control of the conscious, but you don't have even an understanding of why you're doing this kind of compulsion or whatever it is.

And then secondly, yes, there is every possibility that there is something really valuable hidden for you here. And what we have to make conscious is what's really going on. And then you can see whether you want to keep doing this or not, and how that squares with your own morality. But let me just read you this little quote. It's in the book. I just came across it earlier. It was St. Maximus. I was just reminded of how powerful this is, I think, because I think it's so easily forgotten in our world in general. And it's not just the Church that has morality as a kind of banner it waves. It's just a kind of interesting quote for, I think, our times in general. But he said—this was him writing on the Lord's Prayer—that

> the spirit has to persuade the intellect to desist from moral philosophy in order to commune with the supra-essential *logos* through direct and undivided contemplation. For when the intellect has become free from its attachment to sensible objects, it should not be burdened any longer with preoccupation about morality, as with a shaggy cloak.

And I just love this idea of morality-preoccupations as a shaggy cloak. And I like to think that Freud would have liked that too. And of course, Maximus is talking about this idea, this sort of direct—and experience of God through—contemplation of the *logos*. And this is very much a patristic idea. It's a sort of a mystical apprehension of God. But I'm reminded of Jung's quote, and I don't know where he has this. He wrote somewhere that the idea of the superego, Freud's superego, is a necessary substitute for an experience of the Self. And I just think it's so marvelous not to equate the Self with God, because self, even from a Jungian perspective, as much as it may connect to God, as Ulanov writes, is also part of the created order. And St. Maximus is talking about apprehension and perceiving of God, of the energies of God. But analogously, this idea is that it's not morality that is the thing. Maximus writes this elsewhere. He said that "the truth does not exist for the sake of virtue. Virtue exists for the sake of the truth." So it's both a guidepost and a byproduct of engagement with the truth.

JL: We had a lot of discussion on the podcast with different people around this, differentiating the superego from conscience, for example. Jung also developed his thoughts in his late essay "A Psychological View of Conscience," where he makes these distinctions and speaks of conscience as the Vox Dei *or potentially the voice of God, differentiating it from these internalized father images or images of authority. And the importance of doing that work, moving from a moral, as a sort of idea of the mass, to ethics.*

PC: I'm thinking of the role of projection, in so much of what is ethical or not ethical, and how we dehumanize others, how we project onto them. So much of the work of depth psychology in the recollection of projection off of people actually allows for a much greater morality, in a way, because you can actually begin to engage with others as others, and not just shadow projections or whatever other complex there might be. The idea that working through these issues actually frees up true conscience, kind of a true ethic of relatedness, makes a lot of sense.

JL: And this is probably too big of a question, but is there something you could say on conscience, on its role in the Orthodox tradition? I understand it's a huge question, but I do think you touch on it in the book.

PC: Just anecdotally, it's something that is considered to be a prompting of God in the heart. It's when someone's struck by a moment of conscience, it's part of how—I haven't looked at this in-depth theologically—but I would myself link it to this notion of the image of God in it (if I'm speaking as a theologian), that the image of God in us has this understanding of what's true in it, embedded in it. And when we, again—I really love the works of St. Maximus, and so it comes up a lot when I talk—go back to St. Maximus, he talks about how the passions arise when we distort our perception of an object and combine that with one of our natural faculties like desire or anger. Again, the natural faculty is good. It's been given by God. The capacity for anger is also the capacity for courage, and desire can be love. But when there's a distortion in your perception of something, then the desire becomes lust or the anger becomes vengefulness: they get what they call—they like to use the word—*distorted*. And I think that conscience is that deep knowing in you that something has been distorted here and you're acting on it. But that's not an area I've examined overly much theologically.

JL: Moving maybe into areas that I know that you have examined deeply in your book: I was thinking about what you just brought up here, Eros, *and the importance of* Eros *and desire, both in the analytic process, but also then the question of its role in a patristic theology. Your chapter four is called* "Eros, *Healing Fire." It's a great title. So, it's speaking a little bit about* Eros *and desire and what you found in your research there.*

PC: Goodness, where to start? When I was working through this research, there were two things that stood out at me, particularly in a Jungian approach. (I studied many of the other psychoanalysts and really benefited from them as well. And I've always employed an eclectic understanding in my own clinical understanding. So that's just parenthetically.) Jung has both this idea in his method that there is a kind of psyche that is given, that we have been given wherever it comes from, psyche is self. And then there's the *telos* of the person, the journey of the person through life and their own arc of destiny. And healing and an analytic—it's basically the path of individuation for them. And I was astonished when I was doing this research—I was really pulled to the works of St. Maximus, and I was actually quite dumbfounded when I understood that a basic tenet of St.

Maximus's understanding was what he called the *logos* of being and then the trope of being—meaning that being is given to us, and then there is the trope of being that is our arc through life, how we go through life, what we do with our own sense of being. So there was a kind of incredible overlap of understanding that made me want to really explore.

The first part, the *logos* of being, the *psyche qua psyche* and self itself, that's one of the chapters in the book where I look at what I think of as the image of God. It's the innate impetus toward healing, it's the blueprint of the Self, as Jung talks about, it's kind of what's given, it's what's there. And the chapter on *Eros* is the next part, which is how you go, what takes people from a kind of—not stasis, because it's not static in that way—but a kind of *potentia* to an actualization. To going out into the world and doing something. It's the innate talent to be an architect, and then it's the drive to go to architecture school, right? It's the potential versus the actualization.

And I think that in both of those—whether it was Saint Maximus or a more modern-day understanding of the person—of course *Eros* is key because *Eros* is, as I discuss in that chapter, understood in a lot of different ways. It's not just sexual, although it certainly manifests sexually, but it's desire moving out into the world seeking connection, seeking relatedness, seeking the object of the desire. And so that seemed quite commonsense within the psychoanalytic world. It makes sense that desire would be so key. What I was surprised to find was how key it was in the theological world as well, that it's the desire for life, for being, for God. It's the seeking of union with the good that then also creates a kind of—it doesn't create but participates in—a thrust of *Eros* that is also about integration and not just—again, I think *Eros* is often confused with lust in our world. And it's not that, it's a deeper, more powerful, broader, richer vein of desire that can unify and can unite and can unite without confusion different aspects, both of ourselves and of the cosmos, as Maximus talks about. So we need that thrust and we need that ability to love. And it's not a sentimental love. It's not a moral love—I would say air quotes around moral—in the sense that it's full of life and it's full of fire and it has to be real. Otherwise it's not *Eros*. It can't just be a kind of lip service to kindness.

It's very much related to this poor sense of self that we were talking about, and the true sense of Self. And of course *God is love*, in the Christian tradition. So it's all whether you're contemplating God, you're immersed in love—and the images of fire abound as well. But it's hard, because you can say all of that, but then how many of us really live that way? And I think that's where the depth psychologists really excel, and there are all kinds of understandings of where *Eros* can get stifled, where it can be shamed, where it can be blocked, where it can be the cause of great fear, where it can be attached to—like Fairbairn's idea that we are cathected to internalized objects—the wrong objects, even if they're destructive. The abusive parent: the child still loves them, because that's their parent. And now, fifty years later, that inner object still is the object of a lot of *Eros*, even though it hurts the psyche of the person, it hurts the person in their life. So it's a very powerful force.

JL: Well, moving to another side, a link that you're drawing between patristic theology and analytical psychology has to do with the belief in the healing impetus of the psyche or the reliance on the healing impetus of the psyche. Because the listeners are aware that that's a fundament of analytical psychology, but you spend time also expanding on that in the book.

PC: I think that is what I was referring to earlier about the *logos* of being—the image of God in the person (from a theological perspective) or in the psyche, the self. And I was reminded of this wonderful quote by Ann Ulanov (paraphrasing a little bit), "the psyche insists that all of its parts be included, all of its feelers and all of its feathers." I always get this wonderful image of a caterpillar with feathers coming along. The psyche can conjure up such strange images for us and seem so alien and Other to us. But this healing impetus is such a gracious way of understanding these strange aspects of the psyche that can crop up and be very uncomfortable. It's part of the case to be made for "that which is not assumed is not healed":

what shows up appears to want integration. It appears to want inclusion. It's not indifferent to its lived-outness in our lives. Like a compulsion or a complex or a symptom that keeps bothering us—on the one hand, if you're having panic attacks, they're absolutely awful and it is devastating. On the other hand, is there something there that is trying to get included and worked out and brought into life in a different way, whether it's a wound or a desire that seems to be too dangerous to have?

So it just seems that in the living of it, there is a desire for inclusion, but I think that is the brilliance of Jung, to say, yes, this symptom is not just a symptom that we want to get rid of so that you're better functioning. People love to say what's quote unquote "normal" or "healthy" these days, but it's deeper and bigger, and I would say better, than that. It's not just about being functional; it's about living. So there seems to be fundamentally a deep desire for life that can then get very distorted because of the hand we've been dealt and the choices we make or some combination of both. So I think it's very important to see that from a depth- psychological perspective. And then just to say, well, that makes perfect sense, because if the image of God lives in us, what's it doing? Just being very practical about it, like what would the point of it be if it means nothing in our lived lives? And this was a way of wondering if this is part of what that is. This is part of the image of God.

JL: And is there this type of openness also in the Orthodox experience or as you experience it? Also I'm thinking now of desire, of the passions, of seeing and putting value to the longings of the body. Often, I guess stereotypically, we look at most Christian traditions as against that or disowning that.

PC: I can speak anecdotally and say that I've had mixed reception. I think there have been times when I have loaded some of these ideas. For example, I remember there was an article on internet pornography addiction and they were talking exactly about this—this is a psychological article—about that this was really a desire for intimacy and connection and should be understood as such. And I took it to a priest and professor and said, what do you think? And he said, that's exactly an Orthodox approach. That's how we would understand it too. And I thought, wow, I wasn't expecting that. But I've also heard others—it depends, priest to priest, church to church, and not because the theology is actually that individual, but I think people take it and understand it in their own ways and in light of their own background—so you can certainly find a great warning against images of sexuality, of passion. I think that they, even in the early Church, talked about how, when trying to do the liturgy or to engage in deep prayer, the demons will send images of erotic temptation to derail you. I don't think that, by and large, in the Church, if someone has something like that, they go, oh, this is great. Let's just see what this image is all about.

But the reason I think the conversation is worth continuing to have is that there is a deep respect for desire. And there is a deep—particularly in the patristics—focus on *Eros* as almost like a power of God. That it's there. So that's true. But then there's of course the idea that that's not meant to be focused. The difference is going to be on the object of the desire, because it's one thing to love another person, but it's relativized by the love of God. It's included within the love of God, which is supposed to be, it's the struggle throughout life to be, the primary love. So it's not, Oh, I love chocolate croissants and I'm just going to eat as many as I can because that's my right and that's my desire and I'm living life fully. And that's not even a very good example, but I mean that the passions are constrained by an understanding of what's supposed to be ultimate. And on the other side, sometimes therapy seems like it just unlooses the passions. And everyone says, oh, good, well, now I'm not repressed anymore. But then, where does it go? Does it have a kind of lifegiving *telos* for the person? And I think that the idea that it just unlooses the passions and doesn't send them anywhere useful is often a religious suspicion of therapy. These are complicated areas to navigate, and they require respect for both sides, because there are also often assumptions about both sides.

JL: Well, we have already touched on such lamented questions for our human existence and how the field of Orthodox theology and Christianity can engage with that. Also, the field of analytical psychology has been already very rich. So, I'm sort of hesitant to add this last question because it's about a huge one, but I think I'll try still.

PC: Okay.

JL: And that is, you are also making a brief excursion on death. I think you write it like that. And trying to look at and describe how analytical psychology and Orthodox Christianity looks at death, and you say biological death is not the whole death. Death is not as an opposite to immortality, but to the true life. That felt very fundamental, and if you could please just say a few more words about that, your exploration of that.

PC: It's tricky, but it was born out of this idea: they say in the Church that Christ has defeated death. But everybody's still dying. So what does that mean? On the one hand, again, speaking theologically, you can say what it means for eternity and the resurrection, and the resurrection of all people to the life to come, and that this isn't the only life, and that there is a life beyond this. But again, Jung would say, well, I don't know anything about life beyond this one; I can only talk about this one. And I think that both Orthodox Christianity and depth psychology could agree that there are—I hesitate to even say people—but just to start by saying that there are people who live dead, even though they're alive, who seem as though they're sort of dead on the inside, even though they're alive. And I think even that's a bit of a straw man, but it's that there are pieces of us that are dead, even while we're alive, or there are pieces of us that are dormant or as if dead. And there are times in our lives when we live, but we feel dead inside. And I don't just mean by dead that we feel nothing, but that we can feel like we're not there. We can feel like we're one step removed from our lives. We can feel like nothing we do helps and nothing ever changes. We can feel despair. We can feel walled off. There are so many ways to experience a kind of deadness, and we can keep living while we're doing that. Inside, biologically, we're living and we're getting up and making coffee and maybe getting the kids to school or getting ourselves to work or whatever it is. But there's that kind of deadness. And we can look at the reasons for why that is. I think despair is usually a big part of it.

But that idea can be changed. Ulanov, in one of her books (I think it was her book on poison ivy), at the end of it, says that the goal of a depth analysis is not health, it's not to acquire the ability to have symbolic thinking, it's not a cerebral exercise or exercise in self-insight; it's to come alive. It's livingness, that sense that you are just deeply alive and connected to life. And I think that that's the analog on the depth- psychological side—to life and to death. And I think on the theological side that there is a sense that people experience in the sacraments, the sacraments of healing and communion and confession, of touching and being touched by a life, a sense of life that is beyond us, that is the uncreated energy, that is a kind of radiance that comes in so that even as you're struggling with your dead parts and maybe are in an analysis or therapy at the same time wrestling out these dead parts, there's also this uncreated life that is being offered to participate in. And that you do, even though you will physically die someday. So it's an interesting place to end, because actually we're back right on the point of there are analogs, but they're not the same, because the Orthodox Church is talking about God's uncreated energies, and you can, if you're not going to psychologize that, then you have to respect that that's what they're claiming. And on the other side, there is the deep psychological work of working through your own dead spaces and into life. You can bring those two together. They're not the same, but they can meet and they do meet, I believe, which is why I was trying to write this book.

JL: Beautiful. Thank you so much for sharing with us. And thank you so much.

PC: Thank you. Thank you so much, Jacob. It's a pleasure.

Jung's Wrestling with Christ: Roundtable with Murray Stein, Ann Conrad Lammers, and Paul Bishop

"I think that it's not likely we're going to see Jung rewriting Christian doctrine in a way that the Church will adopt institutionally. But I think, on an individual level, what people get out of Jung may help them in their adult, their mature, their conflicted faith. Anybody who's lived a long life has a complex faith, not a simple one. And Jung can be there with you while you're doing that."

—Ann Conrad Lammers

JL: Well, it's great to have you all here, Paul, Ann, and Murray. Now we get this chance to discuss and have a conversation about Jung's wrestling with Christianity. When starting this podcast, I reached out to Murray to ask him if he would be open to having a conversation with me about these matters. And it seems like there is not only myself who is wrestling or struggling or engaging with these questions, because the following of the podcast has been growing significantly. So, it seems like there is something in the collective as well that speaks to the fact that what we're talking about is of value, and is of interest, also for individuals not living in Jung's time, but today, with all the complexities of collective life and individuation.

I would start with the first question. A few weeks ago, I had a conversation with a Jungian analyst. His name is Jason Smith, and he released a book called Religious But Not Religious: Living the Symbolic Life. *He said something to me that I think could work a little bit like a leitmotif and help us introduce this topic of Jung's wrestling with Christianity. He said the following:*

> *I think so much of Jung's work is his wrestling with Christianity . I think if you want to understand Jung, you need to have some understanding and engagement with Christianity. You certainly need to read the Bible. In understanding Christianity, I think it helps to know Jung, because he gives some perspectives that cannot be had in other disciplines. At the same time, it is also necessary for me to be able to try to engage Christianity on its own terms, not on Jungian terms, to try to meet it in terms of what it says it is, and not what Jung says it is. And so there's a tension in that. In wrestling with Christianity, I'm also wrestling with Jung.*

I would like to start to go the full round, and ask each of you for your personal reflections on the statement, but also if you could share something short about your own—if it's wrestling or engagement—with Jung in regard to the question of Christianity . And how you view Jung as a guide into Christianity. And I would like to ask if Murray would start us off.

MS: Well, I would like to begin by saying I didn't find Jung as an entry point to Christianity. I started with Christianity, and then I found Jung. I grew up as a Christian. My father was a Christian minister. I grew up with the Bible. The Bible was more familiar to me geographically than the many places we lived—Jerusalem, Bethlehem, Jericho, Galilee, etc. We moved around from parish to parish when I was a child. So I did not come to Jung either looking for answers to questions I had about Christianity or trying to find an entry into Christianity. I was a Christian. I still am a Christian. So I was able to read Jung's writings on Christianity with a little distance.

I'm trained theologically, like Ann is—Ann and I actually shared a teacher at Yale, a wonderful theologian and scholar and philosopher—so my background is biblical and theological and literary. When I read Jung, I read him with this background, a theological background, which is quite different from his. That said,

I do appreciate Jung's views on Christianity. I wrote my dissertation at the University of Chicago, on Jung and Christianity. It was later published as *Jung's Treatment of Christianity*. There, I asked the simple question, "what was Jung trying to do with Christianity?" I decided he was trying to treat it as he would a patient in his psychoanalytic practice. Jung wrote a lot about Christianity. He saw that Christianity had gotten stuck in its individuation process and needed to take another step in the direction of integrating two things that were left out or repressed in Christianity, namely evil and the feminine. He was proposing a God-image that included them.

I think Christianity has come a long way, particularly in the respect of integrating the feminine into its theological and liturgical life. When I went to Divinity School at Yale, there were almost no women studying to become ministers. These were women who would become workers in the Church, in education, but none were planning to become ministers. Today, about half the students at Yale Divinity School are women, and they're preparing for the ministry, because there's a place for them in the ministry in the Protestant churches, and to the top levels. I think there's been a significant shift also in the question of the feminine in the Bible. I think Christianity has moved and is continuing to move toward inclusion of the feminine. With regard to the problem of evil, I think we need to discuss that separately.

JL: Thank you, Murray. Ann, would you be fine to go next?

AL: I'll give it a go. Yes, like Murray, I was raised in a clerical family. My stepfather, who was my father for most of my growing up time, starting age four, was an Episcopal priest and a holy man, which is difficult to live with in the family, because his vocation was so powerful and his commitments were so demanding. But it was, and as I age—I've lived a lot longer in my life than he lived in his (he died in his fifties)—I appreciate more and more of what he taught me by example and by actual verbal teaching.

I came to Jung in my thirties, maybe around age thirty. How did I land there? I wanted to—I'd gone through a divorce, which is always a painful thing, and I had a sense of vocation to a healing profession, and I knew somehow, I had the instinct, that it needed to be based on both psychology and theology. I began looking for seminary teaching, a seminary course that I could take, and the very first thing that struck me was a course on Christian theology and schools of depth psychology.

And there I was, plunked down into Freud, Jung, Sullivan, and the existentialists. And it was Jung that really grabbed me. I began reading, independent of anything that was assigned, and whether or not I was able to understand it. I started just absorbing. I was reading Jung's *Psychology and Religion*, his Terry lectures. I was reading *Answer to Job* long before I had the tools to grapple with it, and a lot of his writings on Eastern religion, too. I just plunged in. And what Jung did for me first off, almost before anything else, was he showed me a way back into the Episcopal Church, which I had left for twenty years in my marriage, as a Quaker. I was a full-fledged member of Scarsdale Friends Meeting, and marching against the war. And I would still march against the war—that's not an issue. But I had been living in a non-structured, non-ritualistic—except insofar as silence is a ritual—a different form of religious community. And I just really missed scripture, hymn-singing, the colors and seasons of the Church year. I missed theology. I missed preaching—actual, scripture-based preaching. Quakerism didn't have a solid center for me anymore.

I needed to get back into the Church of my childhood. But how to do it without being a child again? I'm thirty, I'm an adult, I've moved beyond where I was when I was a teenager. What do I do? How do I get back into this Church of ancient rituals and dogmas and teachings? Well, Jung gave me the path. He gave me an intellectual—a respectable—way to embrace what I'd grown up with, seeing it through a new lens, looking at it differently. Because he respected the ancient rituals and the ancient teachings. He may have taken them all apart and looked at them from a different angle than any of my childhood teachers would have looked at them. That didn't matter. He told me how to get back.

So, there I am, entering seminary with a deep appreciation of Jung and also thirst for theology. And I've been kind of working both sides of that street ever since. I carried it on, that tension and that dialogue. I carried it through my seminary education, and then into my doctoral work at Yale, which is where Hans Frei is the common denominator for you and me, Murray. By the way, as a Barthian, Hans had very little patience with Jung. He tolerated my insistence on doing a dissertation that was devoted to Jung. That was alright. He said, I appreciate your approach to Jung saying "well, yes and no." Which is what I needed to do in the study of Victor White's relationship with Jung, because I could not write about Victor White and C.G. Jung unless I respected both of them equally, and shared both of their basic assumptions, to the degree that one can share both of their basic assumptions and not fall apart inside. I struggled not to fall apart inside while I was doing that dissertation. But anyway, I got it accepted, I got the doctorate, and it's been with me in some fashion ever since. And here it is again today.

As I've remained a Christian and a worshipping member of an Episcopal parish, I'm more and more aware that we didn't need Jung—we Christians didn't need Jung to tell us about the problem of evil. We've got the Hebrew prophets. And some of what Jesus is reported to have said is consistent with the blessings and curses. Blessings and curses on the one hand, and on the other hand, which is the Hebrew rhetoric. We've got this, and we've got that. Reading Isaiah—some of the passages that don't get used in church very much—he ricochets between God's voice telling the people that they are his beloved and he will never abandon them, and they are a polluted rag and they deserve to be burned in the fire. And it's just—well, it's all there, and it's kind of horrifying. And then we have Jesus in the Gospel of Luke: the beatitudes that are in Luke alternate between blessings and curses. There is woe: "Woe unto you." Jesus happened to love Isaiah. It's all there in our tradition, actually.

Jung underlines the gospel of fear, to such an extent that it really took me a very long time, in my loyalty to Jung, to realize that the gospel of love is also there. It's real. Compassion toward one's fellow beings is a reality that we need more of. And I'm finally at the place where I can say that I'm consciously choosing to believe the gospel of love. I know about the gospel of fear. I've seen the darkness. I've seen enough of it. But this is my choice now. And I think that—I'll shut up now because I've talked enough—I think that it's not likely we're going to see Jung rewriting Christian doctrine in a way that the Church will adopt institutionally. But I think, on an individual level, what people get out of Jung may help them in their adult, their mature, their conflicted faith. Anybody who's lived a long life has a complex faith, not a simple one. And Jung can be there with you while you're doing that.

JL: Paul, would you . . . ?

PB: Yes, thank you very much, Jakob, for inviting me. What does Jung do for me, as it were? Well, in relation to religion, I think I put it into the framework of Jung as being such a great pedagogue, and the *Collected Works* really being a little form of education in themselves, in all kinds of areas—world literature, German literature, French anthropology, and religion as well, obviously, as a very important part of that. And I think the term that I would use, that I think Jung gives one a sense for, which is perhaps missing today, is the sense of the sacred. And that Jung is very, very helpful as a thinker who has kept, as it were, the torch of the light of the sacred going, in a period where otherwise it's very difficult. I would associate it, I think, with a term that I find particularly interesting with Jung, which is where he talks about the archaic. Jung's insistence on the archaic dimension of life: I would see it as being his formulation of a term that is more widely known as the sacred. And after all, he wasn't the only one who was interested in that: Otto Rank's work on the hero; Freud in *Totem and Taboo* is very Jungian or proto-Jungian, if you like, in parts. So I think that's undoubtedly one of Jung's major contributions today.

Of course, it also makes it difficult for his reception, precisely the sacred and archaic (and we might have an opportunity to come back and talk about this). I take your point in particular, Ann, about the significance of ritual and symbol as something that Jung had a very, very fine, keen appreciation of, and that reading Jung helps sharpen one's own sense of the aesthetics of the sacred, if you like. And I think that's more powerful, now that we have access to *The Red Book* as well.

Where I'd like to ever so gently part company, perhaps, with you is on the question of dogma. And whether Jung is doing something—I'm sure it's compatible with Christianity—and it might even be parallel with it—but it seems to me there's an important aspect of it that is not Christian at all because it's about Jung's lack of faith. But the way I have received it is he is someone who says, and very frankly deals, with the problem of not being able to—with all the caveats around *Memories, Dreams, Reflections* (they have a function as a parable, if you like)—it's that account of Jung going to his first communion, and this profound sense of disappointment. And I think what I find so interesting about Jung is that on the one hand, he's coming out of this Nietzschean tradition, which says, "God is dead"—in other words, he thinks it's impossible for us to believe anymore. He comes out of that tradition. He has the experience of that. But, at the same time, he's wrestling with God, he's wrestling with religious issues. He doesn't chuck it all out. He doesn't go down the nihilist line. Instead he's doing something that is—well, I don't know: *sui generis*. That's Jung. He's doing his own thing.

And I suppose that on the question of dogma, I suppose that the question I'd want to put in is, isn't it always the case that when Jung gets involved in a discussion with religion, that the religious people back off? And that being the case with the correspondence with Fr. White. They share an awful lot of common interests, but at the end of the day, there is a sort of bifurcation that's there. And I suppose it's teasing out at what point that bifurcation takes place. (Which I would see as one of the things that still needs to be done in terms of research, which is to understand what is the process that Jung goes through in coming to terms with this lack of faith, and then at the same time, constructing something that can hold that emptiness, hold that lack, and turn it into something that is positive.)

JL: Well, I think this connects to another question I'm sitting with here, but I would like to ask first if there's any one of you, Ann or Murray, who wants to respond to anything that's been said?

AL: I do. The word *dogma* slipped out of my mouth. It was not a serious assertion of Jung's position vis-à-vis dogma because I know , as you do, he hates the stuff. He hates that kind of hierarchical, top-down authority. He hates being told what to believe. He respects the history. He studies it closely. It has his attention, but not his uncritical acceptance.

PB: That's why I think *dogma*'s a great word (*chuckles*). Because I think that's exactly the point where, if one's talking about a theological dogma—take the one that Jung is so fascinated with because of the announcement that happens in 1950, the dogma of the Assumption of the Virgin. Jung gets totally excited about that. But surely his understanding of it, as he discusses it, is something that is parallel to, compatible with, but surely not identical with, what a practicing Roman Catholic would understand by it.

MS: I think it has to do with his understanding of symbols. One thing that Ann said struck me: Jung helped her back to the church of her childhood, but in a different way. I think I had that same experience, because if you relate to the Church doctrines—call them doctrines or dogmas—as symbols, you can take them up in a different way. This is the way Jung took them in the Terry lectures, for instance. There he talks quite a bit about dogma and his appreciation of it as being archetypal. The dogmas represent archetypes, so one can appreciate them in that way, as symbolic.

Did Jesus rise from the dead? Yes or no? If you were there on Sunday morning with a camera, would you have been able to capture it? Jung would say, no, but it's a great symbol. The theologians I know would say something like that, but they would also say something important happened that day. It transformed the disciples eventually into apostles. The historical Jesus became the divine Christ for them. This was a matter of faith.

Jung says to Victor White in one letter, "I was reading a paper of yours, and I had to ask myself, do I have faith or a faith, or do I not? And I had to answer, I do not. But I have respect. I have respect for all the religions and all the symbols." And that's the way he would relate to Christianity, as an expression of archetypal symbols.

JL: Murray, isn't that also sometimes where Jung is criticized? Yes, there is something about bringing the symbols alive again, and seeing the symbolic in what happened. But there's also, which often has been expressed, that Jung psychologizes. He psychologizes and turns religion or Christianity, in this case, into something of a psychological or subjective process.

MS: To that charge, I would say yes and no. He does psychologize in the sense that he takes religious doctrine and turns it into a psychological concept. He makes a translation or an interpretation, on the one hand. On the other hand, when he talks about arche-types and the transgressivity of archetypes, he would say, "I don't know." The symbol may be a representation of something ontologically real but beyond what we can know or prove as valid. That's beyond our capacity. He leaves that possibility open. So there's a door into the metaphysical. But he isn't going to step through it very far. He does see the door and he does open it a bit in his work on synchronicity . . .

AL: Murray, I think in what you said about symbols, you might have slipped into discussing metaphors. A symbol can be actually the real flower, as well as what it represents. And the actual physical resurrection, of course we weren't there to see it, but Jung doesn't actually rule it out by saying that it's symbolic. He can't.

MS: I don't think he would rule it out. But what do you think, Ann?

AL: What do I think?

MS: About the resurrection?

AL: I don't take it precisely as Jung took it, because what I read in Jung is that we can win through to a resurrected body—it has something to do with individuation, it has something to do with the interior struggle with the opposites. And I think that that's reductive. (I'm sorry, Jung, but I think it's reductive, and self- serving.) There is something irreducible about that event, and I can't see inside it. It's like a light that blinds me. And I don't attempt to say that it was physical, but I can't rule out that it was. I don't know.

MS: Well, I don't think that that's different from what Jung might say. He doesn't know either. And his definition of symbol is it's the best possible representation of something that we can't see any better than that.

AL: Yes.

MS: I agree with you that symbols are not metaphors. Metaphors are much more creations of the rational mind. They resemble symbols but they don't have the two sides, the concrete and the transcendent. In a symbol we feel the allure of transcendence in the real.

AL: Yes.

MS: Symbols have a mystical quality, a numinous quality. Jung says very early on in his career, in the *Zofingia* lectures he gave to his college mates, that a religion without mysticism is dead. He's discussing the theology of Albrecht Ritschl, the famous nineteenth-century German theologian. Ritschl's theology is rather rational and he discards the numinous or mystical aspect, in fact religious experience entirely, as of interest to theology. Jung on the other hand certainly appreciates that mystical experience, which he later would call the numinous following Rudolf Otto. And, what's more, he doesn't reduce the numinous to personal psychological complexes or wish fulfilment. He leaves it at the symbolic level and says we don't fully know what the symbols really represent. It's beyond our knowing.

JL: I feel like we could go deeper on this and follow this stream, but one of my roles would be to keep the time, so that's why I would like us to move on to the next question, and then come back to this, because I can see that these things will tie into each other. And the second question I would like to ask of you connects to something you also said in the introduction, Murray, about your research on Jung and Christianity. You said, what did Jung want to do with Christianity? What did Jung want to do? And you gave an answer to that.

But I think part of my own wrestling, and maybe a few others', is to try to reconcile this question. At times when you read Jung, maybe the younger version of Jung, you have a sense that maybe he wants to reform Christianity, or analytical psychology, or, in the early days, with the conversation with Freud, he says psychoanalysis has a role to sort of vivify and rejuvenate Christianity. We have Jung's early vision of the Basel Cathedral, and some of the old being destroyed but also a question of rejuvenation, of bringing in the new life into Christianity. So, is Jung a reformer, or does he then try to transcend Christianity? And is analytical psychology an attempt by Jung to dream the myth onward, as he said? The Christian myth onward? Or is it actually a break with Christianity?

PB: I'll go first, only because, as I always say to my students, if you go first, then you don't have to worry about having to go in at a later stage. (*Chuckling*) I'm going to try to follow my own advice, but if I may go back to our previous discussion about symbolism, because it seems to me that this is really key to Jung's role. And I think, Murray, that you're absolutely right to talk about the importance of mysticism for Jung, and Jung was a great appreciator, particularly of German mysticism; Meister Eckhart is the figure that comes to mind there as significant. And then, of course, that's a good case study of saying, well, what on earth is Meister Eckhart about, and it shows maybe just how complex these questions are that Jung is struggling with.

It seems to me that Jung is doing a number of things in relation to religion and the symbol. First of all, going back to *Transformations and Symbols of the Libido*, he says, "The symbol, considered from the standpoint of actual truth, is misleading indeed. But it is psychologically true."[49] That's the point, isn't it, because it was and is the bridge to all the greatest achievements of humanity. So we have a kind of cultural thing that Jung is proposing here. The symbol is not literally true, but it has this function that enables us to be creative. It's the bridge to the greatest achievements of humanity.

The second movement, it seems to me, is does the symbolism still work? Because he then goes on to say, This will be the cause of moral autonomy or perfect freedom. This would be the course of moral autonomy, of perfect freedom, when man could without compulsion wish that which he must do, and this from knowledge, without delusion through belief in the religious symbols.[50]

So, it seems to me a different take on the symbol, because belief in religious symbols is seen to be a delusion in some way, albeit a creative one.

Then, and I think this ties in directly to your question, then, Jakob, which is what Jung thinks about the symbolism of Christianity. And this idea of *can we believe it anymore* is very much there in the lecture that he gives to the Guild of Pastoral Psychology—a movement, organization still going in London—in 1939. Well, he says this:

> We can't turn the wheel backwards. We can't go back to the symbolism that is gone. No sooner do you know that this thing is symbolic than you say, "Oh well, presumably it's something else." Doubt has killed it. Has devoured it. So, you cannot go back. I cannot go back to the Catholic church. I cannot experience the miracle of the mass. I know too much about it. I know it is the truth, but it is the truth in a form in which I cannot accept it anymore.

---

[49] C.G. Jung, *Psychology of the Unconscious: A Study of the Transformations and Symbolisms of the Libido*, ed. William McGuire, trans. Beatrice M. Hinkle. (Princeton, NJ: Princeton University Press, 1992), ¶ 353.
[50] C.G. Jung, *Psychology of the Unconscious*, ¶ 354.

> I cannot say this is the sacrifice of Christ, and see him anymore. I cannot. It is no more true to me. It does not express my psychological condition. My psychological condition wants something else. I must have a situation in which that thing becomes true once more. I need a new form.

And that's the call of a reformer, isn't it? "I need a new form." That's what it seems to be Jung is doing with Christianity.

MS: He says in a letter to Victor White that new wine needs new wineskins. Jung did find his own myth. He went on a search for it and asked: what is my myth? Following upon his experiences in active imagination, he created what he called *Liber Novus*. *Liber Novus* is his New Testament. He discovered his myth through his dreams and active imagination experiences, and that's the ground he stood on. Now that we have *The Red Book* in print, we can see passages that are directly related to his experiences. I think he did create a religion for himself that is not so different from Christianity, but it is his religion.

I once had a conversation with Peter Homans, who was my dissertation advisor and main professor at the University of Chicago and taught Jung at the Divinity School, in which I asked him if he was doing what Jung did. "Are you creating a myth for your own life?," I asked. He replied that he didn't feel capable of creating a religion for himself. He recognized the difficulty and enormous effort that would take. When you look at what Jung did to create *Liber Novus*, who's going to do that? How many people in the world are going to be able to do something like that? Very limited.

AL: Murray, in creating *Liber Novus,* Jung was not evangelizing. He was creating it for himself, sharing it with a very limited, very limited group of people. And it's not until decades after his death that, with a certain amount of misgiving, it was finally published. Well, wonderful that it was.

But it wasn't his idea to create a religion and gather a community around him to worship with him.

MS: No, absolutely not.

AL: In fact, one of the things that I think Jung fails to grasp, and doesn't even try to grapple with in his dialogue with Victor White, is the meaning of the body of Christ as a social community. For Victor White, that was essential. And he tried so hard to get Jung to see. At certain points in their correspondence you see him trying to show this to Jung. Jung had no patience with it. That was not what he was going for. And because he didn't appreciate that aspect of Catholicism, in any of its forms (it doesn't have to be Roman Catholicism; there's the English version, too, and other forms), he was not inside. He had one foot in, one foot out.

But you're right, Murray, that that was a therapeutic stance for him. He needed to have one foot in, one foot out in order to take a therapeutic approach to—what does it mean, actually—Jakob, what does it mean to dream the Christian myth onward? Who's doing the dreaming? And which part of the Christian Church are we talking about? It's a Church that's undergone enormous splits, and it matters whose dream it is. I've known senior Jungian analysts, teachers in their own right, who had such a hostile projection onto everything Christian, that it was quite chilling.

Who's doing the dreaming? I'm really stumped. I really don't know. When I set out to do my dissertation, I wanted to do something on the relationship between psychology and theology. Well, that was going to mean Jung's psychology. So, I had my psychologist picked out. But theology? That's huge. Who was going to represent theology? Which theology? It was a Jungian analyst in the area of New Haven who said, have you read Jung's letters to Victor White? That got me started; and then it was a case study of Jung and White. But we've got to have individuals in mind. Whose voices are we invoking with this broad question of dreaming the Christian myth onward? Which myth?

JL: Well, that's a quote from Jung. It's Jung's expression of "dreaming the Christian myth onwards." And to me, what's striking, living in this historical time, in Europe, is how in this part of the world the Christian Church seems to be absolutely lacking a dream. The music doesn't seem to be in the Church anymore, or it seems like the Church is not where the energy is moving, where the dream is happening.

In contrast to that, the practice of being a Jungian analyst working here in Berlin: the queues for psychotherapy are long; Jung is sort of in vogue again. There's something in Jungian psychology that holds a certain energy, and to me these two things: Jungian analysis and what it offers, and Christianity, are deeply tied together.

Well, it doesn't have to be. Jungian psychology works very well for someone who is Muslim, or from another religion as well. It can work perfectly well as a therapeutic technique. But at times, Jung is expressing that, the hope of his is to reform Christianity, or the hope to dream the myth, the Christian myth, onward. I'm fantasizing, and it might be childish, but I fantasize at times about, what would have happened if Jung had fully owned his Christian faith? Or put differently, if Jung had touched his forehead to the ground, if Jung would have expressed himself as a Christian ?

I think you would agree that the Church needs Jung, that Jungian psychology has something to offer the Church. But I also do believe that Jungian psychology needs the Church. As we've been touching upon in our conversations, this question of lack of community or the difficulty that Jung might have had with aspects of Christianity that had to do with a social aspect of it. So, I think that there's a tension here.

MS: Well, to Ann's question—who's dreaming the myth onward?—a number of thoughts come to my mind. One might be tempted to look to the theologians to dream the myth onward. They're in the tradition. Their dreams would provide the impetus for evolving the doctrines further, applying them further, enlivening them with some new libido, some new symbolism, and so on. Looking there, we'd be disappointed. Karl Barth was a great theologian and he brought a lot of life to theology.

His dialectical theology was very alive. I remember studying Barth, and all those footnotes were very exciting. And as you say, Hans Frei was a Barthian. So Barth really captured the theological imagination in his time.

But did he dream the myth onward? Not really. He revitalized dogmatic theology, no small task, but it was all backward looking, not evolving further.

Can we look to psychologists to do that work? These would be theologically-minded psychologists, people who are not necessarily in the role of the theologian. I don't know of any. Dreaming a myth onward means in Jungian terms taking seriously the dreams that you have had. Suppose you have a symbolic dream in which some aspect of the Christian *mythos* has a place, and you take that dream seriously, you put it to work, you apply it in your life, you do active imagination with it to develop it further, how does it change your life? What difference might it make for Christianity?

Christianity is a universal religion, and it has to capture the global mind. It somehow has to transcend the personal and offer something that takes the collective mind and spirit of Christianity a step further. There are some thinkers who have tried to do that—Teilhard for one. The idea is that Christianity has to evolve just as individuals have to evolve. They have to keep on growing. If you stop, and just look to the past, you become stagnant. That's what Jung says: you can't go backward; the collective has to go forward. And that means dreaming the dream onward, taking the *mythos* and working it further along the lines of individuation.

PB: I just wanted to come back to this sense of urgency and worry, which I find there in Jung when he talks about, for example, in his paper, "Psychology and the Unconscious," when he talks about Nietzsche. He says, "The case of Nietzsche shows, on the one hand, the consequences of neurotic one-sidedness"—let's leave that on one side for now—"and on the other hand, the dangers that lurk in this leap beyond Christianity."

MS: Yes.

PB: "Nietzsche undoubtedly felt the Christian denial of animal nature very deeply indeed, and therefore he sought a higher human wholeness beyond good and evil. But he who seriously criticizes the basic attitudes of Christianity also forfeits the protection which those bestow upon him. He delivers himself up unresistingly to the animal psyche. That is the moment of Dionysian frenzy." And that's a very early paper, isn't it?

I think it's about [1917], but again, in that paper he presented to the Guild of Psychology, he makes very much a similar point, where he talks about the dangers that are involved. He says, "To be extra ecclesiam," he says, "is very, very dangerous. You are no more protected. You're no more in the *consensus gentium*, no more in the lap of the old compassionate mother. You are alone. And you are confronted with all the demons of hell. That is what people don't know." So there seems to me a sense of great worry, urgency, anxiety, a sense of danger that's involved with giving up of Christianity as well.

JL: Well, I also think it's important, maybe, to stress reformation, although Jung said, you're looking for the new, I would think, as a Jungian analyst as well, that he thinks about going back in order to go forward. Or that there's a sort of renaissance—

PB: . . . Absolutely.

JL: And there is a voice out there. I would say there is a voice out there, actually, that is doing a lot of good for Jungians and for Christians. And that doesn't mean that I fully support what he says, but that is the Canadian Jordan B. Peterson, whom some of you may be aware of, who's a psychologist who is very fond of Jung, and he has millions of followers on YouTube, and he has high-level conversations with leading theologians and people from the Church, about Christianity and Jung. In the last decade many people find Christ and Christianity through Jordan B. Peterson into Jung back to Christianity. So, he's a voice. He's not a theologian, but he's a very powerful voice in the culture right now. There's a lot of discussion happening around Christianity, and around Jung, but it's in the public discourse. Maybe it's also happening within the Jungian field, within the Church.

PB: I just wanted to mention as well, in terms of voices, the one who has contributed to the debate, someone whom I have found very useful, is Eugen Drewermann, and Eugen Drewermann seems to be a good example of someone coming out of the Catholic Church who engages very, very deeply with Jung, and then of course, in turn, Drewermann leaves the Church. And that's why I see it more as a tension between Jungianism and Christianity, albeit a very, very fruitful one. I suppose I'd put it like this: are they, at the end of the day, Christianity on the one hand, Catholicism, the Church, on one hand, Jung and analytical psychology on the other—are they actually playing the same game? Do they actually want the same outcomes? And that's not to judge either of them as positive or negative. It's simply to say, are they actually doing the same sort of thing?

MS: It's similar to the question that I've been dealing with, and with some colleagues. Is the goal of individuation the same as the goal of Eastern meditation? Is the final result the same? If you find a fully individuated Jungian and put them beside a fully enlightened Zen Buddhist, do they look alike? Or are they significantly different? These are interesting speculative comparisons. There would be differences, of course, but I think they share something, a glimpse of something beyond, certainly beyond the rational. Everybody, all the religious traditions, will say that thinking can't get you there. It has to come from somewhere else: you have to have a moment of vision or enlightenment. Christianity has said clearly that philosophy will take you so far, but then you need revelation. You need something beyond the rational. And how does that come to you? Well, Jung offers an answer to that: look at your dreams. Do active imagination. Let your mind enter into this other realm, use this other faculty called imagination. This is what he does in *Liber Novus*. If you follow the hints, the symbols, you will come upon the numinous center, the Self. The claim in Christianity is that the revelation has come to us and is complete. It is finished. And now, what do we do with it? Okay, so, that is a bit of a problem. Once you say it's all finished, and it's a matter of just repeating the lessons learned in church, the whole thing gets rather stale. That's why the churches are empty. They're repeating something that's been said and said and said, and people are looking for something more alive and fresh. There is a great demand for spirituality, and the churches aren't meeting it.

JL: I think this connects, Murray, to a question, and it might even be one of the last questions that we have time for today, and that is again a question about community. It's been brought up in many of the conversations I had with different scholars and analysts and also with you, Murray, when you said, what can we learn from Christians? You said something also about community, about faith, and Jungians, at times, struggle with the question of community.

There is a critique that's often raised, also, about Jungians as a group of esoteric elitists, or disconnected a little bit from reality at times. A psychology for the wealthy few. Also if we look at the people who came to Jung there was also people who came from a pretty wealthy background. It wasn't maybe the poorest that showed up in a Küsnacht, which is fine, but to me it also relates to the question of Jesus Christ, actually, and Jung's ambivalent relationship to Christ.

We discussed, all of us individually, in our conversations, the question of imitatio Christi, *and Jung's rendering of that. And he is sort of clear on not imitating Christ: no, no, no, don't imitate Christ. Find yourself, become who you are. But isn't there also a risk in this? Isn't Christ also speaking of the community? Isn't Christ also a symbol of what connects my individuation with others'? Isn't there something in the image of Christ that is not only a symbol for my own Self or potential wholeness, but actually more a symbol of our shared wholeness, our wounds and our difficulties in living a limited life here on earth?*

I wonder if there's a risk, sometimes, in that Jungian psychology reduces the social cause of Jesus Christ, and the loyalty to the kingdom of God, to some sort of ideal of individual self-actualization.

MS: Community in the Christian sense is not present in the Jungian world. Jungians do get together, they listen to lectures together and have discussions, but there is nothing like the sense of a numinous presence in the community. One doesn't look for it there. One looks for it in the inner world. I think the word community is misused to refer to any kind of gathering or group of people. That isn't what Christians mean by community. They mean that where two or three are gathered, the Holy Spirit is with them. That's community. It's a qualitative difference. And we don't have that in the Jungian associations. We don't look for it there.

AL: The other thing that is meant, in most Christian denominations, by community, or at least by the body of Christ, is those who share participation in Christ through baptism and through the eucharist, at least those two sacraments. And that also does not play into Jungian—the Jungian world.

JL: And would you say, is there a risk of moral and religious reductionism in Jungian psychology?

AL: How do you mean, Jakob?

JL: I mean by leaving out anything related to community and too much emphasizing your inner work on your dreams, not speaking of God or Christ or any shared images of the sacred—by focusing too much on what differentiates us from one another but not our similarities, on what holds us together.

AL: I think Jung was rightly afraid of the collective. He saw it as inferior, tending toward unconsciousness, mass-think, collective-think. And his fear of the collective has transmitted down through the generations . . .

Isn't the transforming of the world part of the Christian mission?

MS: Absolutely, yes. But you have to be careful about that notion of transforming because politics easily corrupts the good intentions of transformers. When religion becomes political, power takes over and love disappears. Politicians choose power, and they'll do anything to get it and hold on to it.

AL: Yes.

MS: The political is a very corrupting element in human life, but you still need it. You need power to transform things. But if you get lost in politics, it all becomes a matter of having power. And that's the problem. Jung said, "Where there's power, there's no love ." And you reminded me of Dante's journey, Ann, when you said that you choose love. That's what Dante discovered in *Paradiso*.

AL: Mm-hmm.

MS: He discovered that what actually moves the sun and all the other stars is love. And it infected him. He became transformed by that. So that was Dante's journey. He was no longer a politician. You can say, I choose love, but you have to be gripped by a vision somehow, don't you? That's where the psyche comes into play. It doesn't just value an idea, but it has to be powerfully psychologically motivated by, we would say, a powerful archetypal energy that you experience that motivates and keeps you, sustains you. Christians would call it the Holy Spirit.

AL: Jakob, you were bringing us back to the question of *imitatio Christi*, and the aspect of the imitation of Christ that involves brother and sisterhood with the poor and suffering. That is an essential part, I think, of the ministry of the Church, when it can remember that that is its life.

MS: That's Francis.

AL: Yes, it's Francis.

MS: Absolutely.

AL: Yes. And how much of that can be lived? And where do we see examples of it being lived, anywhere, either in the Church, which tends to get seduced by the world anyway, or in the Jungian world? Do we see that identification with the poor and preferential placement of the poor anywhere in the Jungian community now? Is that part of our vision?

MS: Well, Jakob, you did something like that in Berlin, didn't you? Psychotherapy on the street.

JL: We were trying to at least—maybe not build a bridge—but trying to keep a relationship to that side of community building. And for me there's been strikingly a lack of that in reading Jung. I do not hear much about the poor. I feel that there is a lack of that discourse. I think there is a danger if this journey inward is not connected to what's actually just in front of us. What's out there.

A clinical example: a patient dreaming about a beggar, and an immediate interpretation could be, from my fantasy Jungian analyst, that this is the beggar in you, this is your inner poverty, and there's something to that. There is something to that. But sometimes a beggar is just a beggar. Sometimes there's also something about you having to look at what's in front of you. And I think that's also where I have had a lot of help of reading Freud, actually, and Freud's emphasis on the reality principle. Obviously, it's a struggle, the tension of holding this, a patient's individuation, and helping them to feel better or feel more whole, and at the same time facing a world that continues to disintegrate in front of our eyes. That's a huge disconnect or cognitive dissonance. And I think that's where I personally believe that Jung, in my understanding of him, needs Christ.

Epilogue

As we have learned, it is in *The Red Book* that Jung offers his psychological rendering of the *imitatio Christi*, presenting it as an analogue for individuation. But before making this theoretical formulation, Jung goes through the experience of being crucified like Christ himself. In "Resolution," the tenth chapter—ending the first of the books, Liber Primus—Jung actively imagines the following scene:

> I: "I see that a terrible and incomprehensible power forces me to imitate the Lord in his final torment. But how can I presume to call Mary my mother?"
>
> Salome: "You are Christ."
>
> I stand with outstretched arms like someone crucified, my body taut and horribly entwined by the serpent: "You, Salome, say that I am Christ?"[51]

This is Jung, if not imitating, identifying with Christ in his last hours on the cross, while being informed by Salome (another important character of his imagination) that he *is* Christ. Later, in the chapter "Divine Folly," Jung begins to work through his experience more theoretically; as in another active imagination, he picks up a copy of Thomas à Kempis's fourteenth-century book *The Imitation of Christ.* He tries to determine whether Christ has any meaning for him any longer, and if so, what it

[51] Jung, *The Red Book*, 197.

might be. Such working through involves a series of dialogues between himself and a librarian, as well as other figures of his imagination. Jung's radically new understanding from this work was that to imitate Christ today means to live one's life as fully and authentically as Jesus did.

For Jung, the *imitatio Christi* becomes not following the traditional rules of morality and the collective, but when necessary, for the sake of conscience, breaking with tradition in pursuit of personal truth and individuation. Jung's rendering of the *imitato Christi* emphasizes the rebellious aspect of Jesus Christ, that one should be oneself not Christian but Christ. "If I thus truly imitate Christ, I do not imitate anyone, I emulate no one, but go my own way, and I will also no longer call myself a Christian."[52]

This radical rendering anew to fit Christ's message with Jung's own psychological disposition can be rather liberating, especially for individuals who, like Jung, grew up with a traditionally moralistic and restrictive Christianity emphasizing a literal interpretation of scripture and Christ. There is a dried-out form of Christianity that fails to give value to subjective personal experience. There are communities in which the imitation of Christ is interpreted too literally. In such contexts, imitating Christ becomes a restrictive moral code of perfectionist ideals around self-sacrifice, with little value given to the feeling-life of a person and the development of a unique personality.

But the other way around, Jung's merely psychological understanding of Jesus Christ, risks becoming too reductive, incomplete—stripping Christ from the gospel of good news, the *evangelion*, the gift of grace. Along such lines it is possible that the person of Christ is overly psychologized, reduced to an archetype, a mere model of individuation—all of which risks being incomplete, no longer radical or transformative at all. What is more, relativizing Christ as one psychological archetype among many archetypes risks too narrowly recasting Christianity's revolutionary universalism—his message of *faith*, *hope*, *love*, and *forgiveness*

[52] Jung, *The Red Book*, 332.

for everyone—as a merely personal story of individual well-being and wholeness.

The story of Christ can surely be read along Jungian lines as a symbolic tale of individual transformation and individuation, but this threatens to miss Christianity's collective vision of a transformed social order through love. To find faith in Christ is to open oneself to the idea that one is loved by God. With such openness comes the possibility of finding compassion for oneself as well as one's neighbor (recall the second greatest commandment: "Thou shalt love thy neighbor as thyself").

Jung's depth psychology emphasizes development of individual personality, and through the process of individuation, making the unconscious conscious, finding the Kingdom of God within. In contrast, Christianity offers a radical vision of society transformed through love, promising the Kingdom of God on this earth, *in this world*—available through grace at any time, for everyone.

Returning to Adolf Keller's poignant question to Jung from our introduction: whether the motif of insight, integration, totality, and wholeness would possess the same "religious binding power" as the need for forgiveness, personal fellowship, and salvation, I believe that *binding power* is to be found in both analytical psychology and the original message and vision of Christianity. A few scholars in this book have shared how they have found unique ways of synthesizing Christian faith and Jungian psychology in their own lives. For others, it is still a wrestling, or perhaps a weaving, to find where the two fields meet and where they collide or need to separate. The weaving creates a pattern within which Jung's psychology, in opening to the Christian depth, is enriched by surrender through faith in an invisible God taking the form of a suffering human, instilling hope and love in the human heart through the gift of grace. There is no room for egoic hesitation in a psychology of the cross; so too must analytical psychologists bow an extra millimeter to touch their foreheads to the floor.

What Christianity offers depth psychology is a big dream and a collective vision that goes beyond the individual. Its social ethos has always been to offer healing not only to the wealthy few, but to the neglected, to the impoverished, to the displaced and despised among us. The people that Jesus still prefers to dine with are those who live on the margins, those who are neglected—if they register at all—in Jungian discourse. Individuals who most likely will never have a chance to enter the analytical room.

Conversely, Christianity's original message can be infused with fresh blood again when the insights, techniques, and symbolic lenses of Jung's psychology are allowed inside. People of the Church, practicing Christians today, can be transformed by opening to the dynamic reality of the unconscious psyche, to dreams and the techniques of active imagination. In so learning and doing, they can give more value to individual life experience and to listening to spiritual as well as bodily erotic longings.[53]

Pope Father Francis, today's leader of the Catholic Church, has openly shared that he underwent psychoanalysis when earlier in life he

---

[53] In his early excitement about psychoanalysis, expressed in a 1910 letter to Freud, thirty-five-year-old Jung articulates an ecstatic vision for the field that, later in life, he would retract:

> I imagine a far finer and more comprehensive task for psychoanalysis than alliance with an ethical fraternity . . . . I think we must give it time to infiltrate into people from many centres, to revivify among intellectuals a feeling for symbol and myth, ever so gently to transform Christ back into the soothsaying god of the vine . . . . A genuine and proper ethical development cannot abandon Christianity but must grow up within it, must bring to fruition its hymn of love, the agony and ecstasy over the dying and resurgent god, the mystic power of the wine, the awesome anthropophagy of the Last Supper—only this ethical development can serve the vital forces of religion. (Jung to Freud, February 11, 1910, *Letters*, Vol. 1, 17–19)

Fifty years on, a student of Jung's wrote him, referencing these comments on Christianity. In a letter dated April 9, 1959, Jung replied: "Best thanks for the quotation from that accursed correspondence. For me it is an unfortunately inexpungable reminder of the incredible folly that filled the days of my youth. The journey from cloud-cuckoo-land back to reality lasted a long time. In my case Pilgrim's Progress consisted in my having to climb down a thousand ladders until I could reach out my hand to the little clod of earth that I am (Jung, *Letters*, Vol. 1, 19)."

went through a difficult phase, and that it was helpful for him. In this area as well, he could set a good example for people in positions of power in the Catholic Church. The psychoanalysis of Catholic as well as Protestant clergy, and the implementation of Jungian shadow-work, might help to humble and temper what appears to be a spiritually overinflated power-elite (given its continued misuse of power and complicity in abuse). Perhaps Murray Stein was right in understanding Jung's project as a wish to treat Christianity, to put it on the couch—and with it a new generation of theologians, priests, and pastors-in-training more open to Jung's prophetic message.

There is *religious binding power* in what both Christianity and Jungian psychology have to offer, and even more so when they are held together, as opposites or a cross, two parts belonging to a larger whole. The question of where Christ and Christianity fit into a new psychology, or where analytical psychology fits into a new Christianity, calls for continuing wrestling and weaving, individually and through continuing conversations such as the ones published in this book. But the wrestling is not limited to Jungian analysts and scholars. It is happening already in exchanges between analysands, through theologians, depth psychologists, individual seekers, and laypeople around the world in Internet forums. It is in our curiosity or despair, in our religious instinct, that we are led, that we formulate questions keeping us in their grip, that we suffer the current of human life washing us to shore where psychology meets the cross.

Dreaming the myth onward

The subtitle of this book is *Conversations on Dreaming the Myth Onward.* In Jung's late writing, both in *Memories, Dreams, Reflections* as well as in *Answer to Job* and *The Undiscovered Self,* he writes how an ample point of departure in the development of Christianity can be found by going back to the original version of the myth. It is Jung coming out again as a Protestant Reformer, offering the renaissance solution of going back to go forward, who summarizes his late thoughts on Christianity's role in our time and in the future:

> Our myth has become mute, and gives no answers. The fault lies not in it as it is set down in the Scriptures, but solely in us, who have not developed it further, who, rather, have suppressed any such attempts. The original version of the myth offers ample points of departure and possibilities of development.[54]

In my understanding, Jung's big dream was not to form a new school of depth psychology, or to found a training institute of Jungian theory and concepts. Jung was, rather, hoping for analytical techniques to play a role in a renaissance of the original Christian message. He saw that this development would happen through the individual's encounter with the *numinous*, whether in its fascinating or terrible form. It is in the rapture of the fabric of our ordinary human life that Christ's message can come through and lead us into a process of individuation, or if you prefer, a process of incarnation.

In *The Undiscovered Self,* he writes: "The Christian symbol is a living thing that carries in itself the seeds of further development."[55] It is this living thing that we come into contact with when we study the roots of the questions Jung put to himself in his wrestling with Christianity. It is a seed that this book has been an attempt to uncover and illuminate, a seed that holds the potentials of dreaming the myth onward.

---

[54] Jaffé and Jung, *Memories, Dreams, Reflections*, 364.

[55] C.G. Jung, *Civilization in Transition*, 245–306.

Bibliography

Giegerich, Wolfgang. *Dreaming the Myth Onwards: C.G. Jung on Christianity and on Hegel*. Vol. 6 of *The Collected English Papers of Wolfgang Giegerich*, edited by Wolfgang Giegerich. London: Routledge, 2020.

Harding, M. Esther and C.G. Jung, TS of lecture "Human Relationships in Relation to the Process of Individuation." *Cornwall Seminar, July 23, C.G. Jung: Unauthorized Notes / by M. Esther Harding*, July 1923. Kristine Mann Library, C.G. Jung Center, New York. https://collections.library.yale. edu/catalog/10076043.

Heisig, James W. *Imago Dei: A Study of C.G. Jung's Psychology of Religion*. Lewisburg, PA: Bucknell University Press, 1979.

Hillman, James and Sonu Shamdasani. *Lament of the Dead: Psychology after Jung's* Red Book. New York: W. W. Norton & Company, 2013.

Homans, Peter. *Jung in Context: Modernity and the Making of a Psychology* . Chicago: University of Chicago Press, 1979.

Jaffé, Aniela and C.G. Jung. *Memories, Dreams, Reflections*. Edited by Aniela Jaffé. Translated by Richard Winston and Clara Winston. New York: Random House, 1961.

Jung, C.G. and Adolf Keller. *On Theology and Psychology: The Correspondence of C.G. Jung and Adolf Keller.* Edited by Marianne Jehle- Wildberger. Translated by Heather McCartney and John Peck. Princeton, NJ: Princeton University Press, 2020.

Jung, C.G. *1906–1950.* Vol. 1 of *C.G. Jung Letters*, edited by Gerhard Adler and Aniela Jaffé, translated by R. F. C. Hull. London: Routledge Kegan & Paul, 1973.

Jung, C.G. *Aion: Researches into the Phenomenology of the Self.* 2nd ed. Vol. 9, Part II of *The Collected Works of C. G. Jung*, edited by Herbert Read, Michael Fordham, and Gerhard Adler, translated by R. F. C. Hull. Princeton, NJ: Princeton University Press, 1968.

Jung, C.G. "Answer to Job." In *Psychology and Religion: West and East.* 2nd ed. Vol. 11 of *The Collected Works of C. G. Jung*, edited by Herbert Read, Michael Fordham, and Gerhard Adler, translated by R. F. C. Hull. Par. 560–758. Princeton, NJ: Princeton University Press, 1969.

Jung, C.G. *The Black Books 1913–1932: Notebooks of Transformation*. Edited by Sonu Shamdasani. Translated by Martin Liebscher, John Peck, and Sonu Shamdasani. W. W. Norton & Company, 2020.

Jung, C.G. *Civilization in Transition*. 2nd ed. Vol. 10 of *The Collected Works of C.G. Jung,* edited by Herbert Read, Michael Fordham, and Gerhard Adler, translated by R. F. C. Hull. Princeton, NJ: Princeton University Press, 1970.

Jung, C.G. "Commentary on *The Secret of the Golden Flower* ." In *Alchemical Studies.* Vol. 13 of *The Collected Works of C.G. Jung*, edited by Herbert Read, Michael Fordham, and Gerhard Adler, translated by R. F. C. Hull. 1–56. Princeton, NJ: Princeton University Press, 1969.

Jung, C.G. "Face to Face: Carl Jung." Interview by John Freeman. *Face to Face*, BBC, October 22, 1959. Video, 38:00. https://www.bbc.co.uk/iplayer/episode/p04qhvyj/face-to-face-carl-jung.

Jung, C.G. *Jung on Ignatius of Loyola's* Spiritual Exercises. Vol. 7 of *Lectures Delivered at ETH Zürich : 1939–1940*, edited by Martin Liebscher, translated by Caitlin Stephens. Princeton, NJ: Princeton University Press, 2023.

Jung, C.G. *Mysterium Coniunctionis: An Inquiry into the Separation and Synthesis of Psychic Opposites in Alchemy.* 2nd ed. Vol. 14 of *The Collected Works of C.G. Jung*, edited by Herbert Read, Michael Fordham, and Gerhard Adler, translated by R. F. C. Hull. Princeton, NJ: Princeton University Press, 1970.

Jung, C.G. "A Psychological View of Conscience." In *Civilization in Transition.* 2nd ed. Vol. 10 of *The Collected Works of C.G. Jung*, edited by Herbert Read, Michael Fordham, and Gerhard Adler, translated by R. F. C. Hull. 437–55. Princeton, NJ: Princeton University Press, 1970.

Jung, C.G. *Psychology and Alchemy.* 2nd ed. Vol. 12 of *The Collected Works of C.G. Jung*, edited by Herbert Read, Michael Fordham, and Gerhard Adler, translated by R. F. C. Hull. Pantheon Books. Princeton, NJ: Princeton University Press, 1968.

Jung, C.G. *Psychology and Religion: West and East.* 2nd ed . Vol. 11 of *The Collected Works of C.G. Jung*, edited by Herbert Read, Michael Fordham, and Gerhard Adler, translated by R. F. C. Hull. Princeton, NJ: Princeton University Press, 1969.

Jung, C.G. "The Psychology of the Child Archetype." In *Archetypes and the Collective Unconscious.* 2nd ed. Vol. 9, Part I of *The Collected Works of C.G. Jung*, edited by Herbert Read, Michael Fordham, and Gerhard Adler, translated by R. F. C. Hull. 151–81. Princeton, NJ: Princeton University Press, 1969.

Jung, C.G. *Psychology of the Unconscious: A Study of the Transformations and Symbolisms of the Libido*. Edited by William McGuire. Translated by Beatrice M. Hinkle. Princeton, NJ: Princeton University Press, 1992.

Jung, C.G. *The Red Book* = Liber Novus. Reader's Edition. Edited by Sonu Shamdasani. Translated by Mark Kyburz, John Peck, and Sonu Shamdasani. New York: W. W. Norton & Company, 2009.

Jung, C.G. *The Symbolic Life: Miscellaneous Writings*. Vol . 18 of *The Collected Works of C.G. Jung*, edited by Herbert Read, Michael Fordham, and Gerhard Adler, translated by R. F. C. Hull. Princeton, NJ: Princeton University Press, 1976.

Jung, C.G. *Symbols of Transformation: An Analysis of the Prelude to a Case of Schizophrenia.* 2nd ed. Vol. 5 of *The Collected Works of C.G. Jung*, edited by Herbert Read, Michael Fordham, and Gerhard Adler, translated by R. F. C. Hull. Princeton, NJ: Princeton University Press, 1967.

Jung, C.G. "The Tavistock Lectures." In *The Symbolic Life : Miscellaneous Writings*. Vol. 18 of *The Collected Works of C.G. Jung*, edited by Herbert Read, Michael Fordham, and Gerhard Adler, translated by R. F. C. Hull. 5–266. Princeton, NJ: Princeton University Press, 1969.

Jung, C.G. "Transformation Symbolism in the Mass." In *Psychology and Religion: West and East*. 2nd ed. Vol. 11 of *The Collected Works of C.G. Jung*, edited by Herbert Read, Michael Fordham, and Gerhard Adler, translated by R. F. C. Hull. 201–98. Princeton, NJ: Princeton University Press, 1969.

Jung, C.G. "The Undiscovered Self (Present and Future)." In *Civilization in Transition.* 2nd ed. Vol. 10 of *The Collected Works of C.G. Jung*, edited by Herbert Read, Michael Fordham, and Gerhard Adler, translated by R. F. C. Hull. 245–306. Princeton, NJ: Princeton University Press, 1970.

Kierkegaard, Søren. *Works of Love*. Translated by Howard V. Honig and Edna H. Honig. New York: HarperCollins Publishers, 2009.

Lammers, Ann Conrad. *In God's Shadow: The Collaboration of Victor White and C.G. Jung*. New York: Paulist Press, 1994.

Sanford, John A. *The Kingdom Within: The Inner Meaning of Jesus' Sayings*. Rev. ed. San Francisco: HarperOne, 2009.

Stein, Murray. *Jung on Christianity*. Princeton, NJ: Princeton University Press, 1999.

Stein, Murray. "Jungian Psychology and the Spirit of Protestantism." *International Journal of Jungian Studies* 3, no. 2 (September 2011), 125–43. https://brill.com/view/journals/ijjs/3/2/article-p125_4.xml.

Stein, Murry. *Jung's Treatment of Christianity: The Psychotherapy of a Religious Tradition*. Asheville, NC: Chiron Publications, 2015.

Stein, Murray. *Solar Conscience Lunar Conscience: An Essay on the Psychological Foundations of Morality, Lawfulness, and the Sense of Justice*. 2nd ed. Asheville, NC: Chiron Publications, 2015.

Thomas, à Kempis. *My Imitation of Christ*. Brooklyn, NY: Confraternity of the Precious Blood, 1982.

Ulanov, Ann, James Hillman, and Sonu Shamdasani. Carl Gustav Jung and the Red Book (Part 1). *The Red Book of Carl G. Jung: Its Origins and Influences*. Symposium presented at the Library of Congress, Washington, DC: Library of Congress, June 19, 2010. https://hdl.loc.gov/loc.gdc/gdcwebcasts.100619mns0900.

Index

A

B

C

D

J

K

N

O

P

Y

Z

www.ingramcontent.com/pod-product-compliance
Lightning Source LLC
Chambersburg PA
CBHW020657270326
41928CB00005B/162
9781685032210